Writing Essays in English Language and Linguistics

English language and linguistics shares many of its writing conventions with other disciplines, but there are certain features – 'ways of doing things' – and expectations that distinguish it as a subject. This book is written specifically to help undergraduate students of English language and linguistics develop the art of writing essays, projects and reports. Written by an author with over thirty years' experience of lecturing in the subject, it is a comprehensive and very readable resource, and contains numerous discipline-related examples, practice exercises and an answer key. It includes chapters on referencing (including plagiarism, paraphrase and guidance on referencing styles), stylistic issues that often get overlooked, and writing a dissertation. The book offers practical guidance and a layout that guides students as they work though their project. It will be an invaluable reference tool that students can read cover to cover or dip into as and when required.

NEIL MURRAY is Associate Professor of Applied Linguistics and a member of the Research Centre for Languages and Cultures at the University of South Australia.

Writing Essays in English Language and Linguistics: Principles, Tips and Strategies for Undergraduates

NEIL MURRAY

CAMBRIDGE UNIVERSITY PRESS
Cambridge, New York, Melbourne, Madrid, Cape Town,
Singapore, São Paulo, Delhi, Mexico City

Cambridge University Press
The Edinburgh Building, Cambridge CB2 8RU, UK

Published in the United States of America by
Cambridge University Press, New York

www.cambridge.org
Information on this title: www.cambridge.org/9780521128469

First published 2012

Printed in the United Kingdom at the University Press, Cambridge

A catalogue record for this publication is available from the British Library

Library of Congress Cataloging-in-Publication Data
Murray, Neil, 1960–
    Writing essays in English language and linguistics : principles, tips and strategies for
undergraduates / Neil Murray.
        p.   cm.
    Includes bibliographical references.
    ISBN 978-0-521-11119-5 (Hardback) – ISBN 978-0-521-12846-9 (Paperback)
1. Linguistics.   I. Title.
    P121.M929 2012
    808′.042–dc23
                                                                            2011033924

ISBN 978-0-521-11119-5 Hardback
ISBN 978-0-521-12846-9 Paperback

For my wife Mitra, for her love and unwavering support over the years, and my children Faye and Alexander, of whom I'm enormously proud

Contents

Acknowledgements

There are a number of individuals all of whom who have impacted positively in some way on the writing of this book and who deserve my sincere thanks. First up is Helen Barton, the commissioning editor at Cambridge University Press, for her enthusiasm for the project and the invaluable guidance she provided during the book's development. I must also thank my colleagues in the Research Centre for Languages and Cultures at the University of South Australia – in particular Angela Scarino for her friendship, support and infectious energy, Kathleen Heugh for her encouragement and great wisdom, and Anthony Liddicoat and Tim Curnow, for their advice and for always giving generously and willingly of their time. I also owe a debt of gratitude to Alexander Murray for his help and expertise in generating some of the graphics in the book, Chris Klinger and Faye Murray for their eagle eyes in helping proof the manuscript, and David Beglar for his suggestions on the text. Special thanks should go to Professor Vivian Cook, for kindly allowing me to use his definitions of linguistic terms in the book's glossary. While every effort has been made to contact the authors of *all* such materials used in the book, in the very few cases where this proved unsuccessful I should be delighted to acknowledge their contributions explicitly in any future editions of the book.

Finally, there is my family, for putting up with my frequent unsocial behaviour and for turning down the television on so many occasions for my benefit. Without their encouragement, love and forbearance I could not possibly have completed the book – and completed it to schedule.

Introduction

When it comes to writing, academic disciplines – particularly those within the humanities and social sciences – have a good deal in common and, for the most part, they share very similar expectations of students' writing. However, despite such similarity, each discipline also tends to have its own particular set of conventions, its own way of doing things, and the fields of English language and linguistics are certainly no exception. The variation that can exist between the writing practices of different disciplines can leave students who are just starting out on course assignments or research projects uncertain about what exactly they should be doing and how. Although libraries or student services units will often produce guides to help them navigate this territory, these tend to be generic rather than discipline-specific; and while individual departments may give their students guidance on how to write within their particular discipline, such guidance is often sketchy at best, providing only a few general pointers and often leaving them with more questions than answers.

This book uncovers, for the intending or newly enrolled student, some of the particularities of writing English language and linguistics essays and research projects. In doing so, it presents discipline-specific guidance on such things as assignment questions, information sources, the nature of evidence, referencing, stylistic issues and formatting, alongside much that is more generic and applicable to other areas of academic inquiry. All examples, tasks and illustrations are English language/linguistics related and many are authentic.

The book has been written in a style which, I hope, is engaging and easily accessible to undergraduate students. In order to clarify explanations, it includes numerous examples, as well as tasks designed to help you test and consolidate your understanding of the ideas presented. It also includes 'tips' – experience-based insights to help you improve your writing and avoid common pitfalls. Finally, there's a handy section on frequently asked questions and a glossary of linguistics terms.

Writing Essays in English Language and Linguistics can be used in different ways to suit your particular purpose:

- it can be read serially from start to finish in preparation for your studies;
- it can be read serially in coordination with the writing of your assignment. In other words, as you reach each stage of your assignment, you can read the relevant section(s) of the book, thereby syncronising the two processes; or
- it can 'dipped into' as a quick-guide reference work as and when you need advice on a particular topic. In this case, you'll probably want to use the more detailed index in combination with the table of contents.

However you decide to use the book, I hope it helps bring you success in your studies.

I would welcome any feedback you may have and, in particular, any suggestions for inclusion in the frequently asked questions section.

Neil Murray
University of South Australia
April 2011

A guide to the book's icons: what do they mean?

Different people will no doubt use this book in different ways to suit their particular needs and learning styles. Whichever style you personally prefer, the following icons and other graphical 'cues' have been used in the design of the book in order to help you navigate through it quickly and easily.

 This icon indicates an example or examples. Whenever you see this icon you can expect to find at least one example of the particular point being discussed.

 Alongside this icon you can expect to find a piece of advice (a 'tip') or an observation designed to improve your writing in some way. Sometimes it may simply contain an anecdotal remark based on experience of students' writing; at other times it may indicate a concrete suggestion for writing more effectively, or an alert to possible pitfalls.

TRY IT OUT!

Whenever you see this it will be appear in a box and be accompanied by an activity or task designed to get you reflecting on and/or practising a particular idea or approach.

PART **1**

THE BASICS

Writing at school and writing at university: are they really so different?

'I just don't really know what to expect. What exactly are the differences between writing at school and writing at university?'

What's covered in this chapter:
Different philosophies, different writing styles
Shifting the balance: reproduction vs critical analysis
Originality, creativity and 'voice'
The emphasis on research and reading extensively
Depth of analysis and depth of argument
Sound reasoning and the importance of evidence
Transparency, clear organisation and accessibility
References and bibliographies
Appendices
Length

Introduction

Actually, despite the title of this section, the truth is that writing at school and writing at university are not really *that* different. Many of the adjustments you'll need to make to your writing will be adjustments of degree and style as much as anything else. The principles of good academic writing are the same whether you're writing as a high school student or as a postgraduate doctoral student.

'So, why do I need a book of this kind?' you're probably wondering. Well, here are a few reasons:

- Due to such things as time pressure, a full curriculum and student capacity, schools vary in the attention they pay to developing academic writing skills.

- Schools, understandably, tend to focus on training you to produce written work that will earn you good AS/A-level grades. They don't normally prepare you specifically for academic writing at undergraduate level. As a result, certain principles of writing are not covered at all or are covered only superficially, with much important detail often being left out – detail that may be crucial to successful assignment writing at university.
- Traditional thinking has been that undergraduates will learn much of what they need to know 'on the job', once they enter university, through observation, a process of trial and error, and tutor feedback. Unfortunately, these days, the ever-increasing demands being placed on tutors' time means that it's becoming increasingly difficult for them to provide their students with detailed feedback on the form (as opposed to the content) of their writing, with the result that students themselves need to be more resourceful. Furthermore, many students who wish to make a good start with their first assignments feel anxious and uncomfortable about handing in essays without a clear grasp of what's expected of them. In other words, they're not happy to take the risk of 'learning on the job' as this may mean below-par marks in the early phase of their university careers.
- While many academic departments, libraries or information services departments offer leaflets on aspects of academic writing such as referencing and plagiarism, these are often only very brief guides – useful certainly, but not really adequate.

So, although you may well already have an understanding of the basics of academic writing, chances are there are still some things you probably don't yet know or about which you don't yet know enough. A quick look through the Table of Contents on pages vii–x should give you some indication of what you do and don't know.

TRY IT OUT! #1

List below what you think some of the differences are between writing at secondary school and writing at university.

	Writing at Secondary School	Writing at University
1.		
2.		
3.		
4.		
5.		

Let's now look briefly at some of the major differences between writing at school and writing at university. As you'll see, the subjects mentioned in

1.1–1.10 below are all closely connected and will be discussed in much greater detail at various points later in the book.

1.1 Different philosophies, different writing styles

At a broad and rather basic level, high school education and university education can be differentiated in terms of purpose. The vast bulk of your education at high school consists largely of developing discipline in your approach to study and building up a body of knowledge that will prepare you for the outside world – both the social world and the world of work – and for the studies you may choose to undertake as an undergraduate student. In contrast, university education exists to build on that foundation with a view to further developing your intellect and powers of analysis, your specialist knowledge of the subject you have chosen to study and your ability to play a role in taking forward that field of study through your own ideas and creativity. This shift of emphasis as you move from high school to university is reflected in the expectations tutors have of your writing. What that means in concrete terms will be discussed in the remainder of this section and, indeed, throughout the remainder of this book.

1.2 Shifting the balance: reproduction vs critical analysis

Although it may be a bit of a generalisation, it's nevertheless true to say that whereas at high school the main emphasis is on absorbing and applying information appropriately according to context (i.e. the particular question or exercise being attempted), at university far greater emphasis is placed on analysing and thinking critically about that information. In other words, there's less stress placed on the simple reproduction of information (the displaying of knowledge), and more on the ability to evaluate or *appraise* it. The nurturing of that ability is very much in keeping with the notion that a university education exists to hone the mind and discipline its students' thinking.

1.3 Originality, creativity and 'voice'

Not only will you be expected to evaluate the information you absorb, you will also need to use it to support your own thinking and bolster your own arguments. If universities exist to develop 'the mind' further and to push the boundaries of knowledge in the various academic disciplines and fields of research, then students must be given free rein to express themselves – to question, to challenge, to disagree, to form their own ideas and propose new ways of looking at things ... right? In other words, they need to 'find their own voice'. Such a process is key to the advancement of any area of inquiry, and without it many of the great discoveries that have changed the way we live and think about the world would never have come about. It's not surprising, then, that universities promote its cultivation as early as possible. However, as we'll see, in order to be creative, it's first necessary to be well informed about what has already been said and written concerning the subject on which you're writing, and to provide a sound rationale for your own ideas (see section 3.3, *How to argue*).

1.4 The emphasis on research and reading extensively

In order to give depth to your work and provide a strong basis for your own ideas, you need to have a good understanding of the relevant issues and to have pondered them and tossed them around a bit – perhaps with your fellow students, as well as your lecturers and tutors. If you're to do this effectively, you'll first need to read around the subject in order to familiarise yourself with the relevant literature and what others have said about it. Only then are you really able to comment usefully and with authority. Lecturers quickly know whether a student is well informed or not, whether they have 'done their homework', and when they are bluffing and waffling! If you've read thoroughly, you're in a position to cite the works you've read and to use them in support of your own views and arguments. Remember, to do really well in your undergraduate assignments, you need to go beyond the standard readings you're assigned and the information you absorb in lectures. You need to engage in your own process of inquiry, in part by reading extensively.

1.5 Depth of analysis and depth of argument

University, then, represents the next stage of your intellectual development. Traditionally, a key element in this rite of passage has been the expectation that you'll gradually demonstrate the ability to understand and present concepts and ideas in much greater detail than you may well be used to. It's no longer good enough to merely put down the first idea that comes into your head, or to assume that, after just one take, your first interpretation of an idea is the correct one. You'll need to research ideas more thoroughly and to consider them more carefully and with a critical eye. And when you comment or pass judgement on them, you'll be expected to provide a carefully and logically thought-through rationale based on your own ideas and those of scholars you've read. Quick and superficial responses are – or should be – a thing of the past.

1.6 Sound reasoning and the importance of evidence

A well-structured piece of writing carries conviction and influences its reader. How? Through clear and well-reasoned argument, familiarity with and consideration of the relevant literature, and the ability to articulate your own opinions effectively. There is, however, one other key ingredient, the glue that sticks all these important elements together: *evidence*. You will have learnt about the importance of evidence while studying for your GCSEs and AS/A-level exams. Without evidence to support them, any statements you make in your writing have little or no value; they're simply opinions, and ten people may have ten different opinions none of which is any more valid than the others unless there is clear and potent evidence to support it. At university, where you'll be expected to be more creative in your thinking, more opinionated and more critical of the ideas and information you hear or read, the importance of evidence becomes even greater. If your ideas are to be taken seriously, they need to be seen to be based on facts and on sound reasoning, which in turn requires the provision of supporting evidence. We will look at evidence and the forms it takes in more detail in section 2.4.

1.7 Transparency, clear organisation and accessibility

The ideas you present must not only be well reasoned and have ample supporting evidence to justify them, they must also be transparent. In the same way that you're expected to show your working when answering a maths question, you must be thoroughly explicit in your presentation of ideas when writing university assignments (see section 2.2). Take very little for granted and assume your reader knows almost nothing. Make sure your writing is coherent and not unnecessarily complex. Be concise and avoid waffle at all cost (you will definitely have heard this before!). You will also need to try and indicate your organisation through a clear system of headings and sub-headings (see section 6.4).

1.8 References and bibliographies

If you are to support your ideas with sound reasoning and convincing evidence, you will inevitably need to refer to or quote other writers you've read and who have influenced your thinking in some way. Using the ideas of other writers in your own writing is often referred to as 'citing your sources'. At the end of your assignments, you'll need to list (in a *bibliography*) all the works (such as articles and books) you've cited in those assignments. There are clearly defined ways of quoting and citing sources in your writing, and of formatting your bibliography, and this book will tell you all you need to know. It will also look at one of the most important things you need to avoid as a university student: *plagiarism* – the practice of using the work of other writers and passing it off as your own (see Chapter 8, and section 8.2 in particular).

1.9 Appendices

You may need to include appendices (singular *appendix*) with your essays. This is additional information that is perhaps too large or slightly incidental (but nevertheless relevant) to the main body of your text, and which is therefore placed at the end of the assignment. You can then refer the reader to it in the appropriate place in your main text.

1.10 Length

Although you will have had some experience of writing long projects at school, generally speaking undergraduate assignments will be longer than those you've become used to. This isn't too surprising considering what we've said about providing evidence, reading extensively, citing other writers, critically analysing ideas and being creative. However, you'll often be required to write to word limits, and that can be difficult. It requires practice – practice at deciding what to include and what to omit, practice at identifying the key and most relevant information, practice at writing concisely and economically, and practice at avoiding waffle and unnecessary padding.

TRY IT OUT! #2

Look at the aspects of university writing listed below, each of which has been discussed in this chapter. Write two things about each one that you would tell somebody about to enter university in order to help them prepare for writing.

Reproduction of information vs critical analysis of information

1. _____
2. _____

Originality, creativity, and developing your 'voice'

1. _____
2. _____

The importance of researching a topic and reading extensively

1. _____
2. _____

Depth of analysis and depth of argument

1. _____
2. _____

Evidence

1. _____

2. _____

Clarity and good organisation

1. _____

2. _____

References and bibliographies

1. _____

2. _____

Chapter 1 Key points checklist

Writing at university means:

- developing your powers of analysis;

- being more critical about what you read and write;

- developing and being prepared to express your own ideas and perspectives;

- thoroughly familiarising yourself with your subject's literature by reading beyond what is assigned to you;

- constructing detailed, well-conceived arguments with a clear rationale and adequately supported with strong evidence;

- producing writing that is well organised and easy to understand;

- including correctly formatted references to the literature;

- creating appendices for information too large or incidental to be placed in the main body of your text;

- writing (often) to strict word limits.

Fundamental principles

'So what are the most important things I need to know ... even before I start writing?'

What's covered in this chapter:
Paragraph essentials: what is a paragraph ... and when should you begin a new one?
Good argument structure: what does it mean and how do you achieve it?
Explaining everything and avoiding assumptions
Supporting your statements: evidence, what it is, why it's essential and how you provide it
Being concise and relevant ... and avoiding waffle
Punctuation, how important is it ... really?

2.1 Paragraph essentials: what is a paragraph ... and when should you begin a new one?

At some time during our school life, most of us were told that when we want to begin writing about a new idea we should start a new paragraph. And if you think I'm going to tell you anything different here then I'm afraid you're going to be disappointed – new paragraphs are indeed started when a writer has a new idea they wish to introduce into their discussion. The trouble is, it can be difficult in practice to know what a new idea actually is. A person might argue, for example, that every sentence expresses a new idea; however, we certainly don't have a separate paragraph for every sentence that we write!

Generally, a new paragraph represents a shift of focus by the writer which is usually the result of one of the following:

- a new argument;
- a new point in a sequenced argument containing a series of logical steps or thought processes;

- a new stage in a process or procedure, or a discrete element of a description;
- an alternative point of view;
- a discussion or explanation of each point or item in a list – one paragraph for every point/item.

We indicate a new paragraph by indenting the first line slightly, usually by about one centimetre or half an inch, as in the following example in which different types of morphemes are discussed:

     Some morphemes like *boy*, *desire*, *gentle*, and *man* constitute words by themselves. Other morphemes like *-ish*, *-ness*, *-ly*, *dis-*, *trans-*, and *un-* are never words but always parts of words. Thus, *un-* is like *pre-* (*prefix*, *predetermine*, *prejudge*, *prearrange*) and *bi-* (*bipolar*, *bisexual*, *bivalve*); it occurs only before other morphemes. Such morphemes are called prefixes.

     Other morphemes occur only as suffixes, following other morphemes. English examples of suffix morphemes are *–er* (as in *singer*, *performer*, *reader*, and *beautifier*), *-ist* (in *typist*, *copyist*, *pianist*, *novelist*, *collaborationist*, and *linguist*) and *–ly* (as in *manly*, *sickly*, *spectacularly*, and *friendly*), to mention only a few.

     Some languages also have infixes, morphemes that are inserted into other morphemes. Although infixes are not common in English, two examples that sometimes appear are *bloody* and *flipping*, as in *abso-bloody-lutely* and *Cali-flippin'-fornia*.

     Then there are circumfixes. These are morphemes that are attached to a root or stem morpheme both initially and finally. This happens more commonly in German than in English. In German, the past participle of regular verbs is formed by adding the prefix *ge-* and the suffix *–t* to the verb root. This circumfix added to the verb root *lieb* 'love' produces *geliebt*, 'loved'.   (Adapted from Fromkin and Rodman, 1998)

Instead of indenting, as in the above example, in recent years it has become increasingly popular in academic writing to simply leave a line as a way of indicating a new paragraph. Look at this example:

Some morphemes like *boy*, *desire*, *gentle*, and *man* constitute words by themselves. Other morphemes like *-ish*, *-ness*, *-ly*, *dis-*, *trans-*, and *un-* are never words but always parts of words. Thus, *un-* is like *pre-* (*prefix*, *predetermine*, *prejudge*, *prearrange*) and *bi-* (*bipolar*, *bisexual*, *bivalve*); it occurs only before other morphemes. Such morphemes are called prefixes.

Other morphemes occur only as suffixes, following other morphemes. English examples of suffix morphemes are *–er* (as in *singer*, *performer*, *reader*, and *beautifier*), *-ist* (in *typist*, *copyist*, *pianist*, *novelist*, *collaborationist*, and *linguist*) and *–ly* (as in *manly*, *sickly*, *spectacularly*, and *friendly*), to mention only a few.

Some languages also have infixes, morphemes that are inserted into other morphemes. Although infixes are not common in English, two examples that sometimes appear are *bloody* and *flipping*, as in *abso-bloody-lutely* and *Cali-flippin'-fornia*.

Then there are circumfixes. These are morphemes that are attached to a root or stem morpheme both initially and finally. This happens more commonly in German than in English. In German, the past participle of regular verbs is formed by adding the prefix *ge-* and the suffix *–t* to the verb root. This circumfix added to the verb root *lieb* 'love' produces *geliebt*, 'loved'.

I would recommend that you check with your tutor or supervisor whether they have a preference for how you should format your paragraphs.

TRY IT OUT! #3

Divide the text below into paragraphs. Reflect on the reasons why you choose to break up the text as you do. Underline the main idea of each paragraph and the supporting detail.

Dialect is defined as a regional or socially conditioned variant of a language. Dialects may vary in their phonological, lexical, grammatical, and pragmatic conventions, but are generally mutually intelligible and often spoken by people who live in the same general geographical region. The difference between a dialect and a language is not clear, however. For example, Italian and Spanish are two different languages that are nonetheless mutually intelligible. Mandarin and Cantonese are not, although they are both considered dialects of Chinese. One whimsical linguist argued that a dialect becomes a language when its speakers get their own army (Foss and Hakes, 1978, p. 5). From a linguistic point of view, every dialect – like every language – is a highly structured system, not an accumulation of errors caused by the failure of speakers to master the standard dialect. To prefer one dialect over another would be to display 'dialectical chauvinism', just as to prefer your own native language to any other would be to display 'linguistic chauvinism'. As linguists such as Labov (1972) point out, dialects such as African-American English vernacular have a logic and a set of rules every bit as complicated as that of Standard English. The differences between dialects have to do with how they negotiate the trade-off between work a speaker has to do (for example, mark plurality twice, once on the pronoun, once on the verb: *he comes versus they come*) and the work a listener has to do (listen carefully and catch each point in the conversation where information is not presented redundantly). African-American English vernacular has some redundancies that Standard English does not (for example, negatives must be marked at least twice, as in *I ain't never lost a fight*) and omits some redundancies required by Standard English (for example, omitted copulas, as in *Stan here right now*). Many speakers of English learn to switch their dialects to suit the occasion, talking Standard English at school, for example, and their home dialect among friends and family. In fact, linguists may be the only people who perceive dialects to be equivalent. The 1997 controversy over the Oakland, California, school system's adoption of Ebonics (more technically known as African-American vernacular English, or AAVE) as a primary language has made this difference in the perceived prestige of dialects painfully clear. On a less-explosive level, George Bernard Shaw explored the difference in the prestige of dialects in his famous play, *Pygmalion*, and its musical version, *My Fair Lady*.   (Adapted from McCabe, 1998)

2.2 Good argument structure: what does it mean and how do you achieve it?

Good argument structure is the key to effective academic writing. If your ideas are well organised, they'll not only be easier to understand but also more effective at luring the reader into a more sympathetic response to them. As the reader buys into each building block of your argument, they'll become more persuaded by it, provided those building blocks are placed correctly in relation to one another. In order to understand more precisely what that means, we need to look at the notion of **coherence**.

Coherence and the logical flow of your reasoning

Coherence refers to the way in which your ideas connect together; the way in which one idea leads into that which follows it, which in turn leads into the next idea, and so on. In a well-written essay or article, these connections are so smooth and obvious that the reader can often anticipate the next building block of the argument even before s/he has begun reading it. The following diagram illustrates in simple terms how a coherent piece of writing 'works':

Imagine each idea as an individual pearl on a pearl necklace; if you take away one of the pearls or replace it with a stone, the circle is broken and the continuity lost. It is no longer a thing of beauty; it has lost its unity, its perfection. Coherence, then, refers to the unity that characterises a well-structured piece of writing.

Coherence, of course, does not happen automatically; like a pearl necklace it too requires the artifice of a skilled hand – and, crucially, careful planning. We shall look in detail at how to plan your writing in section 4.3.

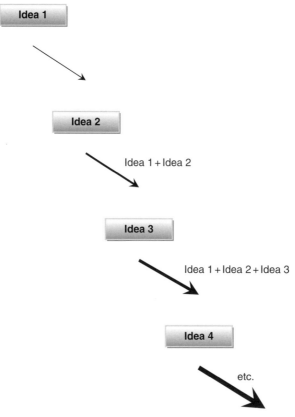

Figure 2.1

2.3 Explaining everything and avoiding assumptions

As you're writing your essay, continually ask yourself the question, 'Would this be absolutely clear to somebody who didn't have access to my mind?' Often, as we write and become increasingly involved in our ideas and eager to get them onto paper, we forget to consider our reader and how accessible our written translation of those ideas is to him or her. The problem is that, as we write our own ideas or read what we've written, we automatically 'fill in' information gaps because we know what we wish to say; we already understand the ideas we're attempting to express. Unfortunately, our reader does not have the benefit of such a vantage point and the onus is therefore on us to ensure that we provide them with all the necessary information in a clear and systematic way; that way they are not left struggling to see the links between our ideas and the rationale underlying them. A good rule of thumb is to put yourself in your reader's shoes: assume very little and explain everything in full, even if at times this feels rather unnecessary and laboured. And, of course, you can always bounce your work off a friend to see if he or she is able to follow your thinking.

The importance of explaining everything in detail lies not only in ensuring that your reader is able to follow your logic or argument structure but also in reassuring them that you understand the concepts you're discussing. After all, your reader is most likely going to be your lecturer and/or examiner!

So, in summary, the importance of providing adequate detail and thorough explanations in your writing lies in:

- helping your reader to follow your train of thought (good planning also plays a key role here, as we've seen)
- enabling them to ascertain how well you understand the concepts you're discussing

2.4 Supporting your statements: evidence, what it is, why it's essential, and how you provide it

One thing you will quickly learn at university is that your lecturers will not take your ideas seriously if those ideas are presented simply as statements of fact without any rationale to back them up. We saw, in section 1.6, how statements made in the absence of supporting evidence amount to little more than opinion, and as such they carry little or no weight. Evidence is a crucial element of mature university writing and it's important, therefore, to consider ways in which you can present your ideas such that they carry conviction and, put simply, convince the reader of their soundness. Each time you back up your claims with sound evidence your work acquires a little more credibility, so that by the time the reader approaches the final paragraphs or pages they will be more readily inclined to be sympathetic to what they read and will have more faith in the integrity of what you've written. That faith will never be unquestioning, but it will be much more readily forthcoming if you've built up a 'track record' throughout the assignment or research project and/or through previous work. Eventually, of course, lecturers get to know those students who produce rigorous, well-constructed, well-supported arguments, and they come to expect it of them!

So, what are some of the forms that evidence can take? Here's a brief overview of different types of evidence (often used in combination) that writers typically employ in their writing in an effort to inject it with rigour and credibility.

Citing statistics

This is one of the simplest ways of providing support for statements; however, there are three important caveats. Firstly, not all types of statement lend themselves to the support of this kind of evidence, and even if they did it would not be stylistically desirable to repeatedly draw on the same type of evidence. Secondly, if you do decide to draw on statistical evidence, you need to be sure that the statistics and the methodology through which they were obtained are sound. It would not be sensible to cite statistics that are known to be questionable or which are self-evidently of dubious validity. Finally, be sure that any statistics you cite do actually serve to support the point you're making. It's surprisingly common for students to take statistics from their original context and apply them inappropriately in a new context. This often occurs as a result of their misunderstanding the nature of the statistics and/or the project that generated them.

 Always make certain that the statistics you are quoting translate to your own context and support the claims *you* are making.

 Today, the IELTS remains the default gate-keeper for British, Australian, and other universities looking to assess the English language skills of their applicants, and its role as such would appear, on the face of it, to be more important than ever given that NESB student numbers continue to grow: Davies cited a figure of 300,000 overseas students studying in the United Kingdom in 2003–04 (Davies, 2008, p. 2), while in Australia the figure for 2006 was 250,000 (Bradley et al., 2008).   (From Murray, 2010)

Data from empirical studies

Much of what applies to statistics in particular also applies to data in general and the empirical studies that generate it. Such data might extend to audio-video recordings, transcriptions or historical documents, for example, and once again their provenance needs to be carefully scrutinised before you draw on them in your own writing.

In discussing English language learners' avoidance behaviour in respect of relative clauses, Liao and Fukuya cite empirical research in the following extract:

 When comparing the errors in relative clauses made by native speakers of Chinese, Japanese, Persian, and Arabian learners in their English compositions, Schachter (1974) found that the difficulty of relative clauses for Chinese and Japanese students, which was predicted by contrastive analysis, manifested itself not in the number of errors made by these two groups of learners, but in the number of relative clauses produced, which was much smaller than that produced by the Persian and Arabian speakers. She concluded that 'if a student finds a particular construction in the target language difficult to comprehend it is very likely that he will try to avoid producing it' (p. 213) ... To pinpoint avoidance behavior more accurately, Kleinmann (1977, 1978) examined four English grammatical structures (passive, present progressive, infinitive complement, and direct object pronoun) produced by two groups of intermediate-level learners of English as an L2: native speakers of Arabic and native speakers of Spanish and Portuguese. Before looking at any potential avoidance, Kleinmann administered comprehension tests to establish the presence of the learners' knowledge of the four structures in question. His results showed an avoidance pattern in accordance with difficulty predictions made by contrastive analysis.   (Adapted from Liao and Fukuya, 2004)

Here's one more example, in which Baldauf and White discuss staffing levels in university language programmes and, in doing so, cite empirical research:

The quality and availability of language program depends on their staffing. In White and Baldauf (1997), staffing levels were reported to have fallen, making it more difficult to teach language programs. The issue was again investigated in the 2001–2005 survey. Table 4.10 presents full-time equivalent (FTE) staff losses by language; Table 4.11 presents staff additions; and table 4.12 presents net losses and gains of staff positions.

In some respects, the changes reflect the kind of natural variation found in university employment, as well as the changes in the patterns of offerings (the loss of a position in Vietnamese and the gain of one in Turkish; the need to staff new programs in Spanish). However, the gains come predominantly in Italian, for which language the Cassamarca Foundation had recently been funding a number of ongoing lectureships. When this unusual activity is taken into consideration, it becomes clear that there has been some erosion of staffing – beyond Indonesian where there has been a drop in programs and student numbers. This seems to have come at the expense of the major languages (German -9.8, French -4.65, Mandarin -4.5, and Japanese -2.18), perhaps because this is where there is full-time staffing in the languages area.
(From Baldauf and White, 2010)

Quoting published works/authorities in the field

This is perhaps the most common way for undergraduate students to support their claims. Often, they'll read the work of a particular scholar, borrow their idea, and then (quite rightly) cite them in their writing. Conversely, the student may come up with an idea of their own, conduct research around it via a review of the literature, and then cite any authorities they identify whose writing lends support to that idea in some way or other.

 Remember for someone else's writing to provide evidence for your own ideas, it doesn't necessarily have to be concerned precisely with the issue that is the focus of your attention. Sometimes, evidence can be sourced from other, different contexts where similar principles may be at work. Often, more able students are able to 'cross-fertilise' in this way and the ability to do so can lead to more colourful, creative and interesting writing.

Gerunds are traditionally seen as nominalizations, meaning that while their internal syntax may be clausal, their external syntax is that of a noun phrase (Jespersen 1940; Lees 1966; Ross 1973; Declerck 1991; Heyvaert 2003; Hudson 2007: Ch. 4). (From De Smet, 2010)

Unlearning – moving from a superset grammar to a subset grammar – is particularly difficult because it cannot proceed on the basis of positive evidence alone: As discussed earlier, the input alone cannot tell learners that English definite plurals lack generic readings (see Schwartz and Sprouse, 1994, 1996; Slabakova, 2006; Wexler and Manzini, 1987). (Adapted from Ionin and Montrul, 2010)

As for acquisition of generic reference by early bilinguals, there is evidence of crosslinguistic transfer from English to Italian, whereas the results concerning transfer from Italian to English are inconclusive (Serratrice, Sorace, Filiaci and Baldo, 2009). (From Ionin and Montrul, 2010)

Dunbar (1996), for example, argues that language evolved as a device to build and maintain coalitions in increasingly larger groups. (Adapted from Weiten, 2010)

Providing examples

Often, providing concrete examples can add substance to what you say and in doing so give it added credibility. If the examples are relevant, poignant and illustrate your point convincingly, they can function as an important source of evidence. Be careful though: often it can be equally easy to provide counter-examples and this can lead to accusations of you having been selective (or biased) in your selection of examples. Such accusations are frequently made against scholars who have selected particular data or statistics, decontextualised them in the way described above and only presented those parts of the data which help support their own position. This kind of practice can severely undermine your work.

 One feature of Estuary English, the use of a glottal stop fort (Fabricus, 2002), is also not unique to that variety but is spreading widely, for example to Newcastle, Cardiff and Glasgow, and even as far North as rural Aberdeenshire in Northeast Scotland (Marshall, 2003). (From Wardhaugh, 2010)

Rational exposition

Rational exposition essentially means convincing your reader of what you're saying through rational argument; that is through meticulous analysis and sound logic. In other words, you attempt to bring them around to your viewpoint through developing a good, watertight argument structure in which each idea follows logically from that which precedes it: Given A, then B must be true; if B is true, then C must in turn be true; and D logically follows from A, B and C; and so on. Of course, for rationale exposition to be effective, not only do you need to be sure that each premise is true, but also that the logical relationships binding them together are absolutely secure. Now look at this example taken from a text which discusses the types of English language provision needed for university students:

 Although there is an argument for saying that proficiency is part of academic literacy and should therefore be developed within that framework, there is also a rationale for distinguishing the two: Even if their language exhibits dialectal forms not in sync with academic and professional standards and expectations, ESB students are, by definition, fully proficient, yet they share a need with NESB students for academic literacy tuition, as we have seen. This fact implies a different if related set of abilities underlying proficiency and academic literacy.

(From Murray, 2010)

I have argued that academic literacy and professional communication skills are best developed in all students as an integral part of the curriculum, where disciplinary idiosyncrasies can be more effectively addressed and learning takes on greater immediacy, relevance, and authenticity for students. Although some students will enter their degree programmes having developed some knowledge of the literacies they will need, courtesy of their secondary school education, levels of such knowledge tend to be highly variable, and many international students will bring with them practices from educational cultures not in tune with the expectations of the Western academic tradition. Embedding academic literacy in the curriculum assumes, therefore, that (a) all newly enrolled students come with little or no prior knowledge and thus commence their studies on roughly equal terms in this regard, and (b) the teaching of academic literacy should therefore be a normal part of academics' teaching responsibilities. Given that all newly enrolled students will need to develop the academic literacies of their disciplines and that such development can happen most effectively when those literacies are strategically embedded in the curriculum at points where they are most relevant, there would appear to be little justification for implementing a PLA designed to test students' abilities in these areas. The same is true of professional communication skills, which should be learned as a fundamental part of becoming conversant in the discipline and as crucial to students' ability to negotiate the particular demands of their academic studies and future careers. As such they would appear to be most usefully taught as a core component of students' undergraduate programmes rather than included as a focus of post-enrolment testing.

Given that there is little reason to formally assess students' academic literacy and professional communication skills, it would appear that English language proficiency is the only sensible focus of PLA, and this raises the question of how such proficiency-focused assessment might be implemented.

(From Murray, 2010)

23

Visual material

Although, generally speaking, it's rare for students of English language and linguistics to draw on this kind of evidence in their writing, one might nevertheless imagine a scenario where, for example, photographic evidence or drawings are used to illustrate a claim that speakers of a given language background tend to articulate a particular phoneme in a certain way, and that by modifying that articulation those speakers can be made to better approximate to a native speaker's pronunciation of that sound. In the example below, the writer provides an illustration which shows those areas of the brain affected by Broca's or Wernicke's aphasia and which are responsible for language.

 Disorders such as aphasia have been helpful in helping researchers understand language acquisition. Aphasia affects those parts of the brain, highlighted in the figure, responsible for language function. It usually occurs suddenly, often as the result of a stroke or head injury, and impairs the expression and understanding of language, as well as reading and writing. Although most people who suffer from aphasia are middle-age or older, it can also affect young children and this is where it can be helpful to language acquisition research. In particular, researchers have been interested in establishing whether and to what extent children who suffer the effects of aphasia pre-puberty are able to recover language function to some degree.

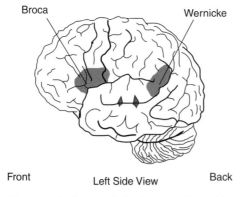

Figure 2.2 Areas of the brain affected by Broca's and Wernicke's Aphasia

Anecdote/personal experience

This type of evidence, while potentially useful and often engaging, needs to be treated with caution. The problem with anecdotal evidence is that, while it may tell the reader something about a particular instance, it's not possible to go on and generalise from that instance. In other words, just because something happened to you, or you experienced something in a certain way, does not mean it happened to someone else, or that they experienced it in the same way. In other words, avoid making overly ambitious claims on the basis of personal experience. Having said that, anecdotes can be one way of helping describe or define a particular situation and of locating a problem within that situation. For example, you may have noticed that many teachers in Japan feel uncomfortable in their English-language classrooms adopting – and having their students adopt – behaviours associated with a communicative approach to language teaching that are out of sync with their Confucian educational traditions but recognised as consistent with good current classroom practice. This unease or tension might motivate you to conduct a small research study of Japanese teachers' attitudes, and as such it would deserve mention, possibly in the introduction to your study. So, my message is that anecdote and personal experience can often be helpful in contextualising a study or discussion, but they should always be used sparingly and treated with caution.

 It is certainly the case that language teaching methodologies have been exported – some would say imposed – around the world on the basis of notions of 'good practice' originating in so-called 'inner circle' countries and often regardless of their cultural fit. This is no more true than in the case of Communicative Language Teaching (CLT), and in particular its introduction into so-called 'Confucian-heritage' countries such as Japan, China and South Korea, where they have since been endorsed by education ministries. Unfortunately, some of the basic principles informing CLT are at odds with Confucian beliefs that guide the behaviours and expectations of educators and students in these (and other) countries. In my early days of teaching on the JET programme in Japan, I personally experienced the all too tangible sense of unease with which teachers adopted CLT principles in their classrooms and the discomfort – even embarrassment – with which students responded to them. Upon reflection, it was an unease that stemmed from knowing that the classroom behaviours these principles engender were out of kilter with what were considered normal and appropriate behaviours both in the educational context as well as the broader cultural context. This dissonance can be such that taboos are broken and it is no surprise, therefore, that educators in these countries are often ambivalent about newly imported methodologies such as CLT.

A good writer of academic texts, then, will 'substantiate' their statements by citing one or more of these types of evidence. But why should they bother? Often we may feel so confident of our ideas and so convinced of the validity of our opinions that it hardly seems necessary to go to the trouble of citing evidence. Once again the answer to this question lies in the principle of assuming nothing; after all, ideas only seem redundant because we assume our reader already knows and believes them. However, once we take the stance that, in fact, everything needs to be explained, the importance of evidence becomes clearer. The fact is that, certainly within an academic context, ideas carry almost no weight at all unless they are backed up by sound evidence. Just saying something is so, doesn't make it so, so why should anyone believe you? Indeed academic integrity in Western educational culture is largely founded on the principle that one should be sceptical of all ideas until they have been shown to be true, and that truth emerges as a result of a questioning process – sometimes referred to as the *Socratic Method*. So, as a writer of an academic text, you must think of yourself as having an ongoing dialogue with your reader and imagine the kinds of questions they might be asking you about what you're writing, with you responding accordingly. Eventually, through sound argument, clearly expressed and reinforced with good evidence, they should feel satisfied and content to go along with what you're proposing.

 As you are writing, imagine you're having a dialogue with a very sceptical reader. Try to pre-empt any possible criticisms by covering every base. This will help keep your work disciplined, watertight and impervious to criticism.

2.5 Being concise and relevant ... and avoiding waffle

Two other golden rules of academic writing are 'Be concise' and 'Be relevant'.

What is concision (being concise)?

Being concise means keeping your writing brief and to the point; in other words, being economical in your use of language and saying only what needs to be said and no more. And beware: this is not a licence to reduce your workload by reducing your ideas or discussion and cutting things down to the bare minimum! Being concise does *not* mean being minimalistic; it means making every word count and being very precise in your thinking and in your use of language such that you are able to say in five eloquent, well-considered and well-constructed sentences what might otherwise take ten sentences.

Remember, few things will irritate your lecturers and examiners more than writing which is full of hot air, has very little substance and says almost nothing. There are no Brownie points for complex, beautifully structured sentences if these are at the expense of substance. In fact, even if your writing has substance, it will not be well received if it is unnecessarily complex. Today, good writing in the academic world – and increasingly in other walks of life – is writing that is crisp, to the point, accessible and without any 'padding'.

What is relevance?

Being relevant means staying on topic, keeping your discussion focused, and not going off on a tangent and introducing ideas that don't key into the aims of your assignment or research project. Particularly when you are discussing complex issues in depth, it's surprisingly easy to get distracted and 'wander' away from your main focus. So, be disciplined and check regularly that you're keeping on track and that your train of thought is transparent and easy to follow.

One way of ensuring that your writing is concise and relevant is to consider the reasons people fail to keep their writing brief and to the point. Here are some of the usual suspects:

- Not having a clear idea in their own minds about what it is they want to say. This is probably because they haven't clarified concepts and clearly articulated to themselves their own beliefs and arguments. You can be absolutely certain that if an idea is not clear in your own head, then it won't be clear on paper either, with the result that your reader will be trying to second guess your thinking (if indeed they bother at all) and, in all likelihood, will give up in frustration. Obviously, that's not the reaction you want when you're striving for a good grade!
- Not planning their writing carefully enough and taking sufficient time to consider how the various ideas they wish to articulate relate to one another and can therefore be presented most logically and coherently. Section 4.3 covers planning in detail, so you'll want to check out that section at some point before you begin writing in earnest.
- Not planning in enough detail.
- Not following their plan carefully enough.

If you can avoid these pitfalls, you'll have gone a long way to ensuring that your writing is on track and doesn't meander all over the place. The payoff will be a reader who is more stimulated and engaged by what you have to say and much less likely to feel frustrated or to fall asleep!

 Consider running your work by a friend or colleague to see if they understand it easily or whether they struggle to follow it and get at your meaning. A good rule of thumb is that regardless of whether or not they have specialist knowledge of language and linguistics, they ought to be able to read your work with ease and at least make educated guesses at the meaning of what you've written. In other words, good writing is identifiable to a reader regardless of their unfamiliarity with the particular subject matter.

Finally, when you review your work before submitting it, try to identify sentences or sections of text where you could be a little more succinct and rework these where possible.

2.6 Punctuation, how important is it … really?

The answer to the above question is *very* important, and for a number of reasons. First of all, written work (and indeed its author) will normally be judged partly on how well their writing is punctuated. A poorly punctuated assignment or research project will often be marked down simply *because* it's poorly punctuated. Furthermore, rightly or wrongly, the ability to punctuate well (or not) is seen as a reflection of the education or erudition of the writer. This latter point is important when you consider that it may influence the way in which your reader evaluates your work and the ideas it contains, regardless of how sound they may actually be in themselves.

But there are also more fundamental reasons why punctuation is important. Most crucially, punctuation helps to make your writing more comprehensible to your reader by dividing it up into manageable chunks and showing the relationships that exist between clauses, sentences and even paragraphs and sections. A sentence, for example, without any punctuation is very difficult to decipher and the process of trying to understand it can be a tiresome and irritating one. Reading a poorly punctuated essay is not an experience lecturers and examiners enjoy, so it's in your own best interests to punctuate well and keep your reader in a good and sympathetic mood!

Punctuation also indicates whether the ideas and/or words you are using to express them are your own or those of somebody else; it can even convey a writer's attitude or feeling – just think of how exclamation marks are used.

This section on punctuation is not designed to be comprehensive; it could not possibly be so when you think that there are books on punctuation that run into hundreds of pages. What I seek to do below is provide you with a few fundamental punctuation rules, – or guidelines – a number of which are the subject of numerous mistakes in undergraduates' work. Examples are presented to illustrate each rule and, most importantly, to give you a sense of how that particular punctuation type 'works'. So let's begin with …

Capital letters

Rule no. 1: *Use a capital letter at the beginning of a new sentence:*

> *The words we know form part of our internalised grammars.*

> *Every language has word classes. They are a universal feature of languages.*

Rule no. 2: *Use capital letters for proper nouns or adjectives (e.g. people, places, book titles, theories, organisations, institutions):*

> *Many Asian languages, such as Thai, Chinese and Burmese, are tone languages.*

> *The syntactic structures of Black English were investigated by William Labov.*

Chomsky's 1959 Review of Verbal Behaviour by B. F. Skinner *heralded a revolution in approaches to language and linguistics.*

Klein's Introduction to Language and Linguistics *is an invaluable resource for students new to the field.*

(Note how 'Language' and 'Linguistics' are both capitalised here because they are part of the actual name of a book, whereas in the previous example they are simply used in a generic way to refer to language and linguistics in general.)

Samuel Johnson is celebrated as the author of the first English dictionary.

Quirk and Greenbaum's Grammar of Contemporary English *is often cited as the definitive reference work on English grammar.*

The work of the Council of Europe was an important influence in promoting a communicative approach to the teaching of languages.

Important research into language testing has been conducted at the University of Lancaster.

Rule no. 3: *Use capital letters at the beginning of main words (sometimes called 'content words') in titles:*

Principles of Pragmatics

A First Dictionary of Linguistics and Phonetics

Syntax: A Linguistic Introduction to Sentence Structure

Rule no. 4: *Use capital letters for titles and the abbreviated forms of proper names:*

Dr Remick Professor Stupor Associate Editor the U.S. TESOL Sir William Jones

Commas

Rule no. 1: *Use commas to separate items in a list. Before the last item in a list a comma is unnecessary:*

Nouns, verbs, adjectives, adverbs and prepositions are often referred to as 'parts of speech'.

Whereas English developed out of Anglo-Saxon, the Romance languages, such as French, Spanish, Italian, Portuguese and Romanian, had their origin in Latin.

Sapir stated that 'Language is a purely human and non-instinctive method of communicating ideas, emotions and desires by means of voluntarily produced symbols.'

> *Some of the methods and approaches to language teaching that have appeared in recent years include Suggestopedia, Communicative Language Teaching, the Natural Approach, the Silent Way and Audiolingualism.*

Rule no. 2: *Use commas to separate introductory phrases from the sentences they introduce:*

> *Despite considerable research having been done in the area, second language acquisition has to date had little impact on pedagogy.*

> *Having discussed the various theories that appear in the literature, McKay states categorically that Accommodation Theory offers 'the best account of any theory currently on offer'.*

> *Although an utterance may not appear to be relevant superficially, we assume nonetheless that it is relevant at a deeper level.*

> *After discussing Speech Act Theory, Harris goes on to consider the work of Grice, Lakoff, Leech and Sperber and Wilson.*

> *Besides formal correctness, it has been argued that appropriateness and attestedness are necessary facets of language use if one is to claim full communicative competence.*

> *Because of the brain's 'plasticity', pre-pubescent children who suffer brain damage are often able to re-learn their first language to some degree.*

> *Given that we all learn a first language, each one of us must come hard-wired with a language acquisition device that enables us to acquire language according to the input we receive from those around us.*

> *In general, bilingual children fall behind in their studies initially, only to catch up and overtake their peers later on.*

Note that in all the above examples, where a comma appears after the introductory word or group of words, it would be natural to pause slightly if one were speaking the sentences. This is one way useful way of identifying when a comma is required.

Rule no. 3: *Use commas after connecting words and phrases which show a clear relationship between two clauses or sentences.*
Such connecting words include:

however, . . .	*nevertheless, . . .*	*therefore, . . .*	*for this reason, . . .*
consequently, . . .	*as a result, . . .*	*similarly, . . .*	*conversely, . . .*
additionally, . . .	*hence, . . .*	*thus, . . .*	*on the contrary, . . .*
similarly, . . .	*moreover, . . .*	*furthermore, . . .*	*for example, . . .*

The theory, then, was fundamentally flawed; however, it did serve to open up new and productive avenues of inquiry.

It is, nevertheless, difficult to conclude from this that certain ethnic groups are inherently better language learners than others.

We express our personality and individuality in our language behaviour via the social categories that are encoded in language variation in the community of which we are members.

Furthermore, the social meaning that is assigned to the variables of accent and dialect is largely determined by so-called stereotypes.

For Wilkins, the term 'notion' incorporates functions. Conversely, Halliday uses the term 'function' to refer to the formal encoding of meaning within a grammar.

Rule no. 4: *Use commas after words and phrases such as* clearly, obviously, sadly, unfortunately, without a doubt, *which say something about your attitude or feeling:*

Unfortunately, Freedman fails to explain adequately how he draws the conclusions he does from his data.

Chomsky has, without a doubt, had a greater impact on linguistics in the last fifty years than anyone else.

Obviously, this research is in need of replication.

Rule no. 5: *Use commas after first(ly), second(ly), third(ly), finally, etc.*

Secondly, the fact that a sound is marked does not automatically render it less important for intelligibility.

Finally, there is the argument which states that grammar cannot be acquired through an explicit focus on form.

Rule no. 6: *Use commas to separate and distinguish additional or incidental information inserted into a sentence:*

Affixes, the subject of section three, are a good example of this tendency in language.

Behaviourism, which was to become part of the theoretical basis of Audiolingual methodology, was most closely associated with Skinner.

It was, needless to say, this coincidence of events within different and very diverse disciplines that led to a shift of paradigm.

Malinowski, an anthropologist of the early twentieth century, coined the phrase 'context of situation' and raised awareness of the importance of context to meaning.

31

Semi-colons

Rule no. 1: *Use semi-colons to indicate pauses longer than those associated with commas but shorter than those associated with full-stops:*

One might speculate that it is because the learner draws variably on his interim competence according to the situational demands made upon it; that his interlanguage contains variable rules as well as invariant categorical ones and in this respect resembles fully fledged languages.

Functionalism in language teaching was taken by many to mean the complete exclusion of any focus on form in the classroom; grammar and the explicit teaching of rules simply had no place.

Language never fossilizes; it constantly changes and adapts in response to the purposes for which its users choose to employ it.

In each of the above examples, you'll notice that there's a very close connection between the idea that appears before the semi-colon and the one that appears after it. The idea following the semi-colon appears to expand on or explain the idea preceding it, and so the semi-colon effectively indicates the closeness of that relationship. Although it's *always* possible to substitute a semicolon with a full-stop, in doing so you lose the opportunity to make that relationship more explicit to the reader.

 One of the easiest ways to think *about* a semi-colon is as something which performs a function that is midway between that of a comma and that of a full-stop.

Rule no. 2: *Use semi-colons immediately before linking words such as however, moreover, furthermore, nevertheless, therefore and instead:*

Scholars of slang generally acknowledge it as an illustration of creativity and vibrancy in language; nevertheless, there are those who still consider it to be a decadent, impoverished form of language.

Native speakers of certain languages other than English are simply unable to hear particular sound distinctions in English; for example, /b/ and /v/ are indistinguishable to many Japanese.

It appears, then, that all children learn a first language unless they suffer some kind of physiological impairment; furthermore, the research suggests that in doing so they all follow an invariable developmental sequence – a natural order of acquisition.

Rule no. 3: *Use semi-colons to separate items in a list, where the list of items is long and/or each item in the list is too long to be separated by a comma:*

People have to be taught to observe, whether it be the doctor learning to observe and 'read' the human body; the artist learning to observe and 'read' great paintings; or the geologist or geomorphologist learning to observe and 'read' the landscape. The language-learning student is no different; they have to learn to observe and 'read' the way in which a particular grammar 'works'.

Compare the above list with that under Rule no. 1 (Commas), where shorter items in a list are normally separated by commas.

Colons

Rule no. 1: *Use colons to introduce explanations or examples:*

Linguistic repetition is a feature of a structural orientation to teaching with its emphasis on knowing: learners are required to practise particular structures so as to facilitate unconscious assimilation.

How to Write Better Assignments: A Student Handbook (a book title)
Reference, Sense and Denotation: An Analysis of Descriptive Meaning (an essay title)

The distinction between a formal and a notional approach can be illustrated by considering the following data from the African language Akan, from central and southern Ghana:

1a	*Kofi ware*	*Kofi is tall*
1b	*Kofi reware*	*Kofi is getting tall*
1c	*Kofi aware*	*Kofi has grown tall*

The essay will look at a number of different learner factors including:

- *age*
- *motivation*
- *aptitude*
- *preferred learning style*
- *previous language learning experience*

The term 'propositional structure' relates to:

(1) the type of 'state' or 'action' described by the sentence;
(2) the 'participant roles' involved in the state or action.

Other phrases that are often followed by a colon include *'for example: …'*, *'Consider this example: …'* and *'There are one/two/three such cases: …'*.

Notice how the statement of each 'rule' in this section on punctuation includes a colon which precedes a series of examples designed to illustrate that rule!

Rule no. 2: *Use colons to introduce quotations:*

> *He acknowledges that his tasks are factual and rational in meaning-content and that they require no procedures for increasing emotional involvement, but adds: 'This does not imply any denial of value to emotional involvement in learning.'*

> *In this regard, Brown argues that:*

>> *For complex social and psychological reasons, they are less sure that they have grasped the topic being spoken of, the opinion being expressed about it, and the reasons for the speaker wanting to talk about it.*

Notice how, in the second of these two examples, the quotation is indented slightly and separated from the main text by a single line. This is because it is a longer quotation – something we shall return to in Chapter 8, *Referencing and Quotations.*

 In order to understand how colons function it can be helpful to think of them as a substitute for language and to ask yourself how one might express their function or meaning in words. With this is mind, we can say that a colon means something like '... and here it is', 'Here we are', 'thus ...' or 'as follows ...'

Parentheses

Rule no. 1: *Use parentheses when citing references in your text:*

> *This phenomenon has been described as 'a normal facet of language development and thus one to which all languages are susceptible, irrespective of whether or not it is perceived as desirable or acceptable' (Franklin 2007, p. 67).*

> *In this regard the 'Track-it' concordancing website* (http://www.track-itconcordancer.com) *has been a particular boon for researchers and teachers alike.*

Rule no. 2: *Use parentheses to identify and enclose information which is relevant to, but additional and slightly peripheral to, the main idea of a sentence.*

> *Searle develops this idea during his discussion of the 'speech act' (a concept originating in the work of philosopher John Austin), and it has since been further refined.*

Rule no. 3: *Use square brackets to enclose information which is not part of the original quotation:*

> *Havelock states that 'it [Murdoch's account] ignores many factors necessary in a detailed description of communication by language'.*

According to the subject's diary, she 'studied English every weekday except Wensdays [sic] for five years'.

(Use the word 'sic' after a word that you have copied to signal that you know it has been spelled, punctuated or used incorrectly and that it is not your mistake!)

Inverted commas (quotation marks)

The use of double or single quotation marks is really a matter of convention rather than rule. In some cases double inverted commas are used as the first level of quotation mark and single inverted commas as the second level (i.e. a quotation within a quotation); in other cases the opposite is true. Given that most linguistics writing uses APA style (see section 8.4), that is what you will see in the examples below.

Double inverted commas
Use double inverted commas to indicate a direct quotation:

According to Cutting, the individualism of pragmatics "underestimates the extent to which people are caught up in, constrained by, and indeed derive their individual identities from social conventions" (2002, p. 120).

In her criticism of Leech's approach to politeness, Thomas argues that there seems to be no motivated way to restrict the number of maxims and that it would be possible to create a new maxim to account for every single regularity in language use. This, she says, "makes the theory at best inelegant, at worst virtually unfalsifiable" (1998, p. 167).

As we shall see in Chapter 8, longer quotations are often inset slightly and follow a free line. These longer quotations do not require inverted commas, despite also being direct quotations.

Single inverted commas
Rule no. 1: *Use single inverted commas to identify a quotation within a larger quotation:*

In discussing the notion of signification, and in particular the distinction between signs and symbols, Lyons states that

> *... there is no consistency in the way in which various authors have defined these terms. For example, Ogden and Richards (1923: 23) distinguish symbols as 'those signs which men use to communicate with one another', whereas Pierce (1940: 104), who also treats symbols as a subclass of sign, defines them '... on the basis of the conventional nature of the relation which holds between sign and significatum'.*

> *(Lyons 1989, p. 95)*

35

Drew states that "there is a limited and quite small number of written genres, and, in the words of Kress, 'the individual can no more create a new genre type than he or she can create a new sentence type'" (Drew 1990, p. 77).

Rule no. 2: *Use single quotation marks when you wish to identify or focus attention on a particular word or phrase:*

Contrary to the view expressed by Cowper, the terms 'variability', 'variation', and even 'variety' have always held certain negative connotations.

Some have used the word 'impoverished' to describe the language learners produce in communicative classrooms that are student-centred.

'Hahesh mi konam' is generally considered to be the Persian equivalent of 'You're welcome' in English.

Rule no. 3: *Use single quotation marks to indicate that a word with an otherwise generally understood meaning, has a more specialised meaning in the particular context in which you are using it.*

In applied linguistics, and second language acquisition (SLA) theory in particular, 'acquired' takes on a particular meaning and is used to describe knowledge of language that has been internalised through a natural process of exposure. It contrasts with learned knowledge, which results from a conscious focus on form.

Rule no. 4: *Use single quotation marks when you wish to indicate that a word or phrase has been misused or applied inaccurately or inappropriately:*

The 'theory' Krashen proposed, in the form of the Monitor Model, was critically undermined in an article by Gregg (1984) in which he argued that because it was not falsifiable, contained ill-defined terms and unmotivated constructs, and lacked explanatory power, it could not properly be termed a theory.

 Single inverted commas are sometimes used to indicate a direct quotation – indeed, single inverted commas are becoming more commonly used in this role than double inverted commas. Ultimately, however, what is most important is that you use the two consistently.

Note: rules 2, 3 and 4 are unlikely to apply in books that use single quotes as their first level of quotation mark.

Hyphens

Rule no. 1: *Use hyphens in compound words (word units of more than one word)*

Compound words can be categorised according to these types:

numerical: seventy-eight, twenty-three thousand, one-fifth, two-thirds *adjectival:* hypo-allergenic, south-east, non-profit, post-natal, high-impact, quasi-legitimate, run-down, up-market, bi-monthly

nominal: bell-curve, super-conductor, well-being, mass-market, by-election, President-Elect

> *Particular subjects on the curriculum can be seen as different sub-cultures in which reality is variously reformulated.* (nominal)

> *The writing of seventy-five second-language students from five first-language backgrounds was monitored and all instances of article use recorded.* (numerical/adjectival)

> *A discourse-based view of language prioritises an interactive approach to analysis of texts. It involves considering the higher-order operations of language at the interface of cultural and ideological meanings and returning to the lower-order forms of language which are often crucial to the patterning of such meanings.* (adjectival)

> *Prabhu's task-based learning prepares learners to engage in a particular kind of problem-solving activity via a 'pre-task'.* (adjectival/nominal)

> *Pragmatics is one area of inquiry that acknowledges the non-linguistic dimension of communication and its importance to meaning.* (adjectival)

It should be noted that compound adjectival and nominal phrases are also sometimes run together without a hyphen. Thus, in your reading you might encounter *postnatal, superconductor,* etc.

Rule no. 2: *Use hyphens after the prefixes* pre- *and* post-:

> *In the post-9/11 world, the kind of rhetoric adopted by governments to speak about terrorism and its sponsors changed dramatically.*

> *McFlannery is currently engaged in post-doctoral research on pidgins and creoles.*

> *Prior to conducting a series of interviews, with a view, ultimately, to analysing the language of child-abuse counsellors, the team were required to obtain pre-approval from the Human Research Ethics Committee.*

> *Before subjects were selected, they were pre-tested in order to determine whether or not they were suitable given the aims of the study.*

> For another example, look at example 3 of rule no. 1 above.

Rule no. 3: *Use a hyphen when you have to split a word across two lines:*

> *Like definitions generally, definitions of applied linguistics have sought not only to describe but are inevitably norma-tive, reflecting how the writer thinks the world ought to be.*

Dashes

Rule no. 1: *Use dashes to enclose information that is incidental or additional to the main idea of a clause or sentence:*

> *In normal circumstances of communication – where there is successful uptake – most language users do not analyse language in this way.*

> *Audio-lingual methods are based on an isolation of language structure – a declarative knowledge which teachers seek to convert into procedural knowledge by pattern practice and the use of drills.*

> *This is defined as background knowledge about the content area of a text – for example, a text about stocks and shares, oil drilling, or about interior design.*

> *Owing to the worldwide political, economic, scientific and cultural dominance of the English language – especially in its function as lingua franca – a tendency towards 'cultural universalism' and 'cultural neutralism' has been set into motion.*

> *Most attempts – and there have been many – to use insights from generative linguistics to inform the design of pedagogical materials, have not been particularly well received.*

 Notice how, in the second and third examples above, it is not necessary to 'close' the additional information with a second dash because this piece of information finishes the sentences (unlike in the first example).

Rule no. 2: *Use dashes as an alternative to the phrases 'for instance', 'for example', 'such as' or 'that is to say', when illustrating a point with specific examples:*

> *Cross-linguistic examples of this kind also exist which may suggest subtly different cultural perceptions: nuclear waste in English is uncountable; the near equivalents in Spanish – desechos radiactivos and residuos radiactivos – are both countable and plural.*

> *Franco speaks of meaning that is a product of the relationship between an expression and the cultural situation in which it is used – pragmatic meaning.*

> *Increasingly, a global vocabulary is emerging particularly, though not solely in the domain of technology – taxi, internet, googling, broadband, cable, mobile, air conditioning, iPod.*

Apostrophes

Rule no. 1: *Use apostrophes to indicate the omission of one or more letters:*

> *It's the spoken language which is fundamental in the sense that human beings normally learn to speak before they learn to read or write.*

(Here, the apostrophe substitutes for the missing 'i' in the word 'is'.)

She's been bilingual since she was eight years old.

(Here, the apostrophe replaces the 'ha' in 'has'.)

After just two years here, they've become fluent in the language.

(And here, the apostrophe replaces the 'ha' in 'have'.)

 Although there will be times when you need to use them (if you are transcribing, for example), you should know that, generally speaking, the use of shortened forms is discouraged in academic writing, as it is generally associated with more casual writing. So, instead of writing 'She's', for example, write the full form 'She is'.

Rule no. 2: *Use apostrophes to indicate ownership or possession:*

The islanders' language differed markedly from that of the nearest mainland community.

Juan's Spanish was more colloquial than his brother's.

The young boy's academic development was initially slowed down as a result of his acquiring three languages simultaneously; however, this quickly changed and he was soon outperforming his peers.

The two young boys' academic development was initially slowed down as a result of their acquiring three languages simultaneously; however, this quickly changed and they were soon outperforming their peers.

Junichiro, Kumiko and Fusako's two-year visit to London left them fluent in English.

In every case, the children's acquisition of past tense consistently followed clear developmental stages.

(Here, 'children' is an irregular plural and is therefore treated as if it were singular – hence the placing of the apostrophe before the 's'.)

 Notice how, in examples 3 and 4 above, the apostrophe is placed differently. In example 3 it's placed before the 's' in 'boys' because there's only one boy whose academic development is being talked about. In example 4, however, the academic development of more than one boy is being discussed; the apostrophe, therefore, should go after the 's'. This is also true of example one, where there is more than one islander. Notice too how, in the fifth example, there is more than one 'owner' or 'possessor' but each is mentioned independently. In this case, the apostrophe should be placed after the last owner mentioned.

TRY IT OUT! #4

In the two passages below, most of the punctuation has been removed. Read the passages carefully and insert any punctuation you feel is necessary.

Passage 1

linguistic scholars engage in a study of our ability to communicate and the means we employ to that end *for its own sake* the roots of this study are found in the basic philosophical quest into the nature of knowledge itself how do we know what we know how do we organise our experience how do we communicate with others this study is sufficient unto itself for most modern linguistic scholars the teacher of english deals with the more immediate task of applying the findings of the language scholars to the training of the young in more effective and more efficient use of their innate language gifts linguistic scholars are interested in the teacher's task as they are interested in all facts of language and its use but for the language scholars it does not loom so large in importance the teachers are by the same token interested in language study but only as one facet of their primary function which is to help students learn the linguistic scholars bear a relationship to teachers of english that is analogous to the relationship of the research scientist to the general practitioner of medicine one seeks information the other seeks to apply that information to the more efficient handling of specific problems

(From Herndon, 1976, p. 5)

Passage 2

the rationalist notes that on an abstract level all languages work in the same way they all have words and sentences and sound systems and grammatical relations and he attributes these universals of language to the structure of the brain just as birds inherit the ability to fly and fish to swim men inherit the ability to think and to use language in a manner which is unique to their species a given language english for example has to be learned but the capacity to learn languages is inherited the child is not a passive agent in language acquisition he actively goes about learning the language of his environment language use becomes almost automatic but what a person learns is more than a set of conditioned habits if you read all the books in the english language you will find very few sentences which are habitually used and are exact duplicates of each other otherwise you would suspect quotation or plagiarism knowledge of a language allows a person to understand infinitely many new sentences and to create grammatical sentences which no one else has ever pronounced but which will be understood immediately by others who know the language

(From Diller, 1978, p. 7)

Chapter 2 Key points checklist

- Begin a new paragraph whenever you introduce a new idea; that is, a new argument, a new point in a sequenced argument with logical steps or thought processes, a new stage in a process or procedure, a discrete element of a description, an alternative point of view, or a discussion or explanation of each point or item in a list.

- Good writing is coherent and demonstrates sound reasoning.

- Explain everything and assume very little. To test the clarity of your writing put yourself in your reader's shoes.

- Support any statements you make with evidence in the form of statistics, data from empirical studies, citations, examples, logical argument, visuals and, where appropriate, personal experience.

- Keep your writing concise and to-the-point.

- Be sure to proof-read for punctuation errors.

Part **2**

GETTING DOWN TO WRITING

Analysing and answering the question

'I'm not always sure exactly what the question means . . . you know, what they want and what I should be doing.'

What's covered in this chapter:
What do assignment questions mean?
Special features of linguistics questions
Different forms of writing . . . and the language you need for them
How to keep focused on the question
Summary: coverage, argumentation and evaluation

3.1 What do assignment questions mean?

There's no point in producing an assignment that's well organised, written in beautifully crafted sentences and demonstrates considerable research and understanding of concepts if what you write ultimately fails to answer the question set. Even with the best will in the world, your lecturer won't be able to pass it. In order to avoid this situation there are a number of simple precautions you can take. First and foremost, before you answer any question, take a little time to think about what the question really means and what it's asking you to do. All too often, students eager to begin an assignment and 'get it out of the way' take only one pass at the question; their first reading of it is what they go with and they tend to miss important words and nuances as a result. Understanding the key elements of assignment questions can help you to produce essays that are relevant and do not miss the point by giving you an analytical tool with which to drill down into the question and ensure your interpretation of it is correct.

1. Element 1: *The subject* – All assignment questions have a subject, which tells you the general area with which the question is concerned.
2. Element 2: *Limiting words* – These are words that indicate which aspect of the general subject area you need to focus on in particular, thereby 'limiting' the scope of your discussion.

3. Element 3: *Direction words* – These are words which tell you what to do within that area of focus. Listed below are some of the most widely used direction words, along with their meaning:

Direction word	Meaning
Analyse	Examine something in detail by breaking it down into its component parts and evaluating those parts and their inter-relationships. Describe, define and/or interpret each part.
Argue	Present the case for or against a particular idea or proposition.
Apply	Show how an abstract idea, concept, principle or model can work *in practice* by solving a problem or explaining a concrete situation.
Assess	Judge, evaluate, critique, determine the value of something.
Comment (on)	Explain, evaluate, critique, make statements about something, consider its implications.
Compare	Discuss one thing in relation to another, consider the similarities and differences between two or more things (situations, propositions, concepts, models, etc.).
Consider	Think about, analyse, offer views on.
Contrast	Discuss the differences between two or more things (situations, propositions, concepts, models, etc.).
Critique	Analyse and evaluate, demonstrating the strengths and weaknesses of an idea, position, etc.
Define	State precisely what is meant by a word or concept.
Demonstrate	Prove or explain an idea, position or phenomenon through argument, examples or experiment.
Describe	Identify main characteristics/features, aspects, qualities and components; provide a detailed account of something; clarify through illustration.
Differentiate	Demonstrate how two or more things are distinct from each other by highlighting their differences.
Discuss	Consider and interpret/evaluate; present, investigate/analyse and evaluate.
Enumerate	Give an item-by-item account of; describe and explain one by one.
Evaluate	Make an informed, well-reasoned judgement on the truth and utility of an argument or idea, a line of thought, a piece of research, a particular behaviour or action, etc.
Examine	Investigate something in detail, evaluate it and consider its implications and those of your analysis.
Explain	Clarify, provide reasons for why things are as they are; identify the factors responsible for a particular situation or outcome.
Explore	Inquire into/investigate a topic or line of thought.
Illustrate	Provide examples, diagrams or a rationale to show that/how something is the case.
Interpret	Show what you understand by; make the meaning and implications of something clear.
Investigate	Analyse, research into, search.

Direction word	Meaning
Justify	Provide a rationale for; provide evidence in support of certain ideas/decisions/interpretations/conclusions.
Outline	Give a brief overview and identify the main features of something.
Relate	Describe, narrate, show how things connect to or affect each other.
Review	Present the main facts about, analyse and critically appraise/evaluate.
State	Specify or explain clearly.
Summarise	Restate in more concise form the main points or ideas.
Trace	Show the evolution, development or history of something.

One thing you'll notice from the above table is that a number of the direction words listed share very similar meanings. Beware though: while in certain cases these words can be substituted for one another, in other cases their meanings may be subtly but significantly different.

Now look at the assignment questions below. For each one, the subject, limiting word(s) and direction word(s) have been identified for you.

1. Outline some of the key differences in men's and women's use of language. Consider the evidence in support of the idea that such differences are biologically based.
   Subject: the characteristics of men's language use and women's language use
   Limiting words: the differences between (men and women's use of language)
   Direction words: outline; consider
2. Using examples, explain the difference between lexical ambiguity and structural ambiguity.
   Subject: types of ambiguity
   Limiting words: differences between (lexical and structural ambiguity)
   Direction words: explain
3. Comment on three features said to distinguish human language from animal systems of communication.
   Subject: the features of different communication systems
   Limiting words: three features distinguishing (human language from animal communication)
   Direction words: comment on
4. Discuss the notion of discreteness with reference to (a) writing and (b) speech.
   Subject: discreteness
   Limiting words: with reference to writing and speech
   Direction word: discuss

TRY IT OUT! #5

Look at these four sample questions. Identify the subject, limiting word(s) and direction word(s) in each.

1. Using examples, explain the difference between a pidgin and a creole and discuss some of the factors that lead to the development of pidgins.
2. Describe what we can learn from the language of brain-damaged people about how language processing occurs.
3. Explain, with the help of examples, how we express politeness through the structure of what we say or write.
4. Discuss the role of motherese in child language acquisition.

3.2 Special features of linguistics questions

As a student of English language or linguistics, you may well be faced from time to time with assignment questions that are of a rather different form to those presented above as examples, and which may involve direction words not listed in the table on pages 46–7. For instance, many linguistics courses frequently feature assignment questions that require you to analyse and comment on language data of some kind. Look at these examples:

Look at the following set of ungrammatical questions and describe what they have in common structurally. Formulate and explain a rule adherence to which will avoid the production of such sentences. (Direction words: look at, describe, formulate, explain)

Below is a transcript of part of an English lesson in a British secondary school. Try to code the acts according to the Sinclair and Coulthard system and show how they combine into moves and exchanges. Describe any problems you encounter. (Direction words: code, show, describe)

(Adapted from Cook, 1989)

Examine the following extract. What can you say about the formation of past tense in Persian and explain how it differs from English? (Direction words: examine, what can you say about [i.e. comment on], explain)

Consider the following extract. Identify which maxims of co-operation and politeness are being flouted and describe its effect on the discourse. (Direction words: consider, identify, describe)

You are probably familiar with playground jingles like:

> *One fine day in the middle of the night*
> *Two dead men got up to fight,*
> *One blind man to see fair play,*
> *Two dumb men to shout 'Hooray.'*

Back to back they faced each other,
Drew their swords and shot each other.

Would you wish to consider such jingles as 'ungrammatical'? If so,
why? If not, how could you handle a linguistic description of the
obviously anomalous nature of such jingles?

(Adapted from Brown and Miller, 1991)

The following task from John Lyons' book *Language and Linguistics* is very typical of the kind of data analysis task typically presented to linguistics students, as Lyons himself observes. He uses a hypothetical language called Bongo-Bongo, which

was deliberately constructed in order to give students the opportunity
of working on a plausible hypothetical language, different from English
in many respects but similar to a variety of other natural languages in
one or other of its structural characteristics. The sentences are given in
a broad phonetic transcription. You should begin by phonemicizing the
data on the basis of phonetic similarity and complementary distribution.
Then see how much of the morphology and syntax you can work out,
paying particular attention to the categories of case, gender, number
and tense/aspect. (From Lyons, 1981)

Similarly, it's highly likely that your linguistics course will include at least some coverage of that approach to the study of syntax known as transformational-generative grammar. Indeed, most linguistics graduates smile wryly as they recall drawing phrase markers and tree diagrams in answer to questions such as:

The following sentences are ambiguous:

(i) John saw the man with a telescope
(ii) John saw the man in the park

Explain the ambiguity clearly and draw a phrase marker for each
interpretation (making it quite clear which interpretation is intended
to apply to which paraphrase). Your phrase marker should use a
notation which consistently distinguishes XP, X1 and X for every
phrasal category. (Adapted from Brown and Miller, 1991)

Using phrase structure rules, draw tree diagrams that break the following
sentences down into their constituent parts. Identify those sentences which
are structurally ambiguous. (Direction words: draw, identify)

One popular assignment task involves students performing specified operations on particular words or grammatical structures – often as a way of raising students' awareness of how grammar 'works', the rules that govern it and its regularity or irregularity.

49

Another form of assignment favoured by linguistics lecturers follows the 'review and discuss' formula. This is where you're given two or three published articles, each typically illustrating a particular perspective on an issue, and asked to compare, contrast and comment on them. We'll look more carefully at what's involved in comparing and contrasting in section 3.3, below; in the meantime, however, it's worth noting that reviewing and discussing a selection of articles comparatively can be quite challenging. Why? Because, before you can do anything, you need to understand each individual article pretty well. You then need to be able to identify where the articles overlap; in other words, you need to identify the themes or main ideas that they have in common. Once you've identified these shared themes, you need to be able to discern and articulate clearly the perspective or 'angle' each article presents in respect of those themes. Only then can you begin to compare, contrast and comment on them in a systematic, coherent and meaningful fashion.

Finally, because linguistics (pure and applied) is about describing language and how language is actually used, answers to linguistics questions are often characterised by the frequent use of examples. This is because in order to demonstrate and/or illustrate regularities – or indeed idiosyncrasies – in language form and use, examples are essential. They make abstract ideas concrete by anchoring them in reality and in doing so give weight and validity to any claims or observations you make. If you think about it, language is an objective phenomenon that lends itself to observation and description in a way that some other disciplines do not; to discuss it, therefore, without drawing on real data or examples is an oversight that can seriously undermine the substance and quality of your work.

3.3 Different forms of writing … and the language you need for them

Although one particular form may dominate, any kind of writing will typically involve you using a combination of different forms including definition, description, classification, cause and effect, comparison and contrast, and argument. You'll notice that these forms are reflected in a number of the direction words listed in the table on pages 46–7 (*argue, classify, compare, contrast, define, describe*). Let's look at each of these different forms in turn and some of the language associated with them.

How to define

Defining terms and ideas is an important part of academic writing for a number of reasons. Firstly, you sometimes find that different writers use similar terminology slightly differently; it's important, therefore, that you make it clear to your reader which interpretation of the term *you* are using. This means citing somebody else's definition or perhaps writing your own. Secondly, defining a term forces you to ensure that you have the meaning of that term clear in your own mind. This is important because if a term's meaning is unclear then the ideas built around it will also be vague, unclear and therefore confusing to your reader. Finally, assignment questions often require you to define a term or idea. Look at the following examples:

> *Explain how syntax differs from (a) inflection and (b) morphology.*
>
> *What is syntactic ambiguity? With the help of examples, show how some kinds of syntactic ambiguity can be accounted for by phrase-structure grammars.*
>
> *Define descriptive linguistics and explain how its approach to the investigation of language is different from a prescriptive one.*
>
> *Define reference and denotation and state how, if at all, you would distinguish between them.*

Handy language for defining
X can be defined as …
(author's name) has defined X as '…'
X is widely understood in the literature to mean …
In this essay I define X as …
I take X here to mean …
X is …
X refers to …
Let us consider was is meant by X/what X refers to
Let us consider the meaning of X

How to describe

Process description

As its name suggests, process description involves giving an account of how a particular process works. For example, you may be asked to describe the processes via which language change occurs or perhaps to describe the training process that students have to complete in order to become qualified secondary school language teachers.

 Using examples, illustrate the process in transformational grammar through which transformational rules allow surface structure forms to be derived from deep structure.

51

Componential description

Componential description involves describing the various elements of which something is made up. A thorough description of a given language, for example, would involve an account of its phonetics and phonology, morphology, syntax and semantics, as well of its orthography, discourse and pragmatics.

 Cite and discuss evidence in support of Carroll's (1981) notion that language aptitude is a composite of several relatively independent cognitive abilities.

Chronological description

Chronological description involves giving a description of how something developed in time, starting with the earliest events and moving towards the present. Within the discipline of linguistics, in fact, a distinction first drawn by Saussure is often invoked between *diachronic linguistics* and *synchronic linguistics* – diachronic being concerned with how a language develops over time (sometimes called historical linguistics) and synchronic with the state of a particular language at a given point in time. So if, for example, you had to write an essay tracing the Great Vowel Shift, this would involve a diachronic analysis, and such an analysis would necessarily involve chronological description in just the same way that an essay describing the spread of English over the last 150 years would.

 With the help of examples to illustrate unfolding lexical and syntactic knowledge, describe the stages of child language development.

Handy language for describing
Process

First(ly), . . .	*Second(ly), . . .*	*Third(ly), . . .*	*Next, . . .*
Then, . . .	*After this, . . .*	*Finally/Lastly, . . .*	*Prior to . . .*
Following . . .	*Subsequently . . .*	*Simultaneously . . .*	*While . . .*

Componential

| *. . . is made up of* | *consists of . . .* | *. . . is constituted by* |
| *. . . is comprised of/comprises* | *includes . . .* | *encapsulates . . .* |

Chronological

before	*subsequently*	*previously*	*at the same time*
after	*prior to*	*later (than)*	*earlier (than)*
next	*simultaneously*	*followed (by)*	*preceded*
in parallel	*in the wake of*	*succeeded*	*concurrently*
later on	*by . . .*	*until . . .*	*during . . .*

How to classify

Classifying information means analysing it and identifying natural patterns or groups within it. For instance, if you're researching world languages, you might want to begin by identifying the world's major language families: Indo-European, Uralic, Altaic, Sino-Tibetan, Malayo-Polynesian, Afro-Asiatic, Caucasian, Dravidian, Austroasiatic and Niger-Congo families. Once you've done that, you can then begin placing languages within each of these families. However, the process of classifying information is not always this straightforward because the categories themselves do not readily jump out at us. Often we are faced with lots of information that we need to make organisational sense of, and this can require very careful examination of that information in order to see the categories that are embedded in it.

This ability to classify is a crucial skill in any kind of writing, and particularly academic writing, because it's one important basis on which we plan and structure the information we've collated as a result of having researched a topic. As we saw in section 2.2, good structure in writing is the key to producing work that is coherent, and therefore easy to read and persuasive. Recognising natural classes or categories in information is actually the most fundamental and perhaps most challenging part of getting started on any writing task, and it's a skill in itself – the more you do it the better you become at it. If you think about it, the kind of review-and-discuss type questions discussed in section 3.2 require you to identify common themes, a process which essentially involves spotting natural categories. As we saw, only once you've done this can you systematically, coherently and meaningfully compare and contrast. This example highlights an important fact about the different forms of writing being discussed in this section, namely that they almost always occur in combination. It's very rare indeed for any piece of writing to involve only description, say, or only classification – a point our next Top Tip reinforces.

 One advantage of classification is that, because it essentially involves defining and thus differentiating different groups or categories, it allows you and your reader to compare and contrast more easily those groups or categories. Not surprisingly, therefore, classification and comparison and contrast are two forms of writing that tend to go hand in hand.

Handy language for classifying

X can be analysed/broken down into three types
X can be categorised/classified/grouped according to …
The first/second/third/next/final or last type/kind/category/division is made up of/comprises …

> *One type ...*
> *Another type ...*
> *Still/yet another type is ...*
> *Three main themes emerge from the data*
> *The literature/these articles embody two main ideas*
> *The ideas expressed here fall into two main schools of thought ...*
> *These views broadly represent two theoretical positions ...*

How to discuss comparison and contrast

You'll remember from our discussion on 'direction words' in questions (section 3.1) that the word 'compare' actually means consider both the similarities *and* differences between two or more things, while the word 'contrast' means only focus on the differences. It may seem strange, there-fore, when essay questions ask you to 'compare and contrast'! Nevertheless, it happens frequently, as the first of our examples below illustrates.

 Making reference to specific linguistic features such as tag questions, compare and contrast the way in which politeness is realised in the language of men and women.

Compare Piaget's and Vygotsky's theories on cognitive development.

Using examples, discuss the similarities and differences between a creole and a pidgin.

When writing an essay on similarities and/or differences, one of three approaches is usually adopted. In the first, sometimes called the *block format*, the features characterising one of the two subjects being compared are presented first, in their entirety. This may be followed by a summary of those features and a transition into the second part of the essay. Here, features characterising the second subject of the comparison are presented in full, again possibly followed by a summary. Finally, a general summary presents the most important similarities and differences, ideally with some personal commentary.

The second approach is called the 'feature-by-feature' or 'point-by-point' format. As its name suggests, this involves discussing how both subjects compare on each feature in turn; normally one paragraph will be devoted to one feature. As with the block approach, the essay will usually end with a general summary of the most important similarities and differences, along with some personal commentary. In contrast, however, because of the nature of the feature-by-feature approach, there will be no intervening summaries.

A final approach is to discuss all of the similarities between the two subjects first, possibly using one paragraph for each similarity, and then discussing all of the differences. Once again, this approach would include a general summary of the most important similarities and differences, along with some personal commentary.

 Often, by highlighting the features that characterise one of the two subjects being compared, we are able to *suggest* that they do not apply to the other, without saying so explicitly. In other words, by stating that a feature, X, applies to one of the subjects, we automatically imply that it does not apply to the other. Look at this example in which, by describing the characteristics of pidgin languages, we learn something about those of creole languages:

> The difference between pidgins and creoles is a clear one. Most importantly, when a pidgin comes to be adopted by a community as its native tongue, and children learn it as a first language, it becomes a creole. Creoles have a large lexicon and a broad array of grammatical distinctions. In time, they become languages as complete in every way as other languages.   (Adapted from Fromkin and Rodman, 1998)

The implication here is that (a) no one learns pidgins as native speakers; (b) they have smaller lexicons than creoles; (c) they have fewer grammatical distinctions; and (d) they are not as complete as other languages.

However you choose to approach comparison and contrast, the important thing to remember is that the methods described here enable you to present your analysis systemically. If it's not systematic it will feel chaotic to your reader and be difficult to follow; as a result, its impact will be minimal ... and so too will your mark!

Handy language for showing comparison and contrast

Similarity	Difference
X and Y are similar in that ...	*... in contrast (to) ...*
X is similar to Y in a number of respects	*Z differentiates/distinguishes X and Y*
X and Y have this characteristic in common	
This is a feature which X shares with Y	*There are marked differences between/ in the way that ...*
There are a number of similarities between X and Y	*Whereas/Whilst/Although X is ...,*
X and Y both show/demonstrate/ display ...	*Y is ...*
Similarly, ...	*Conversely, ...*
In the same way, ...	*... we are not comparing like with like*

> *Likewise, . . .*
> *both X and Y (are) . . .*
> *neither X nor Y (are) . . .*
> *. . . juxtaposing X and Y . . .*
> *It is difficult to make valid comparisons between X and Y*
>
> *both . . ., but neither . . .*
> *. . . corresponds to . . .*

How to discuss cause and effect

Most university essays require you to talk about causes and effects in some shape or form. In writing an essay you may well find yourself discussing some or all of the following for example:

- the reasons why something happened;
- how certain consequences might have been avoided;
- the reasons for decisions;
- the implications of particular actions;
- potential problems associated with a certain view or course of action;
- the significance and/or implications of taking a particular stance on something – either theoretical or practical.

All of these things have to do with causes and effects. Sometimes the very title of an essay will require you to address a cause–effect relationship. Look at the following examples:

 Describe and identify the reasons for the challenges involved in reconstructing dead languages.

Discuss the causes of aphasia, its consequences for language function, and the significance of brain plasticity in treatment of the disorder.

Drawing on the literature, provide an account of the main determiners of success in the acquisition of a second language post-puberty.

> **Handy language for explaining cause and effect**
> *X means/meant that . . .*
> *because of X, . . .; it was because of X that . . .*
> *therefore, . . .*
> *consequently; as a consequence of X, . . .; X is/was was a consequence of Y*
> *X was a result of Y; as a result of Y, X . . .; because of the fact that . . .*
> *resulting in . . .; resulting from . . .*
> *hence . . .*
> *thus . . .*

X is caused by Y
X is the effect of ...; has an effect on
X led to Y
X contributed to Y
E had the effect of ...
X was due to the fact that ...
X determines whether ...
for this reason, ...
X was the motivation for Y
from this it follows that ...

How to argue

It's almost inevitable that on many occasions during your degree programme you'll have to argue a case in writing for or against a particular
notion or proposition. Sometimes, entire essays or dissertations require you
to take a particular stand or perspective and to support it through sound
argument backed up by good evidence in the form of research data,
reference to the relevant literature, powerful analysis and logic. Even essays
with titles that do not explicitly require you to argue a case for or against a
notion or proposition will very likely involve many instances of argument
within them. The same is true of dissertations. In fact, if you think about it,
being able to argue well involves many of the skills and abilities covered
elsewhere in this book such as researching thoroughly, citing the relevant
literature, planning, presenting your ideas coherently and making the right
stylistic choices.

Argument, then, is a form of writing that is fundamental to your ability
to perform as an undergraduate student and as such it's crucial that you
become good at it.

 Not only is the ability to argue considered an important part of a university
student's development and evidence that they're in control of their subject
matter, it's also a crucial part of the development of any discipline in that
it pushes the boundaries of knowledge, questions current thinking, offers
new ways of approaching ideas and provokes discussion and debate.

Look at these sample questions:

*Given that people say 'more sugar' and 'more books', it is perfectly logical
that they should say 'less sugar' and 'less books' (and not 'fewer books', as
traditional grammars dictate). Do you agree? If yes, why? If not, why not?
With the help of examples, argue the case that auxiliaries should represent a
separate word class rather than be classed as verbs.*

57

'Slang should be regarded as a sign of creativity in language use rather than one of decadence.' Agree or disagree with this statement, providing evidence to support your view.

Being clear about what you want to say

In section 2.2, we looked at the importance of coherence to creating powerful and effective arguments in your writing. However, before you can begin to think about how to stitch your ideas together in a way that ensures they flow well, you need to be absolutely clear about what it is you want to say. If you've not got your own thinking clear, you've a poor foundation upon which to organise your writing and, as a result, it'll probably end up being vague, imprecise, difficult to follow and thus unconvincing to your reader. Good argument, therefore, is first and foremost about clarity of thought. Knowing what it is you want to say, developing a view or perspective and being able to give shape to what may start out as quite disparate ideas is part of the process of 'finding your voice', discussed in section 1.3.

Presenting your arguments most effectively

Once you're clear about what it is you want to say, you can really begin to think about how to present your argument most effectively. A good argument will normally follow a series of steps as follows:

Step 1: Place your argument in context.

If your argument is to have any real meaning and significance then it has to 'fit in' somewhere; it has to relate in some way to existing knowledge, to ideas that are already in circulation. Those ideas give you a stepping off point for your argument; they place it in context and therefore make clear its relevance and significance. As we saw in the last Top Tip, it's this very process which ensures that disciplines don't stand still but continue to develop.

Step 2: Survey the literature.

Obviously, in order to place your argument appropriately in context you need to know something about that context; more importantly, you need to show your reader that you know something about it. How do you do that? By discussing others' ideas and arguments. This means that you need to do your research and familiarise yourself with the literature in which those ideas and arguments appear. The ability to cite or quote this literature is a crucial part of developing a strong and convincing argument because by demonstrating that you have a grip on the issues with which your argument is concerned and the perspectives and opinions associated with them, you'll give your reader greater confidence in the soundness of your own ideas.

Step 3: Articulate your argument.

Having established the context or framework for your argument, you next need to articulate or 'spell out' the argument itself. As we saw in section 2.2, this requires you to plan the building blocks of your argument carefully so that it's well reasoned and each idea follows from those that precede it. If these links between your ideas are sound, then the argument which they collectively make up will also be sound. And don't forget, always support any claims you make with evidence.

Step 4: Acknowledging and addressing the arguments/counter-arguments of other scholars.

It's important always to bear in mind that creating a powerful argument isn't merely about presenting your own view; it also involves acknowledging the perspectives of other scholars and, where necessary, neutralising any arguments that run counter to your view. In doing this, and doing it effectively, you again show that you're familiar with the literature and also that your own view is well informed. This is important, because if your reader can see that you've covered all bases in forming your view, then they'll regard it as far more credible. As you read through the literature, it's inevitable that you'll come upon authors whose views conflict. While you may not be able to resolve the conflict, you need to show your reader that you're aware of those views and understand the arguments by analysing their logic, the nature of the evidence provided, and any hints of bias or prejudice that may distort the authors' judgement. In other words, you have to observe how and to what extent their arguments are as sound as those you're striving to construct!

Step 5: Using persuasive language.

'Carrying' your reader with you and making them sympathetic to your argument is not only about being logical and showing an awareness of the literature, it's also about the language you use to express your ideas. The main point here is that you need to employ language that is persuasive, and that can involve a number of things. One mistake new undergraduates frequently make is that of overstating the case; in other words, making claims that are too extravagant and cannot be adequately supported with evidence. Put simply, extravagant claims quite rightly appear unreasonable in the eyes of your reader and therefore will lead them to call into question your ability to be measured in your thinking. This, in turn, means that they are less likely to take anything else you say seriously; at the very least, they'll view it with a more sceptical, critical eye than they otherwise might. Extravagant claims, then, put your reader on high alert – a situation you really want to avoid. One way of doing this is to tone down your language. Look at these examples:

Ways of toning down your language

Instead of saying . . .   say . . .

Instead of saying . . .	say . . .
Conversation analysis is a technique that is *only* useful for exploring spoken language in more institutional, ritualistic settings.	Conversation analysis is a technique that *tends to be* most useful for exploring spoken language in more institutional, ritualistic settings.
The existence of a critical period means that those who begin learning a second language after their early teens *will never* sound like a native speaker.	For those who begin learning a second language after their early teens, *the likelihood is that they will not* achieve full native-speaker competence.
It is absolutely clear from the data that women are less domineering in conversation and favour cooperative or supportive participation.	*The data suggest that women are* less domineering in conversation and favour cooperative or supportive participation.

Other words and phrases that can help you tone down your language include: *perhaps, possibly, it is/would be impossible/unrealistic to claim that, it seems as if, it might be argued that, an important caveat* and *one might tentatively say.*

Be careful not to use too many of these words and phrases in your writing, otherwise you'll dilute what you say to such an extent that it'll be virtually meaningless. It's important to remember that these words and phrases should not be used as a way of hedging and being vague or deliberately ambiguous (see Hedging below, p. 64) but as tools that can help you to (a) be more discerning in the claims you make, and (b) reflect on their accuracy. The fact is that 'absolute' words such as *only, never, always, everything, everyone, all, completely* and *entirely* cannot be used very often because there are usually exceptions to rules, trends and beliefs.

Finally, you may wish to look ahead to Chapter 9, where we look in more detail at issues concerning writing style.

Let's briefly recap what we've said so far. When you present an argument, it needs to:

- be placed in context;
- show awareness of the relevant literature;
- be clearly articulated;

- be well reasoned and logically watertight;
- acknowledge other perspectives;
- be concise, to the point and unambiguous;
- use persuasive language;
- avoid extravagant claims.

It can take a new undergraduate time to develop the ability to construct a good argument and early efforts at academic essays often suffer from a number of common problems. Let's now briefly look at some of these pitfalls in the hope that by having them flagged here you'll be more alert to them and therefore better placed to avoid them in your own writing.

False syllogisms/non-sequiturs

A false syllogism is when the wrong conclusion is drawn from two premises. In other words, the conclusion does not follow logically from the statements that precede it. This is sometimes referred to as a non-sequitur, meaning *doesn't follow*. When this happens a writer is said to have committed a logical fallacy. Compare:

Major premise:	*All Scandinavian languages follow an SVO (subject–verb–object) order in their sentence structure*
Minor premise:	*Danish is a Scandinavian language.*
Conclusion:	*Danish follows an SVO order in its sentence structure.*

with:

Major premise:	*All Scandinavian languages follow an SVO order in their sentence structure.*
Minor premise:	*English follows an SVO order in its sentence structure.*
Conclusion:	*English is a Scandinavian language.*

In the first example, the conclusion follows from the two premises; in the second example it does not. It is, therefore, a false syllogism based on a misunderstanding of the major premise that all languages that follow an SVO order are Scandinavian – they are not. To say that all Scandinavian languages follow an SVO order is not the same thing as saying that all SVO languages are Scandinavian! Equally, to say that all Panasonic TVs are plasma TVs is not the same thing as saying that all plasma TVs are Panasonic TVs.

Be careful: arguments based on this kind of faulty logic can fatally undermine your work and it can be surprisingly easy sometimes to slip up in your reasoning. When you construct your arguments, be sure to check that each statement follows logically from those which precede it. If in doubt, check with a friend or lecturer.

Begging the question

Begging the question is another type of logical fallacy and it's sometimes referred to as circular reasoning. Put simply, begging the question means assuming as true the very thing you are trying to prove. Here's a commonly cited example of begging the question:

1. *The Bible is the infallible word of God.*
2. *The Bible says that God exists.*
3. *Therefore, God exists.*

Here the reasoning is circular: although the writer is trying to prove that God exists (3), they've already assumed it in the first premise (1). In other words, if the Bible is 'the infallible word of God', then God must exist. So why bother with stages 2 and 3 of the argument? Premise 1 actually requires just as much evidence as the main question, namely whether or not God exists! This faulty argument, then, tries to convince us that God exists without providing any proof. Hardly convincing! Yet, you'd be surprised how often this kind of poor reasoning appears in students' essays.

Look at the following examples taken from a student's assignment:

> *All people learn to speak a language because language acquisition is based on a genetic capacity in human beings. This genetic capacity has arisen through the forces of evolution over millions of years and is demonstrated by our ability to acquire a language.*

> *Providing comprehensible input is necessary for language acquisition. It is necessary because without it, nothing can be learned.*

In both these examples the argument is circular and nothing is proven. In the second example, the second sentence says the same thing as the first sentence, so the second sentence doesn't provide any independent evidence that the first sentence is valid. The whole thing is circular.

Again, as you're working through your ideas, make certain that the logic underpinning them is sound and keep a careful lookout for any circular reasoning when you check your work. Remember, errors in reasoning will rarely span three simple sentences situated one after the other as in the above examples. Often they will span a number of sentences, paragraphs or even pages and may therefore be more difficult to spot.

Over-generalisation and under-generalisation

Over-generalisation means making statements so general that they simplify reality. When people over-generalise, they assume that, because something is true in certain instances, it must be true in all instances. During the process of learning their first language, for example, children frequently over-generalise as they discover how the language works and, over time, gradually refine the L1 grammar. A good example of this is the past tense regular verb ending *–ed*. Children hear words like *watched*, *played*, *laughed*, *washed* and *bathed* and assume that we form the past tense by adding *–ed* onto *all* verbs – although, of course, they don't think in terms of 'past tense', they just notice and mimic the most salient feature of past-tense verbs! This means that irregular verbs end up as *eated*, *goed*, *sitted* and *rided*. Gradually, however, as the language acquisition process takes its course and they refine the rules of their L1 grammar, they begin to notice the exceptions to the general *–ed* rule and produce the past tense more accurately.

Although I've given you an example of the way in which children over-generalise, it's a practice that is certainly not confined to children – a fact to which all too many undergraduate student essays bear testimony! Here are a couple I've recorded:

> One thing is clear: it is not possible for anyone to develop full-native speaker competence in a language that they began learning post-puberty.

> The definite article 'the' is always used before proper nouns that are unique or one of a kind. For example, we talk about the Eiffel Tower, the Atlantic Ocean, the Taj Mahal, the Sydney Opera House, the Berlin Philharmonic Orchestra, the QE2 and the Royal Academy. (But what about London Bridge or Buckingham Palace?)

Generalisations can be a quite powerful way of persuading a reader provided they're accompanied by clarification and evidence. When no such clarification exists, you open yourself up to accusations of over-generalisation. As a writer you need to be highly disciplined and scrutinise any statements you make extremely carefully in this respect.

Over-generalisation is a good example of 'all-or-nothing' language (see section 9.4). As we shall see, statements that are too broad or absolute should be used sparingly and only if evidence is presented to justify them. In the absence of such evidence they may well be regarded as reckless, viewed with scepticism and considered to be of dubious validity. Rarely are things absolute; there are usually exceptions to be found once you delve beneath the surface.

While over-generalisation is quite common in new undergraduate students' writing, students also sometimes make the mistake of under-generalising; in other words, they're reluctant to make claims that might *feel* too ambitious even if the evidence appears to warrant them. This is a pity because it can make them appear unsure of themselves and lacking in confidence and result in a paper that will have less punch than it otherwise would. So, while it is, of course, important to be cautious about generalising, provided you are confident that your facts and/or analysis are sound, don't be afraid to stick your neck out!

Overstating the case

When people 'overstate the case', they make claims beyond what is actually the case or beyond what the evidence strictly permits. Although, in this respect, it's similar to over-generalisation, not all instances of overstating the case are instances of generalisation. For example, the statement 'Our subject exhibited no sense of pragmatic awareness in the L2 whatsoever' would almost certainly be overstating the case (most normal people have some sense of pragmatic awareness) but it would not constitute over-generalisation. Overstating the case is considered bad practice in academic discourse generally, and one way of avoiding it is to hedge – a practice that can be used to good effect but which can also be abused. Let's now, then, look briefly at hedging.

Hedging

Hedging means using language that is cautious and indicates the uncertain status of ideas or your attitude toward them. By using cautious language you can be measured in what you say and avoid overstating the case by indicating clearly to your reader your stance on a particular subject, or the strength of the claims you're making. We looked on page 60 at ways of 'toning down your language' and making it more cautious: Here are some other words and phrases that writers typically use to do this:

> *seem, tend, look like, appear to be, think, believe, doubt, be sure, indicate, suggest, assume, would, may, might, could, probable/probably/probability, possible/possibly/ possibility, perhaps, conceivably, typically, certain, probable, possible, assumption, it could be the case that, it might be suggested that*

 The data suggest that motivation plays a crucial role in language learning.

> *It is possible that Miguel's success in learning English, Swedish and Japanese to a native speaker-like standard reflects an aptitude for language.*

> *It is certainly conceivable, therefore, that interference from the subjects' first language was the reason for their near-universal misuse of the particle.*

Hedging, then, can be a legitimate and useful device in academic writing. At its worst, however, it can be used by students (and others) to be deliberately obscure and ambiguous. This tends to happen when:

- they want to avoid committing to a particular position or view. Often this is because they're uncertain how a commitment to one or other position will be received by their audience (in the student's case, their lecturers or examiners!) and they don't want to be penalised for supporting the 'wrong' position. Sometimes, if they know their work will be seen by two lecturers who have opposing views, they may attempt to keep both happy;

- they're conceptually unclear about what the positions actually are and therefore feel unable to commit to one or other of them;
- they have not clarified in their own mind what their view is on the issue.

 It's generally possible to say that adjectives usually precede nouns.

(Here, the words *generally*, *possible* and *usually* water down the writer's claim to such an extent that it becomes almost meaningless. This student has told us practically nothing!)

Our research seems to suggest that there may be a connection between previous language learning experience and speed and success in learning a new language.

(Either the research suggests it or it doesn't. This writer needs to nail their colours to the mast and commit one way or the other!)

There appears to be some evidence to suggest that there may be a relationship between gender and the use of certain kinds of question tags.

(Appears? May? Certain kinds of . . .? This is too vague and fails to tell us anything concrete and useful.)

TRY IT OUT! #6

Look at these three examples of poor hedging as they appear above. Rewrite them so that they are acceptable. Don't worry about whether or not they are factually accurate.

Original: *It's generally possible to say that adjectives usually precede nouns.*
Modified: _____

Original: *Our research seems to suggest that there may be a connection between previous language-learning experience and speed and success in learning a new language.*
Modified: _____

Original: *There appears to be some evidence to suggest that there may be a relationship between gender and the use of certain kinds of question tags.*
Modified: _____

 Remember: there's a difference between hedging in order to avoid committing yourself or to camouflage ignorance and hedging in order to remain measured and objective. Used for the wrong reasons, hedging results in writing that is vague and unclear and as such it is not in keeping with the idea of academic writing as clear and concise. Furthermore, hedging in order to avoid committing yourself is not consistent with the idea of 'finding your own voice' (see 1.3 and 8.1) and developing the confidence to take a *well-informed* stance on issues. In essence, then, poor use of hedging can make you look unclear and lacking in confidence, conviction or commitment.

Bias

For an argument to be persuasive it needs to be seen to be fair and objective; that is to say unbiased. Objectivity is one of the golden rules of all academic writing. There are a number of ways you can avoid introducing bias into your writing.

- Try to keep yourself honest. Sometimes, if you feel strongly about an issue and have a particular perspective on it you can fall prey to tunnel vision; you only see what you want to see and other contrary ideas can get too easily dismissed. Periodically take a step back from your writing, view it as your audience might and ask yourself whether your arguments and the statements that comprise them are reasonable and well founded.
- Provide evidence for your statements. In the absence of evidence your claims look 'thin' and unsubstantiated. A lack of evidence might be interpreted as naivety, blind faith or over-confidence, all of which can lead to accusations of bias.
- Present counter-arguments and try to refute them through sound reasoning. This demonstrates not only that your presentation of the facts is not one-sided but also that you have enough confidence in your own ideas to be able to show how they stack up against the ideas of other scholars. Writers who fail to acknowledge views contrary to their own usually either are not open-minded enough to recognise those views as worthy of consideration and thus mention or lack belief in their own views.
- Use measured language. This reassures your reader that you're keeping a healthy emotional distance from the ideas you're discussing. Avoid words and phrases such as *ridiculous, pathetic, unforgiveable, no thanks to, unbelievable* and *was misguided enough to think that.*

 Top tip: While your writing should appear objective and unemotional, this doesn't mean you can't have your own view, only that your view should be seen to be well informed and balanced. In fact, having a view, finding your own voice and demonstrating confidence is encouraged at university, where it's seen as an important part of your educational development (see also section 1.3).

TRY IT OUT! #7

Look at these examples of biased language. Rewrite them using more measured language.

1. Linguists today realise the absurdity of the behaviourist view of language acquisition.
2. Audiolingualism and Communicative Language Teaching had nothing in common.
3. CLT's principle of 'function over form' meant that, in the early days at least, the teaching of grammar was completely absent from language classrooms.
4. It is clear from the evidence that it is impossible to develop native-like proficiency in a second language if learning begins post-puberty.
5. The fact that we can sometimes understand a concept without being able to express it in words proves that the idea that all thought is constrained by language is false.

Red herrings

A red herring is something that is irrelevant to your discussion although it may well be dressed up in a way that suggests it *is* relevant. Red herrings are essentially a distraction and as such serve little useful purpose other than to divert attention away from a weak argument or perhaps to demonstrate a writer's strength of feeling. Often writers will go off at a tangent if they feel particularly strongly about an issue and want to 'get it off their chest', even if it's not directly relevant to the discussion at hand. Red herrings, then, can indicate (a) that you lack conviction in your own argument, (b) that your objectivity is questionable, and (c) that you are unable to stay on track and keep focused. Beware: red herrings will generally lead to red ink on your essays bearing the words 'Irrelevant!' or 'Keep on track'!

 Although extensive reading is popular in some circles, we have many other ways to teach students to read, such as skimming, scanning and intensive reading.

(The existence of other ways of reading is not only off topic, their existence doesn't constitute a valid argument against extensive reading either.)

There is merit in providing negative feedback on students' written work. I recommend that more teachers do so because too many teachers today simply don't take their jobs seriously enough.

(Comment: providing negative feedback appears to be unrelated to teachers taking their jobs seriously.)

False analogies

In an analogy, a speaker or writer infers that, because two concepts, objects or events are similar in certain respects, then they will also be similar in another particular respect. The thinking is: 'A and B are basically similar; therefore, if A has property X, then B must also have that property.' People use analogies such as the following very freely:

> *Learning to play the piano is like learning to ride a bike.*

> (A speaker who says this probably means that once you've learnt the skill of playing the piano, you never forget it – just as you never forget how to ride a bike once you've mastered the skill.)

Analogies are used by writers to make their arguments more powerful and convincing, to clarify ideas, or to explain in familiar terms something which may be unfamiliar to their readers. Unfortunately, however, the inference that because two things are similar in many respects they will be similar in all respects is not always justified and this results in a *false analogy*. When someone commits a false analogy they are sometimes accused of 'comparing apples and oranges'; in other words, the 'comparison isn't valid'. Here are two examples of false analogies:

> *Learning to speak a language is a complex skill and, as such, is much like learning to play a musical instrument.*

> (These two skills are different in many ways. For instance, everyone learns to speak a language well, but not everyone learns to play a musical instrument. Also, motivation (in the normal sense of the word) isn't needed for first language acquisition, but it is needed when learning to play a musical instrument.)

> *Words, we have said, are like coins with meaning and word class on one side and sounds on the other.* (From Aitchison, 2003)

> (Although we may understand what Aitchison is saying, in fact words and coins don't have much in common (and words also don't have 'sides'!)

So, the lesson is not to push your analogies too far! Just because two subjects have one or two things in common doesn't make them analogous. Whether or not an analogy is justified depends on the number and strength of known similarities between the two things being compared, and this is something you have to judge. Finally, be very sparing in your use of analogy as its overuse can make your writing feel too 'literary' or flowery and this is not in keeping with writing in the field of linguistics – unless of course you're discussing the use of analogy in spoken or written discourse!

 Top tip: Remember: the different types of writing described in this section often overlap. Language change, for example, not only involves process description but also chronological description – it happens gradually, over time.

Developing arguments: common pitfalls to avoid

False syllogisms/non-sequiturs   *Red herrings*
Begging the question   *False analogies*
Over-generalisation   *Hedging*
Bias

3.4 How to keep focused on the question

There are two main ways to ensure you don't wander away from the question and produce a response that is irrelevant or only partially relevant. The first is to periodically check that your thought processes are keying into the question. Often, as you brainstorm ideas and begin conceptualising your essays and developing arguments, your thoughts will meander in many different directions. As you work through and investigate an argument or line of thinking, the chain of ideas that make it up becomes longer and more complex; each new idea adds a link to the chain and, eventually, it can be difficult to see how the final idea (the completed chain) relates to the question! You may well have to backtrack and work out how you got to where you are and what the connection is between the first and last links in the chain. If you keep adding new links without checking with yourself how they all fit together and address the question, you'll come unstuck and produce an answer that has no clear focus or direction.

Handy language for arguing

Stating and supporting a view	Refuting a view/argument
The data suggests that ...	*There is little evidence to corroborate this view*
It can be argued that ...	
The argument runs as follows:	*There have, however, been doubts/ criticisms expressed over this view*
X argues that ...	
The evidence in support of this position is ...	*This position would appear to be untenable*
The available evidence certainly corroborates/supports this view	*The evidence suggests overwhelmingly that this argument is flawed*
Another argument in favour of X is ...	*There are certainly grounds for scepticism*
This indicates that ...	

Acknowledging other perspectives
X provides a rather different perspective
This, however, is not the view/position taken by X
X, in contrast, suggests otherwise
Those who support X claim that …
Opponents of X often use/cite the argument that …
Some argue/claim/assert/maintain that …
This view is not without its merits

The second way to ensure you remain focused on the question is to develop an essay plan. This is an essential part of good writing because it helps to discipline your thinking and gives you a global picture – or overview – of your entire essay and the opportunity, therefore, to see whether and how all the various ideas of which it's comprised gel together to answer the question. We'll look in more detail at how to plan writing in the next chapter.

3.5 Summary: coverage, argumentation and evaluation

In summary, we can say that in producing a piece of writing, you need to ensure that you have dealt adequately with the elements of coverage, argumentation and evaluation as follows:

Coverage – Have you covered all the main points relating to the title of your essay, and have you avoided digressions and kept the discussion on track and relevant?

Argumentation – Have you argued your case well according to the accepted canons of your field and the principles of style that apply, and have you provided sufficient objective evidence?

Evaluation – Have you demonstrated the ability to conduct a reasoned evaluation of the claims, ideas and theories mentioned in your essay, and to identify their relative strengths and weaknesses?

If you can honestly answer 'yes' to these questions, then it's likely that your essay will be well received and rewarded accordingly.

Chapter 3 Key points checklist

- A good strategy for analysing assignment questions is to identify (1) the subject, (2) the limiting words and (3) the direction words in the question.
- Be absolutely clear on the meaning of the direction words.

- Familiarise yourself with the particular forms of linguistics questions and what they require.
- Make sure you have a clear understanding of the types and purposes of different forms of writing and associated language: definition, description, classification, comparison and contrast, cause and effect, and argument.
- There are five key steps to a good argument: (1) place your argument in context; (2) survey the relevant literature; (3) articulate your argument clearly and logically; (4) acknowledge and address the arguments and counter-arguments of other scholars; (5) use persuasive language and avoid extravagant claims.
- When building an argument, avoid common pitfalls: false syllogisms/non-sequiturs, begging the question, over- and under-generalisation, overstating the case, hedging, bias, red herrings and false analogies.
- Make sure you keep focused on the question by working to an essay plan and periodically stepping back and evaluating what you have written.
- Finally, check your writing in terms of *coverage*, *argumentation* and *evaluation*.

The writing process

"What's the best approach, if I want to write a really good essay?"

What's covered in this chapter
Information-gathering: brainstorming, researching and selecting material
Note-taking
Planning
Drafting, checking and revising

The most important part of writing a good essay actually comes before you've even put pen to paper – in the preparation. In fact, good preparation is the key to producing good writing of any kind. There are three key stages you need to go through in preparing your essay. The first involves brainstorming, researching the topic and sourcing relevant material; the second involves making notes on what you've read; and the third is the process of taking your ideas and building them into a well-designed plan. Let's look at each of these stages in turn.

4.1 Information-gathering: brainstorming, researching and selecting material

Brainstorming

Brainstorming is a kind of free thinking about a particular idea, problem or topic. It consists of focusing on that idea, problem or topic and coming up with a creative response or solution, pushing ideas as far as possible and not censoring ideas that may seem silly – after all, 'silly' ideas often generate creative and interesting ones. The essential function of brainstorming is to open up as many possibilities as possible without having preconceptions or limits; you can then decide which are most reasonable or useful for your purposes.

Tips for effective brainstorming
- Be clear on the focus of your brainstorming.
- Open your mind up to all possibilities; avoid preconceptions.

- Don't censor any ideas: go with them and see where they lead.
- Write down any ideas that come to mind.
- Don't interpret or analyse your ideas initially.
- Try to be alert to possible relationships between the ideas you generate.
- Once you've completed your brainstorming and are unable to generate any further ideas, analyse and evaluate what you've written down.
- Explore the best ideas using further brainstorming or other more conventional methods.

Researching and selecting material

The information you need for your assignments will typically come from three main sources:

1. your lecture notes;
2. a general course reading list and/or a topic-based weekly reading list, which may include relevant search engines, websites and links;
3. your own research using electronic and hard-copy library resources, and perhaps discussions with tutors in your department.

Whereas, once upon a time, the business of researching a topic consisted mainly of physically going to your university library, using a card indexing system and scanning library shelves for relevant books and journal articles, today things are far easier thanks to information technology – or IT as we've come to know it. While there's still a need to use the library, a lot of 'leg work' can be done from the convenience of a desktop or laptop computer that has access to the Internet. Today, virtually every university has Internet access and, chances are, you'll also have your own home access.

Using electronic resources

Your university pays subscription fees so that you and your fellow students can have access to electronic books ('e-books'), electronic journals ('e-journals'), indexes and collections of journal articles, reference works and digital collections. Your fees help fund these subscriptions, so make sure you use the enormous wealth of information they make available to you!

When you begin your degree studies, it's quite normal not to know the best places to locate different kinds of information and it's only through experience and a certain amount of trial and error that, over time, you become better and quicker at finding what you want. Although your tutors

73

may well direct you to particular sources relating to English language and linguistics, many students will initially locate relevant sources through multi-disciplinary databases such as the Web of Knowledge (isiknowledge.com), Cambridge Scientific Abstracts (CSA; www.csa.com), and OCLC First-Search (Online Computer Library Centre; www.oclc.org/firstsearch). Let's look briefly at what each of these has to offer.

Web of Knowledge: this is a citation and journal database that gives you access to:

- *Web of Science* – comprises three databases: Arts and Humanities Citation Index, Science Citation Index and Social Sciences Citation Index. It provides over 30 million references to research from over 9,000 journals.
- *Arts and Humanities Citation Index* – indexes articles in the arts and humanities from over 1,400 journals from 1975 to the present. Its subject areas include philosophy, language and linguistics.
- *Social Sciences Citation Index* – covers nearly 1,800 journals across disciplines from 1956 onwards, and including applied linguistics.
- *ISI Proceedings – Social Sciences and Humanities* – indexes the published literature of the most significant conferences, symposia and seminars from 1990 to date. Subject areas covered include history, literature and philosophy.
- *Journal Citation Reports* – provides citation data showing high impact and frequency of use from 1997 onwards in subjects including applied linguistics.

Cambridge Scientific Abstracts: this is a database providing access to over 100 databases within Arts and Humanities and including:

- *BHI: British Humanities Index*
- *CSA: Linguistics and Language Behavior Abstracts*
- *ASSIA: Applied Social Sciences Index and Abstracts*
- *Communication Abstracts*
- *IBSS: International Bibliography of the Social Sciences*
- *PsycARTICLES*
- *PsycBOOKS*
- *PsycCRITIQUES*
- *PsycINFO*

OCLC Firstsearch: this is a gateway to databases, e-journals, e-books, and archived content, including:

- *Anthropological Index*
- *Anthropological Literature*
- *Anthropology Plus*

- *Arts and Humanities Search*
- *Education Index*
- *Humanities Abstracts*
- *Humanities Index*
- *Periodical Abstracts*
- *Philosopher's Index*
- *Proceedings First Social Sciences Abstracts*
- *Social Sciences Index*
- *WorldCat Dissertations and Theses (WorldCatDissertations)*

Additional databases of potential relevance include:

- *Central and Eastern European Online Library*
- *Dictionary of Old English Corpus*
- *Eighteenth Century Collections Online ECCO*
- *International Philosophical Bibliography*
- *Middle English Compendium*
- *Oxford English Dictionary*
- *Oxford Reference Online*
- *Oxford Scholarship Online*

Note: linguistic Bibliography/Bibliographie Linguistique is one of the most comprehensive linguistic bibliographies and includes a wide range of periodical sources from all sub-fields of linguistics.

The library

One of the tricks to using electronic sources effectively is to know what's available to you online, and it is your library staff who are best able to advise you on this. As electronic resources become an increasingly important part of conducting research, librarians are having to increase their knowledge of what's on offer so that they're in a position to help students such as yourself. They continually update themselves as new and better search engines and software packages become available and they're therefore a rich and valuable source of information. Increasingly, librarians are becoming specialists in particular discipline areas, sometimes even sitting on the boards of academic schools or faculties with whom they're aligned. This allows them to update academic staff on new resources available and to listen to any requests for additional resources. Most libraries today provide hard copy and electronic guides that explain how to use the library services and get the most out of what is available. In addition, many also produce guides on matters such as referencing conventions and how to avoid plagiarism, and academic writing style (see Chapters 8 and 9). Finally, if your library does not hold a copy of a book you want, they'll normally be able to arrange an inter-library loan.

 At the beginning of the year and periodically during the year, most libraries offer guided tours of their facilities and resources. By attending one of these tours early on in the course of your studies and spending a few minutes learning how to find information, you'll become a much more efficient researcher and save yourself many fruitless and frustrating hours later on.

Tours typically include instruction on how to use electronic catalogues to locate a book, periodical or journal in hard copy or e-journal/book format, procedures for borrowing books and gaining access to resources available elsewhere, an explanation of the Dewey decimal system or the Library of Congress System (the two most common ways of organising hard copy resources on library shelves), and an explanation of the photocopy facilities available, procedures for using them, and copyright regulations.

English language and linguistics journals

As a student of English language, linguistics or a related field, you will find that there are many journals available to you, a large and increasing proportion of which will be available online as well as in hard copy. Below is a list of some of the more popular and respected journals listed alphabetically. As you become familiar with these journals and with your field of study, you'll begin to develop a feel for which ones are of most general use to you and which are most useful for particular topic areas.

> **English Language and Linguistics Journals**
>
> *Annual Review of Applied Linguistics*
> *Applied Language Learning*
> *Applied Linguistics*
> *Applied Psycholinguistics*
> *Applied Semiotics*
> *Bilingualism*
> *Cognitive Linguistics*
> *Computational Linguistics*
> *Computer Assisted Language Learning*
> *Corpora: Corpus-Based Language Learning, Language Processing and Linguistics*
> *Corpus Linguistics and Linguistic Theory*
> *Critical Discourse Studies*
> *Discourse and Communication*

ELT Journal
English Language and Linguistics
English Linguistics
English Studies
English World-Wide
General Linguistics
Intercultural Pragmatics
International Journal of Applied Linguistics
International Journal of Corpus Linguistics
International Journal of the Sociology of Language
International Review of Applied Linguistics in Language Teaching (IRAL)
Journal of Applied Linguistics
Journal of English Linguistics
Journal of Language Contact
Journal of Linguistics
Journal of Neurolinguistics
Journal of Phonetics
Journal of Pidgin and Creole Languages
Journal of Pragmatics
Journal of Semantics
Journal of Sociolinguistics
Language
Language and Communication
Language Acquisition
Language and Cognitive Processes
Language in Society
Language Learning
Language Policy
Language Testing
Language Variation and Change
Linguistic Analysis
Linguistic Inquiry
The Linguistic Review
Linguistics and Philosophy
Pragmatics
Second Language Research
Semantics and Pragmatics
Studies in Language
Syntax and Semantics
TESOL Quarterly
Theoretical Linguistics

A note on using Internet sources

Although the Internet is a truly remarkable tool for any student researcher, it has to be treated with real caution. The quality of information it provides is highly variable and it's therefore essential that you ensure that the source of any information you use is sound and clearly identifiable (after all, you'll need to cite any sources you use and this means providing information that will allow your reader to locate it should they wish to do so – see Chapter 8). If you're using online journals or e-books then you don't have to worry as you can be sure that anything appearing here will have gone through a strict peer-review process; however, information obtained through blogs, forums and personal websites, for example, while it may be interesting and stimulate thought, is best treated with a big dollop of scepticism, for most of it will not have been formally verified or approved and may well amount to little more than personal opinion. As such it may be inaccurate and/or biased, and the author may have an agenda that is unknown to you. Newspaper articles may be used to support ideas, although you need to remember that even these are subject to the opinions of individual writers and the ideological leanings of the newspapers' editorial boards.

One rather disturbing feature of students' writing in recent years has been the increase in references to Wikipedia. Students often mistakenly think that because it's a kind of encyclopaedia, then it must be a reputable and valid source that can therefore be safely referred to in assignments. Not so! Anybody can contribute to Wikipedia, and while readers can and may identify and correct inaccurate or misleading information and so help ensure some measure of veracity, this in no way guarantees that what you read is rigorous and presents the facts accurately and objectively. My advice, and that of most academics, is 'Steer clear of Wikipedia in your academic work and, where possible, stick with recognised scholarly sources.'

 When deciding whether or not to use an Internet source, it can be helpful to ask yourself these questions:

- Who is the information provider?
- Are they likely to be reliable? (Is the information likely to be accurate and objective? If so, why; if not, why not?)
- Does the content feel objective or subjective and emotive?
- Does the website and its content feel serious or casual, light-hearted and/or uncritical?
- Why has the information been provided? For example, is it there to educate, to gain support, to convince you to do or believe something? In other words, do the authors have an agenda other than to provide you the reader with clear and objective information?

- Is there evidence of respected academics having contributed to the website?
- Are there any online security alerts advising caution when accessing the website?

Below is a list of useful linguistics-related websites that you can feel fairly confident about using. However, even with these sites you still need to exercise discretion when deciding what information to incorporate into your work.

Some useful linguistics websites

The Linguist List – www.linguistlist.org
Website for the mailing list: professional communication and networking for the worldwide community of linguists.

Linguistic resources on the internet (SIL International) – www.sil.org/linguistics/topical.html
An extensive and very handy list of internet resources categorised and including: fieldwork, grammar and syntax, language rights and language policy, languages and language families, lexicography and dictionaries, morphology, pedagogical resources, phonology, semantics and semiotics, speech and phonetics, text analysis and corpus linguistics.

iLoveLanguages – www.ilovelanguages.com
A huge catalogue of language-related internet resources featuring over 2,000 links. iLoveLanguages states that these links 'have been hand-reviewed to bring you the best language links the Web has to offer'. Just navigate to the categories that interest you.

Lexicon of Linguistics – www2.let.uu.nl/Uil-OTS/Lexicon
Searchable database of linguistic terminology updated with new terms in the areas of Generative Grammar (Minimalism) and Phonetics. Includes bibliography.

Corpus Linguistics Websites – www.athel.com/corpus_linguistics.html
A list of links to websites dealing with corpus linguistics.

Unilang Community – home.unilang.org
Provides a home for everybody interested in any aspect of language(s) or linguistics.

The sci.lang FAQ – www.zompist.com/langfaq.html
Answers to frequently asked questions about dialects, languages and their relationships, linguistics and phonetic systems.

Multilingual Blog – www.multilingualblog.com

News and opinion articles on sociolinguistics, bilingualism, translation, technology and other aspects of linguistics.

Linguistic Exploration – www.ldc.upenn.edu/exploration
Multidimensional exploration of online linguistic databases.
Introduction to Linguistics – www.uni-kassel.de/fb8/misc/lfb/html/text/startlfbframeset. html

Excellent for those new to linguistics and covering language acquisition, learning disorders, linguistics, universals, early development of the English language and phonetics.

Lingformant – http://lingformant.vertebratesilence.com/2006/09/24/new-linguistics-websites
A discussion forum for linguists with topic-based categories including animals and language, applied linguistics, historical linguistics, language and gender, language and the brain, language in society, language preservation, origins of language and technology and language.

TRY IT OUT! #8

Go to the Mantex website at www.mantex.co.uk/ou/resource/eval-01.htm.
This website provides information and links that will help you evaluate the quality and reliability of web resources.

As we'll see in Chapter 8, you will have to cite all of your sources, including electronic ones, in your list of references at the end of each piece of written work you produce. Using the above information can help save you from an embarrassing confrontation with your lecturer!

Deciding whether information is relevant to your purpose

As you locate information that looks broadly relevant to your particular purpose, you need to have a quick and efficient way of deciding whether, in fact, it's going to be helpful to you. There are a few ways you can do this:

- If it's a book, Ph.D. thesis, journal article, newspaper article or other document, look at its title.
- Look at the names of the author(s). If they are known to be associated with a particular subject or area of research that is relevant to your purpose then it may well be that the source contains something of use to you.
- In the case of a book, read the information on the back cover. This will often give you an idea of its contents.
- Read through any tables of contents.

- If there's a preface or foreword, read it. It may well give you some insight into the nature of what lies in the pages that follow.
- For articles, read the abstract. An abstract is a summary of the article that appears immediately after the title on the first page and is typically around 200 words long (see section 10.4).
- Glance through bibliographies. If there are names listed whose work is relevant to your purpose, then this suggests that parts of the book/article may well also be relevant. And remember: references that appear in works that you decide to use can be very useful pointers to further relevant information.
- Quickly flip through the book's pages. You should find that your eyes naturally alight upon key words that are relevant to your purpose.

 Never cite a journal article having only read the abstract. Make sure you read the article – or the relevant parts of it – in its entirety. Shortcuts can be tempting, especially when you're under time pressure, but they can also lead to embarrassing errors!

4.2 Note-taking

General strategies

Having located and selected the information you need, you'll want to record it. To help make this process as painless as possible there are a number of strategies you can use. Let's look at a few of the most popular and productive ones.

Take a quick first pass at the text

As a general rule, it's a good idea to get an overall sense of the material before you begin to take notes on it. This can help you avoid a situation where you get a kind of tunnel vision, lose perspective and record much more than is necessary because you don't have a sense of where the discussion is going and which parts, therefore, are really most important to you and thus worth noting down. It's easy for almost everything to seem relevant or important if you don't have an overall framework in which to view it! By reading through the material once before taking notes you'll find that you automatically select material for attention and this reduces the burden on you.

Make a visual representation of the main ideas in the text

When you take notes, it's important that you organise them well. Try to develop a system and use it consistently. Not only does this help you to recall what you read at a later date and after you may well have read a good deal of other material, it also serves as a visual representation of what you've read – a kind of conceptual map that illustrates how the ideas you've recorded sit in relation to each other. How you take notes is a fairly individual thing and different people have different preferences. Some of the most popular methods of recording information are the same as those used for planning writing, and we will look at these in the next section: 'Planning'.

Mark and annotate the text

Before they record anything, some people like to mark sections of the text as they read in order to highlight those ideas they feel are most relevant, useful or interesting to them. Often they'll identify important extracts with a line down the side – one line for important and two lines for very important – or by using a highlighter pen. Sometimes, they'll annotate the text with comments, questions and reminders to themselves.

Use symbols and abbreviations

Let's be honest, no matter how interesting ideas may be, noting them can be a pretty tedious affair. Using abbreviations and symbols can significantly reduce the tedium by speeding up the note-taking process. Which abbreviations and symbols you use is a matter of personal preference; what matters is that they work for you. The following, however, tend to be widely used by students. Some of the abbreviations listed are commonly found in the work of students and scholars of writing in the fields of English language and linguistics.

Some useful abbreviations and symbols

Abbreviations

def = definition	ex or e.g. = example
lang = language	i.e. = that is; in other words
stds/ss = students	NC = Noam Chomsky
av = average	agrs = agrees
fb = feedback	diagrs = disagrees
L1 = first language	FLL = first language learner
L2 = second language	SLL = second language learner
TL = target language	SLA = second language acquisition
no.s = numbers	stats = statistics
esp = especially	signif = significant
fig = figure	diag = diagram
w/out = without	intl = international
v. = very	TGG = transformaltional
etc = etcetera/and so on	generative grammar

Symbols

$=$ equals; is the same as	$\neq$ does not equal/is not the same as
$>$ is more than/larger than	$<$ is less than/smaller than
$\therefore$ therefore; as a result	$\because$ because
$\uparrow$ to increase	$\downarrow$ to decrease
$\rightarrow$ leads to; causes	$\leftarrow$ is caused by; depends on
$[$ includes	$]$ excludes
$+$ or $\&$ and; also; plus	... continues; and so on
£ pounds	% percent
# number	~ for example or approximately
Δ change	k million
@ at	/ per
	% percent

 Whichever system you choose for your note-taking, try to use it consistently; that way it will function like a code and you will understand your notes whether they were written last week, last month or last year.

Recording your sources

As you locate, read through and take notes on material, it's absolutely essential that you're meticulous about recording your sources. When it comes to incorporating the ideas of others into your writing, you must be certain about where those ideas originated and able to pass this information on to your reader. You do this through in-text references and a comprehensive bibliography at the end of your work. We'll discuss how to do this in Chapter 8. In the meantime, just remember that every source you use needs to be documented as follows:

- The title of the source
- The name(s) of the author(s)
- The name of the publisher
- The date of publication
- The URL (web address), in the case of Internet-sourced material

It's an excellent idea to discipline yourself into recording this information immediately before you begin taking notes; putting this important bit of house cleaning on the backburner and forgetting it altogether is all too easy to do. As many a student will tell you, there are few experiences more frustrating than having to backtrack later and waste time locating sources you once had right under your nose!

4.3 Planning

So, you've located the information you want and you've taken notes on it. The next step is to take all that information and shape it into a lesson plan. This is a critical phase of the writing process: get it right and chances are you'll produce a decent piece of writing; get it wrong and things can quickly go pear-shaped.

If you are to produce writing that flows smoothly as a result of the ideas it expresses having been organised in a coherent fashion, then you need to know *before you start writing* exactly what you intend to include and where. In other words, you need to plan. It's almost impossible to write a comprehensive, in-depth and well-organised essay in the absence of a good plan.

So, what is a 'good' plan? A good plan is one which, when you look at it, gives you at a glance a good idea of what's going to be discussed and in what order, as well as the relationships that exist between the ideas featured in your essay. Ideally, if your plan is thorough and you're not writing under time pressure, anybody looking at it will be able to ascertain, quite accurately, what the final written essay is likely to look like.

Types of plan

How people plan their essays is quite a personal thing – different people have different preferences. What's important is that you find a method that suits you and with which you're comfortable. There's no 'correct' method, although a good plan needs to have a pattern to it – a symmetry if you like; after all, if there's no pattern, then there's not really any method at all! Below are two main types of plan which students tend to adopt.

Spidergrams

In a spidergram, the development of the essay proceeds from the centre outwards. In the centre is the essay title, from which the main ideas radiate. Each of these then subdivides into further strands as the main ideas are developed with the inclusion of supporting detail. These strands then further subdivide as more detail (including specific examples) is added. This process continues until all information has been incorporated, with those ideas appearing on the periphery of the spidergram representing the highest level of detail or specificity. Lines may then be drawn between strands to indicate organisational and conceptual relationships.

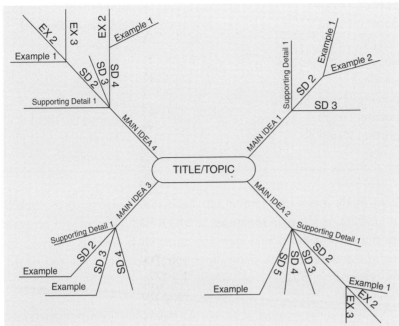

Figure 4.1

Horizontal step diagrams

Horizontal step diagrams move from left to right as the level of detail increases. The main ideas, which appear leftmost, will generally be ordered according to their appearance in the essay. This means that the first main idea to be presented in the essay will appear at the top left of the diagram and then develop rightwards as it's fleshed out with supporting detail. The subsequent main ideas will then follow suit. As you develop each of the different nodes of your plan, it will become more and more comprehensive until it gives you a very clear visual 'picture' of what the essay itself will look like once it has been written.

MAIN IDEA 1	MAIN IDEA 3
Supporting Detail 1	Supporting Detail 1
Supporting Detail 2	Supporting Detail 2
Example 1	Example
Example 2	'Supporting Detail 3
Supporting Detail 3	Example
	Supporting Detail 4

MAIN IDEA 2	MAIN IDEA 4
Supporting Detail 1	Supporting Detail 1
Supporting Detail 2	Supporting Detail 2
Example 1	Example 1
Example 2	Example 2
Example 3	Example 3
Supporting Detail 3	Supporting Detail 3
Supporting Detail 4	Supporting Detail 4
Supporting Detail 5	Example 1
Example	Example 2

Whichever method you use – and it may be an alternative to these – you'll need to indicate on the plan the order in which each element will be dealt with. In the case of horizontal step diagrams, such order is likely to be inherent in the design: those main ideas which appear at the top of the diagram are dealt with first.

 It's worth noting one other advantage of a good plan. If you want to include additional ideas at a later stage, the presence of a plan makes it much easier for you to locate where in your essay those ideas fit most aptly whilst at the same time minimising any disruption to the flow of your discussion. For the same reason, try to be as thorough as possible when you're brainstorming, researching the question and collating information. It's always more difficult to 'squeeze' information in comfortably later.

I always tell students that planning is the most difficult part of writing because that's when you have to get clear in your mind how all the pieces of the jigsaw relate to each other and decide how you can best stitch them together so that they present a clear and accessible argument to your reader. Once you've done this and got a clear conceptual blueprint, the rest is relatively easy. You know what you want to say and where; you've just got to go through the mechanics of actually doing it. Of course, you still need to use appropriate language and try to inject some style into your writing if you really want to grab your lecturer's attention and make an impact.

 Never feel that planning is a waste of time. It's a very solid investment of your time that will pay out huge dividends if done carefully and thoughtfully. It'll save you the frustration of having to continuously rework parts of your text because you haven't thought through its organisation in advance or did not consider all the issues carefully enough at the outset. You can end up having to squeeze in information retrospectively; information which may not fit into your text comfortably unless you restructure part of what you've written. That restructuring can sometimes turn out to be a major undertaking and leave you wishing you'd spent more time initially on planning. Consider explaining your plan to another person as this can be a good way of identifying organisational problems or areas you don't understand well.

TRY IT OUT! #9

Choose one of the three questions featured in the Try it Out! activity in section 3.1, page 48. First remind yourself of the subject of the question, the limiting words and the direction words. Then, using one of the techniques described above, create a plan for the essay.

4.4 Drafting, checking and revising

If you want to produce a really polished piece of writing then it's highly unlikely your first attempt will be the one you submit to your lecturer. You'll want to have one or more practice runs. The writing you produce in each of these practice runs is called a draft. Drafting is a good way of reflecting on your ideas and their presentation in your writing and gradually refining them, so that when you eventually submit the final draft you do so in the knowledge that it really was your very best effort. As you reflect on a draft, ask yourself the following questions:

- Does the text flow well? Will my writing and the ideas I express be easy for someone else to follow?
- Are my arguments sharply focused and clearly stated?
- Is my writing concise and to the point or do I waffle in places?
- Have I divided my writing adequately into paragraphs, and are the paragraphs correctly formatted?
- Would it make things clearer to my reader if I had sub-headings?
- Is my spelling correct (a spell checker can be useful here)?
- Have I made any grammatical mistakes?
- Have I accidentally omitted any words or letters?
- Is my language precise enough?
- Is the style of my writing appropriate? For example, is it too casual or pompous?
- Would a diagram or some other visual be helpful – for example in the presentation of research data?
- Have I acknowledged all references and formatted them correctly?
- Does the title really reflect the content of my writing?
- Is my spacing correct?

When it comes to your final draft, you'll also want to ensure that your bibliography is correctly formatted and includes all references cited in the main body of your text.

Note: many of the items listed above are dealt with in detail in other sections of this book; for example, paragraphing (Chapter 2), coherence and the flow of text (Chapter 2), argument structure (Chapter 3), referencing conventions (Chapter 8), and writing style (Chapter 9). For a more comprehensive checklist that you can use to edit your work, turn to section 9.18.

 It's an excellent idea to have a friend check your draft to see whether they can follow what you've written and to identify and mistakes that you may have missed.

Chapter 4 Key points checklist

- Key steps to writing a good essay are brainstorming, researching and selecting relevant material using lecture notes, 'recommended reading' lists, and both physical and electronic resources (databases that list and give access to electronic books and journals and linguistics websites, for example).

- Familiarise yourself with the most popular and respected English-language and linguistics journals.

- Invest time in learning how to access and use the electronic and other resources available to you.

- Be discriminating in your use of Internet sources and make sure they are reliable and trustworthy.

- Take notes on your sources systematically and efficiently. Mark and annotate texts and use visual representations, symbols and abbreviations where helpful.

- To save yourself headaches later on, always be methodical and fastidious in recording your sources. As you use a source, note it down there and then. Don't postpone it!

- Never begin writing until you have a clear written plan that reflects a well-organised, coherent essay.

- Use a 'draft, check and revise' model to ensure a high-quality piece of writing. In particular, check for good flow and a clear focus, concision, precision, appropriate paragraphing, headings and sub-headings, spelling and grammatical errors, appropriate style and correct referencing.

CHAPTER 5

Writing an introduction

'I always find it really difficult to get going . . . you know, to think of what to write at the beginning of an essay. I know it's important to start well, and it always takes me ages, but I still end up with something boring.'

What's covered in this chapter:
The purpose of an introduction
How an introduction achieves its purpose
The thesis statement: what it is, where to place it and how to write it
Indicating organisation and approach
Length
Paragraphing
When is the best time to write an introduction?
Handy language

5.1 The purpose of an introduction

Why is it that many students find it so difficult to write the opening few sentences or paragraphs of an essay? The simple answer to this question is that being able to write a good introduction is actually something of a craft. Most of us have been told at school how important it is to get an essay off to a good start with a powerful introduction, yet the writing of many undergraduate students suggests that in practice this means little more than a statement of intent, a brief summary of what they're going to discuss in the essay. In reality, an introduction needs to do far more than this. Once you know more precisely what an introduction is, what it seeks to achieve and how it can most effectively be made to serve its purpose, you'll be able to craft far more effective introductions, and with greater ease.

Essentially, an introduction frames the discussion that's to come in the body of your essay; it prepares the reader by providing a context – reference points or hooks – that helps them to engage better with that discussion. That

89

context is usually created by making reference to the relevant literature and/or by discussing a problem or observation that has arisen as a result of your or somebody else's experience (of language use, language learning or language teaching, for example). Once a context has been established, it needs to be made clear to the reader what you plan to discuss in your essay and how it fits into that context.

So, an introduction is a kind of launching vehicle or stepping-off point, which helps the reader get a contextual fix on your essay and certainly gives an indication of the main focus of the discussion to come. Often, it will also give a brief indication of the route you're intending to take in your discussion; it will, if you like, map out the general direction of the discussion – what, in more precise terms, you plan to discuss, how and in what order.

Finally, in performing these functions, an introduction prepares the reader by (hopefully) building a sense of anticipation and a desire to read on.

The main functions of an introduction
An introduction should:

- contextualise your discussion by locating it within the relevant literature and, possibly, your or others' experience;
- provide a clear indication of what will be discussed in the body of the essay, how and in what order (i.e. it should serve as a kind of navigational tool to help orient the reader in advance and as they read through your essay); and
- quickly and effectively engage and stimulate interest in your reader so that they have a real desire to read on.

5.2 How an introduction achieves its purpose

Showing where your discussion fits in

Now to the trickier bit: how do you make sure your introduction fulfils these functions effectively? Let's begin by going back to the idea of context and the need to locate the main focus of the essay within a broader setting. By a 'broader setting' is meant an historical, academic, conceptual or experiential setting, or possibly a combination of two or more of these things. The **historical setting** refers to those events surrounding the particular event, idea or development you're going to discuss. The **academic setting** refers to the literature relevant to your discussion and what others have said about the areas you plan to cover or which have an important bearing on them. The **conceptual setting** refers to the way in which your own discussion/notions relate to particular concepts and ideas already discussed in the literature. The **experiential setting** refers to the real-world experiences you or others have had and which play a role in motivating and informing your upcoming discussion.

Put simply, your introduction shows how your own discussion relates to what has already been said about the subject and in doing so highlights the importance and relevance of your own contribution.

5.3 The thesis statement: what it is, where to place it and how to write it

As part of the process of providing a context for your discussion, you will, then, at some point, be indicating to your reader something about the focus of that discussion – a statement of intent, if you like. This is called the **thesis statement**, and all introductions need one.

Perhaps the simplest thesis statement – one you may well have used many times – begins with the words, 'In this essay, I will . . .' or 'This essay looks at . . .'. It's simple and it certainly does the job; as such, there's nothing essentially wrong with such a thesis statement. However, while it may be perfectly fine for a high-school essay, as an undergraduate student you should be trying to develop a more sophisticated and subtle writing style, and to add more variety of expression to your repertoire. How can you do that with a thesis statement?

One strategy is to avoid such an explicit statement of intent as 'In this essay I will . . .'. Instead, try to make it obvious to your reader what you're planning to discuss without stating it in such direct terms. Take note though: I'm not suggesting you be vague or unclear, but rather that you be more colourful in the way you express your intent. Before we look at some ways of doing this, it would be helpful to consider where in your introduction it's best to place the thesis statement. Although, in theory, it can go almost anywhere, it typically appears either at the beginning or the end of the introduction, and there are good reasons for this.

Placing the thesis statement at or near the beginning of the introduction or at the end gives it more impact. By placing it at the beginning, with little or no prefatory discussion, you 'hit' the reader with it head-on. Once you've made clear what it is your essay will focus on, you'll need to follow up with some contextual framing which will give meaning to your focus; it will explain or justify it. Look at this example, in which the thesis statement has been underlined:

 This essay takes a critical look at arguments for and against the use of native speaker models in the teaching of English as a foreign or second language. In recent years, as a result of the growing role of English as the world's lingua franca, a significant number of applied linguists, and to a lesser extent language teachers, are beginning to question the legitimacy

of a model of spoken English which is actually spoken by a minority of those who use English to communicate. The reality is that today more non-native speakers use English to interact with one another than native speakers, and they do so using their own varieties yet negotiating meaning perfectly effectively. For some this begs the question of why, therefore, native speaker varieties should any longer be held up as ideals to be aspired to. In contrast, there are those who feel that while these non-native speaker varieties may be widely used for business, political, educational and other purposes, they are somehow an aberration of the 'correct' or 'pure' forms of English and should not be encouraged. The issue is one over which the English language community has become increasingly polarised.

Placing the thesis statement at the end of your introduction, in contrast, builds a sense of anticipation and allows you gradually to 'draw your reader in' and guide them to the thesis statement, which slowly unfolds as they read through the introduction. It can be helpful here to think of a funnel, wide at the top and gradually narrowing at the tip. The top of the funnel represents the start of your introduction. Here, you begin to lay the groundwork for your discussion by establishing in broad terms the contextual setting into which it fits. If you imagine that there was no title, at this stage your reader may well have little or no idea about what precisely you're going to be discussing in the essay. However, gradually, that contextual information becomes more specific as you narrow your focus and home in on the particular aspect of the subject that will form the basis of your discussion in the body of the essay. And, eventually, at the narrowest point of the funnel, you let on to the reader exactly what it is your essay will focus on. This is your thesis statement, and its significance should be immediately apparent in light of the background information you have provided. Consider the following example:

 The onset of the communicative paradigm in language teaching in the 1970s represented a significant departure from previous methods and approaches in that it positioned centre-stage the notions of language as communication, language in context, authenticity and appropriateness. Suddenly, competence in language was seen not merely as knowledge of the form of the target language but, more importantly, the ability to deploy that knowledge appropriately and fluently in the real world in order to 'get things done'. Form was now regarded as serving function, and knowledge how took precedence over knowledge that. Language learning curricula and syllabi were recast in order to reflect this new emphasis and the notional-functional syllabus was born – a syllabus which defined learning goals in terms of those things the learner could actually do with language.

This essay will discuss those factors responsible for the success of the communicative approach to language teaching since its inception over thirty-five years ago.

Explicit thesis statements

A thesis statement can be either explicit or implicit. An explicit statement is one where you state overtly what you intend to focus on in your essay. The 'In this essay I will ...' statement mentioned earlier is an example of an explicit thesis statement. Here are some other examples:

This essay takes a critical look at ...
This essay will consider whether ...
This essay seeks to shed light on the question of ...
In the following pages I will ...
The following pages outline/discuss/report on/consider the similarities and differences between ...

Implicit thesis statements

An implicit statement is one that makes clear the purpose of the essay without stating it overtly. Have a look at this example, which is an implicit alternative to the explicit thesis statement used in the above introduction on the emergence of the communicative paradigm:

 The fact that the communicative approach to language teaching remains with us thirty-five years after its inception is reason to ask what it is about the approach that underlies its success.

You will see from this example that the writer never actually says they're going to discuss the reasons for the success of the communicative approach to language teaching; however, it's amply clear from the way in which the context has been created ('the funnel effect') what the discussion will focus on. In fact, if your introduction is well constructed, even before your reader has reached the thesis statement it may well be that they're able to guess the main focus of your discussion. As they approach the tip of the funnel they should be predicting – hopefully accurately – what the essay will be about. As a writer, you need to ensure that such predictions are always accurate, and you do this by providing tramlines in the form of a skilfully developed contextual backdrop. In the above example, it's interesting to note that even if the final sentence were omitted, the main focus of the essay would still be clear enough to the reader.

Occasionally, writers use questions to frame their implicit thesis statements. This is not a strategy you should use regularly, and of course not every introduction and/or essay topic lends itself to this kind of thesis statement. However, it can on occasion provide a useful alternative. Listed below are a few questions I've come across in students' essays – some undergraduates' and some postgraduates':

- *Is this position really justified?*
- *Did structuralism and the audio-lingual methodology associated with it really deserve the criticism it received?*
- *Will the notion that non-native speaker varieties of English can constitute legitimate models of learning ever really acquire currency among the language-teaching community at large? And more to the point, would students themselves accept such models as acceptable targets of their learning?*
- *Given that language learners have always learnt languages with varying degrees of success, regardless – or in spite of – the teaching methodology used and the theories of language and learning underpinning it, the question perhaps needs to be asked, 'Is it not perfectly reasonable to subscribe to an eclectic approach to language teaching?'*
- *This begs the question of whether transformational generative grammar has had any significant impact on foreign language pedagogy.*
- *In view of the often contradictory nature of its findings, to what extent should language teachers and materials designers allow SLA research to inform their activities?*
- *It is often claimed that native-like proficiency in a foreign language can only be achieved if learning begins prior to puberty. However, does the evidence really exist to support claims of a so-called 'critical period' in language learning?*

Now, although, you will not always want to use implicit thesis statements in your writing, they do make it easier to avoid the kind of less interesting, less sophisticated expressions of the 'This essay looks at ...' variety. Nevertheless, direct thesis statements placed early on in your introductions can also be more varied and may include expressions such as:

> *The following discussion sets out to ...*
> *The discussion that follows analyses the question of ... and provides an account of why ...*
> *..., and it is on the pros and cons of that approach that this essay will focus.*

Finally, be careful about using words such as 'attempts' (*This essay attempts to ...*) as these can suggest that you're not convinced you've succeeded in achieving your purpose. This does not inspire confidence in your reader!

TRY IT OUT! #10

Look at this essay title:

'Discuss the reasons why structuralism in language teaching was superseded by functionalism.'

> *Listed below are the main points to be included in an introduction to the above essay. Using this information to create a contextual backdrop for your upcoming discussion, write two versions of the introduction, one with the thesis statement at the start of the introduction and the other with it at the end. Think carefully about how your thesis statement will link the contextual information to the body of your essay, and how you can make it engaging for the reader.*
>
> - *Historically, language-teaching methods and approaches have largely reflected developments in language-learning theory.*
> - *As one learning paradigm goes out of favour and another replaces it, approaches to the teaching of language also change.*
> - *Structuralism was critically undermined by Noam Chomsky, who replaced an empiricist theory of learning with a rationalist one.*
> - *Cross-disciplinary insights into language and language use, emanating from philosophy, psychology, anthropology and sociology, also played a key role in fuelling the shift from a structural to a functional view of language.*
> - *The functional view of language brought with it a change in what were regarded as the appropriate goals of language learning.*
> - *Reinforcing these theoretical and pedagogical shifts in our understanding of language and language teaching were a series of significant social, political and technological developments that occurred in the 1960s and 1970s.*

The middle ground

Finally, there is what might be termed a compromise strategy used in the presentation of a thesis statement. Here, an indication of the focus of the essay is given early on in the introduction, and confirmed at the end of the introduction via an explicit statement of intent. Look at these brief examples:

The idea that foreign languages are better learnt through doing – through actual communication – than through rote memorisation and the practice of grammar rules is not without its critics, many of whom point to their own success in learning foreign languages via such traditional methods. In fact, the evidence suggests that success in foreign language learning is possible irrespective of – or in spite of – the methodology employed, and likely has more to do with factors such as learners' first language, aptitude, motivation, personality and preferred learning style. In other words, despite a search for the holy grail of language teaching, there can, in fact, never be such a thing as an approach which is all things to all men – something which perhaps goes some considerable way to explaining the current popularity of eclecticism among language teaching professionals . . .

With this in mind, in the pages that follow, criticisms commonly levelled at the learning-through-doing approach will be considered carefully with a view to establishing whether or not they are soundly based and a necessary part of language-learning classrooms.

In recent years, the debate over whether or not it is preferable for teachers of foreign languages to be native speakers of those languages has become increasingly polarised, with theoretical and anecdotal evidence being harnessed on both sides of the divide, in an effort to 'make the case' and 'win the argument'. As a consequence, the role of the non-native speaker teacher in the foreign language classroom is a regular feature of conference discussions and debates, journal articles and other fora, and it is an issue that simultaneously calls into question the increasingly common practice, by materials writers and publishers, of including non-native accents in listening materials. This essay casts a critical eye over arguments commonly presented for and against the use of non-native foreign-language teachers.

5.4 Indicating organisation and approach

As we saw in section 5.1, an introduction will often map out the route you're going to take in your discussion, specifying what will be covered and when. In other words, it will give the reader a brief preview of the organisational structure of your essay. This can be extremely useful as it makes it easier for the reader to understand your discussion and appreciate its relevance and significance, for they're better able to fit whatever they're reading at any particular moment into the broader picture or scheme you have given them at the outset, in your introduction. Generally speaking, this preview will immediately follow a thesis statement that is positioned at the end of the introduction. If the thesis statement appears early on in the introduction, the preview will probably still appear at the end, after the context has been established. Look at this example in which the preview follows a thesis statement (underlined):

 The discussion that follows will look at four key pragmatic theories in terms of their contribution to our overall understanding of language and their implications for the way in which languages are taught. It will begin by briefly outlining Austin's Speech Act Theory (1962), Grice's Co-operative Principle, Lakoff's Politeness Principle, and Sperber and Wilson's Relevance Theory, before going on to consider their potential pedagogical relevance. The discussion will then focus on current language-teaching methods and materials with respect to the way in which they account for – or fail to account for – the realities of pragmatics in language use and their importance to the accurate expression and interpretation of meaning. Finally, consideration will be given to ways of incorporating into syllabus design those insights offered by the theories.

TRY IT OUT! #11

Below is a brief list of the main items to be included in an essay entitled 'Explain and discuss Krashen's Monitor Model. Consider, in particular, the reasons for its prominence in the 1980s, the contribution it made to the language acquisition debate and to classroom pedagogy, and its ultimate failure to withstand scrutiny as a sound "theory"'. The items are listed in the order they'll appear in the essay. Write a short paragraph indicating the organisational structure of the essay.

- A brief overview of the theoretical context in which the model was proposed.
- A description of the Monitor Model in terms of what it sought to do and the five hypotheses of which it comprised:
  - the acquisition/learning hypothesis
  - the monitor hypothesis
  - the natural order hypothesis
  - the input hypothesis
  - the affective filter hypothesis.
- An explanation of how the theory informed language-teaching pedagogy, and in particular Krashen and Terrell's Natural Approach.
- A statement of why it attracted the attention of applied linguists and appealed so strongly to language teachers and materials developers.
- A detailed look at weaknesses inherent in the Monitor Model.
- An assessment of the lasting impact of the Monitor Model.

5.5 Length

One question I'm frequently asked is how long an introduction should be; what percentage of the entire essay it should account for. My first response (which students usually like because it's unambiguous and doesn't require too much pondering!) is to give a rule of thumb: 'The introduction should account for roughly 10 to 15 per cent of the entire essay.' My second response tends to be rather less welcome: 'an introduction should be as long as it needs to be' (which provokes considerably more head-scratching). Really, though, the second answer is the better one … so what does it mean? Well, provided it fulfils its purpose, as described above, a paragraph can, in theory, be almost any length. In some cases it may need to be only a few lines, while in other cases it may require a page or more. However, you must always bear in mind the fact that the introduction is precisely that – a preface to the main discussion, and as such it would be odd were it to account for, say, 30 per cent of the entire essay. One way to keep the length under control is to ensure you do not make the common mistake of discussing issues better dealt with in the body of the essay.

5.6 Paragraphing

Another common misunderstanding concerns how many paragraphs an introduction should contain. The idea many students seem to have that it should consist of only a single paragraph is simply mistaken. The rationale for beginning a new paragraph (see section 2.5) is as valid for introductions as it is for any other section of your essay. The chances are your introduction will contain two, three or more main ideas and will therefore warrant a series of paragraphs, not just one.

5.7 When is the best time to write an introduction?

Experienced writers often suggest that the best time to write an introduction is after you've completed the remainder of your essay, dissertation, etc. Why? Because that way you can ensure that it reflects accurately the order and content of what follows and in doing so better fulfils its purpose of preparing the reader for what is to come. Unless you have a clearly articulated plan and follow it in a highly disciplined fashion, it's all too easy for your essay to get derailed as you wander away from the topic. This can result in you reaching the end of your essay and finding that the beginning and the end do not match up neatly. As we'll see in section 7.6, the notion of 'matching up' is most clearly manifested in the relationship between the introduction and conclusion.

5.8 Handy language

Although there's an enormous variety of words and phrases that can appear in introductions, the box below contains a selection that may be of help to you as you shape your introductions. As you use alternative forms that don't appear in the box, add them to the bottom of the list and then use it for quick reference purposes.

Introductions: Handy language

This essay will consider whether ...
This essay casts a critical eye over ...
This essay will shed light on the question of ...
This essay will look at the reasons why ...
This essay will compare X with Y
..., and it is on the pros and cons of that approach that this essay will focus.

2	Main idea 2	HEADING 1
2.1	First supporting idea	HEADING 2
2.2	Second supporting idea	HEADING 2
2.3	Third supporting idea	HEADING 2
2.3.1	First development of third supporting idea	HEADING 3
2.3.2	Second development of third supporting idea	HEADING 3
2.3.3	Third development of third supporting idea	HEADING 3
3	Main idea 3	HEADING 1

As you can see, the tiering of ideas in the above diagram reflects the basis on which lesson plans are designed (see section 4.3); however, although in your plan you may wish to include additional tiers, I would not recommend doing this in the essay itself as it can become too unwieldy and make things seem unnecessarily complex – remember, headings are there to help not hinder. I would, therefore, suggest a maximum of three levels of headings.

 Of course, the main heading is actually your essay title! The best strategy here is to leave any decision about the title until you've completed the essay; only then will you be in a position to consider what you've written in its entirety and choose a title that accurately reflects the content of your work.

Line spacing

Different lecturers and departments can have different policies on line spacing, and while some may have no policy at all and are happy leave it up to the individual student's preference, others are much stricter and expect you to conform to specific guidelines. Generally, 1.5 or double spacing is preferred, in part because it gives the text an airier feel and allows lecturers or examiners to mark or annotate (make comments on) your work more easily.

Margins

My comments on spacing apply equally to margins. Here too there is often variability between different lecturers and departments. Most, however, expect students to leave margins of around three centimetres in their written work. Apart from improving the appearance of your work, it also gives lecturers or examiners space to write remarks.

Footnotes

A footnote refers to additional information that is found at the bottom of a page (at the 'foot' of the page) and which is referred to in the main body of the text, usually on the same page and using a superscript number (^{1}, ^{2}, ^{3}, etc.) to link the reference to its referent. Look at the following two examples:

Example 1

From the body of the text:

Although some argue against the existence of true synonyms (Clark, 1987), to many of us the words *sofa* and *couch* mean the same thing; so do the words *pail* and *bucket*.[1]

Footnote:

[1] However, some words are more suited to certain contexts, and synonyms alter the meaning of the sentence itself (even if the words are identical in meaning). However, Shakespeare's romantic quip, "A rose by any other name would smell as sweet," loses some of its poetic charge in, "A rose by any other nomenclature would smell as sweet." Again, the fact that meanings and words are not exclusively linked to one another leaves room for a separate examination of each domain.

(From Gleason and Ratner, 1998)

Example 2

From the body of the text:

Over its three-year implementational phase, this project, entitled 'Developing Multiple Literacies', yielded increasingly higher levels of awareness in faculty and graduate students not only about the nature of AL2 abilities, but also about pedagogical needs that must be met and opportunities that can be pursued in order to foster students' L2 learning to academic levels of performance.[2]

Footnote:

[2] The entire three-year project is extensively documented on the Department's website, www.georgetown.edu/departments/german/curriculum/curriculum.html. It has been referred to in a number of publications, particularly Byrnes (2000a and 2001b), and Byrnes and Kord (2001).

(From Leaver and Shekhtman 2002)

Notice how footnotes generally appear in a smaller font than that used in the body of the text.

Why is some information placed at the bottom of the page as a footnote? Usually because despite being of some interest and relevance, it's nevertheless slightly incidental to the point discussed in the main body of the text and to which it refers. A footnote is rather like a conversational aside and its status as such is reflected in its positioning, where it cannot interrupt the flow of the main text.

These days, footnotes appear to be increasingly discouraged and many departments ask students to try, as far as possible, to incorporate all ideas in the main body of the text. Usually, with some creative sentence structuring this can be achieved; however, there are occasions when it becomes almost impossible. Only then should you consider whether the idea is valuable enough to warrant its inclusion and therefore justify a footnote. In any case, you should check with your department or lecturer to see what their preference is and adjust your practice accordingly.

Page numbers

It's good idea to number your pages. It may seem like a small thing but it can be frustrating for a lecturer to have to figure out the correct sequence of the pages of an essay that have become disordered for some reason; after all they don't know your essay as you do and the process of reconstructing it may not, therefore, be as simple as you think, particularly in the case of a lengthy piece of writing!

Figures

Occasionally, you may wish to present an idea, or perhaps some data, visually, using a chart or other form of graphic. If you decide to do so, make sure that the graphic serves a useful purpose and is not merely there for aesthetic reasons. The only sound reason to include any graphic in your writing is to add clarification by illustrating something you've discussed, thereby making it more accessible to your reader. Often, ideas or data are more easily appreciated and digested when presented in visual form rather than as text, and will frequently have greater impact as a result. As a student of linguistics or a related discipline, chances are you will, at some stage, conduct a small-scale study or research project as part of your degree (see Chapter 10). It's likely that in writing up that project you'll want to present some of the data you've collected in graphical form – most probably as a table or graph. If you do decide to include a figure, be sure to give it a snappy title that reflects what it illustrates. And if you use more than one figure, give each figure a number – Figure 1, Figure 2, etc. – as follows:

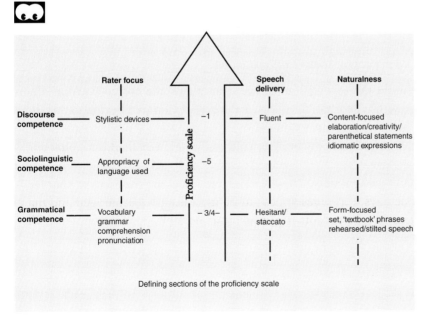

Defining sections of the proficiency scale

Figure 6.1   (Adapted from Pollitt and Murray, 1996)

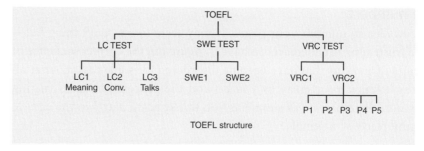

TOEFL structure

Figure 6.2   (Adapted from Brown and Ross, 1996)

By numbering your figures in this way, when you make reference to them in your text your reader is left in no doubt as to which figure you are referring.

As you write the body of your essay, refer regularly to your plan. By doing so, you'll stay on the straight and narrow and will not be tempted to digress, ramble and produce sections of work that are irrelevant and are not tightly knit with the rest of your text.

Examples

When writing about languages and linguistics you will almost inevitably want to cite examples of language structure or language use (see also section 9.16 for a discussion of formatting conventions). When presenting these examples it's good practice to use a hanging indent, which looks much neater. A hanging indent is where all subsequent lines align with the first line. Compare the following:

> (1) Could you please lend me your pen?
>   I don't appear to have my pen on me.   √
> (2) Could you please lend me your pen?
> I don't appear to have my pen on me.   X

Notice how the second line of the example in the correct version aligns exactly with where the first line of the *actual* example begins, rather than with the *number* of the example.

Having completed the body of your essay, next you'll need to think about your conclusion and the question of whether or not it would benefit from being preceded by a summary. These and related issues are the focus of chapter 7.

Chapter 6 Key points checklist

The body of your essay is everything that appears between the introduction and the conclusion. It should:

• typically account for around 70–80 per cent of the entire essay, although this can vary;

- consist of a series of main ideas and more detailed supporting ideas that together form the core of your discussion and demonstrate a coherent argument structure;
- be well laid out and presented and include: sections and sub-sections/titles and sub-titles, where necessary; a systematic numbering/lettering system for headings; correct line spacing; adequate margins; footnotes, if appropriate; page numbers, figures, where necessary and where they serve to elucidate ideas; and examples to illustrate points in your discussion.

Writing summaries and conclusions

'I've never really understood the difference between a summary and a conclusion. Conclusions are kind of like introductions for me: I'm never sure what to write, and it usually feels like I'm just repeating what I've already said. So what's the point?'

What's covered in this chapter:
What's a summary and how's it different from a conclusion?
Are summaries always needed?
Where should I include a summary?
Summaries: handy language
What exactly should I be doing in a conclusion?
Tips for more effective conclusions
Conclusions: handy language

7.1 What's a summary and how's it different from a conclusion?

A summary is a brief restatement – or recap – of the main points you've presented in your discussion. Although it will often precede the conclusion, it's also sometimes presented as part of the conclusion. In either case, though, it's a way of reminding your reader of the main ideas you discussed so that the conclusion can be read and understood more easily with those ideas fresh in their mind.

As the quotation that begins this chapter indicates, students sometimes confuse summaries and conclusions, so let's begin by making a simple distinction between the two. A summary, because it's merely a restatement of ideas already mentioned, adds no new information. A conclusion, on the other hand, *does* add new information: it takes the ideas discussed in the body of your writing and then implicitly asks (and explicitly answers) the question, 'What general observations can we make about those ideas? What do we learn from them? What do they tell us?' In other words, a conclusion makes general statements about the ideas presented in your main discussion; statements containing ideas that will most likely not have appeared elsewhere in your writing. The new information comes not from adding to those ideas but by commenting on them.

Now take a look at these two examples of summaries.

 In this final chapter of Part II I have attempted to show how prior knowledge can, by diverse routes, give rise to the identification and control of genres. I have alluded to the important role of schemata in discoursal processing and production, but I have also observed that schemata alone reflect a microcosmic cognitive world dangerously adrift from communicative purpose and discoursal context. I have also noted that hard evidence for the value of genre-based approaches to the development of communicative competence is not yet readily available, although indirect support for such approaches comes from a number of areas: from schema-theory itself, from explorations into the power of prior texts, from acquisitional psychology and from the limitations of a narrowly expressivist view of reading and writing developments.

(Adapted from Swales, 1990)

This essay has considered the importance of pragmatic competence to communication and levelled criticism at methods frequently used to develop language learners' pragmatic competence on the grounds that they frequently fail to develop in learners an understanding of the pragmatic conditions that determine whether or not a given utterance is acceptable to other users of the language as an act, or the performance of an intended function. This means that whatever learners glean of the relationship between form and function – between what is said and what is meant – its applicability is largely restricted to the particular instances of its use they have experienced in their learning. Consequently, they are deprived of the kind of productivity that comes from an understanding of general principles and the process of discovery that such understanding enables. The quite recent growth of pedagogical pragmatics has sought to address this problem but takes a largely inductive approach in which the observation of particulars leads to an understanding of general principles: over time, through regularly engaging in awareness-raising activities of the kind outlined, learners will gradually induce the broader principles that govern the choices we make in language in order to effectively and appropriately convey meaning. It has been suggested, however, that learners can simultaneously benefit from a deductive approach through which an appreciation of those general and universal principles that govern language choices and our ability to be appropriate is instilled in them early on. By raising their awareness of these general principles, we increase the likelihood that they will notice and learn their particular realisations in English.

You'll notice that in the first example the summary is from the chapter of a book (on genre analysis), whereas in the second example, it's from an essay. Nevertheless, the summary principles guiding both are exactly the same.

109

7.2 Are summaries always needed?

Unlike an introduction, body and conclusion, summaries are not usually considered an essential and necessary part of written work. That's not to say that you don't need to worry about them. What it means is that you're able to use your discretion about whether or not to include a summary – or summaries – in any particular piece of writing you are producing. It's important that you use this discretion because a decision *not* to include a summary where one would be useful in helping the reader to follow your thinking and 'join the dots' of your argument means that your work will not be as accessible to the reader as it would if a summary *were* included. Remember, the more accessible your writing, the more enjoyable it is to read … and the less frustrating. Anything you can do to get the reader on your side will only benefit you when it comes to that all-important grade!

So how do you use your discretion in deciding whether or not to include a summary in your written work? Once again, the answer to that question is 'Put yourself in your reader's shoes and ask yourself whether the complexity of the ideas you have presented and/or the length of your written piece will make it difficult for the reader to move easily from the body of your essay to the conclusion without the help of a summary. And be honest with yourself; be as objective as possible and, if necessary, get a second opinion from someone who is not too close to your work. If the answer to this question is 'no', then a summary is probably not necessary – although it can certainly never hurt to include one anyway. If, on the other hand, the answer is 'yes', then you probably ought to include a summary.

7.3 Where should I include a summary?

As we saw in section 7.1, a summary typically appears towards the end of your essay and immediately prior to the conclusion. Sometimes it will appear as a separate section, and sometimes as part of the conclusion, immediately preceding your concluding statements. In an extended written piece, such as a long essay or dissertation, you may feel that more than one summary is necessary. You may, for example, decide that it would be helpful to locate one at the end of each main section or main idea, particularly if it is especially complex and involved. This is not uncommon by any means and there's certainly no rule preventing you from doing so.

 Where possible, if you do decide to include more than one summary, try to be consistent. If, for instance, you decide to have a summary at the end of one main idea, it's a good idea to include one also at the end of the other main ideas; that way your work has a balanced feel to it.

7.4 Summaries: handy language

There are a number of phrases and sentences that can be useful in introducing summaries. The box below highlights some of the more commonly used ones.

Summaries: handy language

In summary, …
To sum up, …
The main points of the above discussion may be summed up as follows: …
The key points raised can be summarised thus: …
This essay has discussed a number of issues. First, …
In arguing for xxx, a number of issues have been highlighted/analysed …
It has been argued that …
Let us briefly review the discussion so far.

7.5 What exactly should I be doing in a conclusion?

We saw in section 7.1 that the conclusion is that final part of your essay where you reflect on the key ideas you've presented and attempt to draw together the various strands of your discussion and come to some kind of resolution. That resolution usually consists of a series of observational statements that comment, often in quite general terms, on what you've presented in the body of the essay, and typically, fall into one or more of the following categories:

- summary statements of the key points of your discussion;
- logical entailments and implications of ideas raised in the foregoing discussion ('Given that we've said/observed X, we can now say Y');
- the identification of issues that have not been addressed, or addressed adequately, and which therefore warrant further discussion;
- questions that arise from your discussion;
- in the case of a research report (see Chapter 10), any limitations of your research; for example, shortcomings with its design and implementation and ways in which these might be addressed in any repeat study;
- in the case of a research report, reference to how your findings compare with those of other studies;
- suggested directions for future research based on your discussion/findings; and
- a link back to your original question/thesis statement, bringing the essay full circle.

Look at the following conclusion. This is the conclusion that followed the summary we looked at in section 7.1; as such it's an example of a summary that appears as *part of* the conclusion rather than as an independent section (see section 7.3). So that you can see how the summary statement and the concluding statement sit in relation to each other, the complete text is included, with the concluding statement underlined.

 In this final chapter of Part II I have attempted to show how prior knowledge can, by diverse routes, give rise to the identification and control of genres. I have alluded to the important role of schemata in discoursal processing and production, but I have also observed that schemata alone reflect a microcosmic cognitive world dangerously adrift from communicative purpose and discoursal context. I have also noted that hard evidence for the value of genre-based approaches to the development of communicative competence is not yet readily available, although indirect support for such approaches comes from a number of areas: from schema-theory itself, from explorations into the power of prior texts, from acquisitional psychology and from the limitations of a narrowly expressivist view of reading and writing developments. At the end of the day, we may come to see that genres as instruments of rhetorical action can have generative power (Himley, 1986); they not only provide maps of new territories but also provide the means for their exploration. Yet the empowerment they provide needs to be accompanied by critical reflection in order to ensure that our students, as they journey forward, are not blind to the social consequences of their own actions and of those who have been there before them. (Adapted from Swales, 1990)

Here is a further conclusion, this time from a student's essay:

Essay title: *What do you understand by the notion that verbs can be subcategorised into a number of 'aspectual types'? How can these types be exploited to account for restrictions in the occurrence and interpretation of 'progressive' verb forms?*

Although this analysis has not covered all possible interactions between aspectual verb types and the progressive, it does perhaps serve to illustrate a few points. Firstly, the notion of aspectual verb types does appear to be a useful one. This becomes apparent when one considers the difficulties its absence would present in terms of attempts to describe and explain restrictions on the progressive. Taxonomies such as those of Vendler and Quirk et al. as least provide us with a framework via which we can systematically present to learners what we as native speakers generally agree upon. Without such a framework, learning becomes inefficient. Such categorisation, however, is not always clear-cut, for native speakers can and do sometimes disagree about what is possible in the language. Comrie states that know 'does not allow the formation of a progressive, even with reference to a contingent state' (ibid. p. 38), whereas Baker views it as acceptable when it implies an intermediate judgement 'based on only part of the available evidence' (ibid. p. 489). Likewise, Vendler quotes Ryle as maintaining that seeing is not a process or state but an achievement (ibid. p. 113). While 'aspectual verb types' may be useful in helping spell out the generalities of co-occurrence restrictions – such as those covered in this paper – between verbs and the progressive aspect based on the properties of their lexical meaning, they should not be taken as indicators of the aspectual properties of phrases or sentences, for the addition of different syntactic constituents around the verb may alter these properties. The sentences John walked [activity] *and* John walked to the station [accomplishment] *(Dowty 1986, p. 39) illustrate the folly of making such an assumption. Taken solely as a guide to co-occurrence restrictions, the notion of 'aspectual verb types' is a valid one. Bearing in mind its potential complexity, occasional problems around categorisation, and a degree of subjectivity about what is acceptable in English, it should perhaps be treated with due caution. However, this is the case with so much of what we teach of language: generalisations or irregularities imply deviation, but this does not demonstrate their lack of utility as teaching and learning tools that provide the basis for later refinements as learners' competence in the language increases.*

7.6 Tips for more effective conclusions

- Say something new! Do not merely summarise what you've already said in the body of your work.
- Make certain that any new information you introduce has a direct bearing on the foregoing discussion and offers enlightenment on it with a view to bringing some kind of resolution.
- Avoid entering into long and complex discussions that would be more appropriately located in the body of your essay.
- Try to link your conclusion back to the introduction of your essay and ensure that it's addressing the original question. By doing this you create a kind of natural closure by bringing things full circle.
- Consider offering *your* view of how you see a particular issue or field of research developing. Alternatively, consider making some suggestions for productive areas of future research. This latter option typically appears at the end of reports on empirical studies; however, there is no reason why it cannot occasionally be used in a regular course assignment provided the context is suitable.
- Generally, it's best to avoid concluding an argument or essay with a rhetorical question. Occasionally, however, a question written as a

statement (in other words, an implicit question) can sometimes work. Compare the following:

> *If students have successfully learnt languages using structurally based methodologies, then should we not continue to use these alongside more communicative approaches?* (Rhetorical question)

> *Given that students have successfully learnt languages using structurally based methodologies, then we would do well to ask ourselves whether there is, in fact, value in using these methodologies alongside more communicative approaches.* (Implicit question)

TRY IT OUT! #12

Look at these two conclusions from two different journal articles. The first is from the Journal of Applied Linguistics*, and the second from* Pragmatics*. For each conclusion, try to identify those features listed in the bullet point list that appears in* section 7.5.

Conclusion

The unique features of metaphor clusters in conciliation talk, as well as features shared with other discourse types, help to generalise from the various cases studied so far. It appears that metaphor clusters occur when some intensive interactional work linked to the overall purpose of the discourse is being carried out. In lectures, lessons and sermons, the discourse work was mainly explanations of difficult or unfamiliar topics, carried out through extended use of one or two root metaphors. In conciliation talk, the central discourse work of reducing alterity is pushed forwards through metaphor clusters, in which metaphors, as 'ways of seeing one thing in terms of another' (Burke, 1945), are also tried out and gradually appropriated across speakers. Other clusters occur as speakers explore alternative ways of feeling and acting, helping participants contemplate and reject often very negative alternatives. In extending what we know about the role of metaphor clusters and how to identify them, this article offers researchers a heuristic tool to use in exploring discourse. Faced with discourse data, a researcher can seek out clusters of metaphors and investigate the interaction around and inside them, with the expectations that the metaphor clusters indicate points where intensive and important discourse work is carried out. Where large amounts of data are involved, identifying and investigating clusters at the various levels of scale gives a way of 'cutting into' data which can help understand the overall dynamics of the discourse while at the same time identifying particular episodes worth investigating in more detail.

Summary and conclusion

At the beginning of this paper, we proposed a general scheme intended to capture and accommodate all kinds of turn continuation – from prospective to retrospective ones, and within the latter, from TCU extensions to new TCUs. Our focus, however, has been firmly on retrospective turn continuations and how these are done in Chinese conversations.

The general scheme is based on four inter-related but distinct parameters all having something to do with an utterance's structure, meaning, and information status relative to their host. The four parameters are: syntactic continuity vs. discontinuity, main vs. subordinate intonation, prospective vs. retrospective orientation, and information focus vs. non-focus. As we have attempted to show, these parameters interact in interesting ways. Together they define different turn continuation methods located along a continuum ranging from the tightly integrated to the loosely linked.

As far as syntax is concerned, continuity or discontinuity is certainly a very important consideration. But it would be wrong to regard it as the only consideration. We have tried to show how syntax interacts in complex ways with prosody and intonation. The two work hand in hand some of the time, but at cross purposes at other times. In the case of Right Dislocation, for example, syntactic discontinuity is off-set by subordinate intonation. Syntax may even on occasion be over-ridden by prosody. A unit may be syntactically continuous with a prior unit, but this alone does not preclude it from attaining the status of a new, separate TCU, provided that it comes with full intonation and is supported by appropriate features of rhythm and tempo. We believe that the study of turn continuation can proceed on a firmer footing if these four parameters are kept conceptually distinct, even though their interaction and combination are clearly very important.

Regarding the communicative functions of turn continuation, within our limited corpus we have been unable to find any systematic mapping between particular forms and particular functions, except the general observation that all retrospective turn continuations offer a means of supplementing or commenting upon the information conveyed in the just-completed TCU. We did find in our small data collection a range of interactional motivations for further talk after the possible completion of a TCU, e.g. pursuing recipient uptake (FFT 2002), showing affiliation, upgrading one's stand in face of potential disagreement, etc. However, as our corpus contains only Chinese data, and a limited amount of data at that, this question must be left to further research.

7.7 Conclusions: handy language

There are a number of phrases and sentences that can be useful in introducing summaries. The box below highlights some of the more commonly used ones.

> **Conclusions: handy language**
>
> *In conclusion, . . .*
> *The evidence presented indicates/suggests that . . .*
> *Based on the evidence available, . . .*
> *This essay began by asking the question . . .*
> *This essay set out to shed light on . . .*
> *To return to our original question, it would appear that . . .*
> *This essay sought to/set out to . . .*
> *Where does this leave us in our search for an answer to our original question?*
> *What is clear, then, is that . . .*
> *What emerges from this discussion is . . .*
> *There is strong evidence, to suggest that . . .*
> *We can conclude from the foregoing discussion that . . .*
> *There is a need for future research/studies to look at/investigate . . .*

Chapter 7 Key points checklist

- A summary re-states, in brief, key points of your discussion, whereas a conclusion 'rounds off' your essay by making a series of broad reflective statements generated by that discussion.

- Whereas a summary may not always be needed in an essay, a conclusion is always required.

- A summary can appear as a separate section immediately before your conclusion or as the initial part of your conclusion.

- In order to assist your reader, it may be necessary to have multiple summaries in longer, more complex pieces of writing.

- A conclusion will normally do one or more of the following: offer summary statements of key points in your discussion; state logical entailments and implications of ideas raised in your preceding discussion; address issues that have not been addressed or which warrant further discussion; present questions that arise from your discussion; identify any limitations of your research/analysis; compare your findings/analysis with those of other scholars; suggest avenues for future research; link back to your original question/thesis statement, thereby bringing things full-circle.

Referencing and quotations

'It's difficult to know how much I should use my own ideas and how much I should include stuff I've read. And then, I'm not sure how to mention the authors; everyone seems to do it differently.'

What's covered in this chapter:

The importance of finding your own 'voice' . . . and the need to use sources

What is plagiarism, why should I avoid it, and how can I avoid it?

What's the best way to paraphrase?

Referencing styles

In-text referencing: how should I quote my sources?

In-text referencing: citing without quoting

The bibliography: what is it, what should it include, and how should I format it?

Increasing your efficiency: using bibliographic software packages

Handy language

8.1 The importance of finding your own voice . . . and the need to use sources

In section 1.3 we looked at the idea of 'voice' and why it's important to you as a student to develop your own voice; that is, your own way of looking at the world: your own views, opinions or perspectives on issues and your own way of expressing them. Having a view and the courage and conviction to express it, either in writing or orally, is one indication of growing academic and intellectual maturity and self-confidence. However, as we saw in sections 1.6 and 2.4, views cannot be expressed in isolation; they must be grounded in the literature and supported with solid evidence. It is necessary to demonstrate that you are well versed in the relevant language and linguistics debates and the various arguments that compromise them, and that you show how your own views relate to them. In doing so, you contextualise those views and therefore give them greater meaning and significance.

117

Remember, it's as important to show an awareness of views expressed in the literature that conflict with your own as it is to show awareness of those that agree with them. Part of establishing your own position and making it credible consists in identifying counter-positions and then arguing against them.

This chapter looks at the importance of correctly citing other writers and ways of doing so. We'll start by looking at plagiarism, a word you've probably already heard many times and a label for what is widely regarded as the cardinal sin of academia!

8.2 What is plagiarism, why should I avoid it, and how can I avoid it?

Plagiarism is the practice of taking somebody else's ideas and using them in your own work without acknowledging their original source. Whether you plagiarise deliberately or not, the effect is same: effectively you are claiming those ideas as your own when, in fact, they are nothing of the sort. This amounts to cheating and the penalties can be severe; they can range from a hard 'rap on the knuckles' and a very firm caution, to failure of a course, failure of an entire degree, even expulsion from your university. This means that just as it's important to demonstrate that you've read the relevant literature on the subject about which you're writing, it's equally if not more important that you're absolutely fastidious about citing the sources you've used. If you need to get an idea of just how seriously universities take plagiarism, just go online and have a look at the websites of a selection of universities. All of them will make mention of plagiarism somewhere, whether it's in the institution's Handbook of Rules and Regulations for Degrees, individual course information or academic support services information. And they highlight it because it's a growing problem, because the penalties are so severe, and because if, ultimately, they find themselves having to pursue a case of plagiarism, they need to be able to show that all students were explicitly alerted to the issue of plagiarism and given strategies for avoiding it. This places the onus on you the student to ensure you implement those strategies. You have been warned!

There are two main ways of incorporating the ideas of other scholars into your work: though reporting them – sometimes called paraphrasing, and through quoting them directly. Let's look at each of these techniques in turn.

8.3 What's the best way to paraphrase?

Paraphrasing means reporting somebody else's idea(s) using your own words.

 A fatal mistake students often make is to think that because they're writing an idea in their own words they don't have to acknowledge the original author of that idea. Not so! Using your own words makes you no less susceptible to accusations of plagiarism; after all, the idea remains someone else's regardless of the words used to express it. Remember: in addition to ideas that you've paraphrased, you also need to reference quotations, statistics and electronic sources.

When you paraphrase you have to make absolutely certain that in changing the author's words you do not also inadvertently change their ideas too and end up misrepresenting them. Remember: sometimes even a single word can dramatically change the meaning of a sentence. As a linguistics student you will learn – if you don't already know – that words we may treat as synonyms in everyday communication will, in fact, often be subtly different, with each carrying its own unique nuance. This means that when you paraphrase another writer, you need to check what you've written *extremely* carefully to ensure that your rendition of their idea(s) is completely accurate. Finally, make sure that you do *not* add quotation marks when paraphrasing.

Following the series of steps outlined in the box below will help you reproduce others' ideas faithfully when you paraphrase.

---

6 Steps to effective paraphrasing

Step 1: Make sure that the idea you are intending to paraphrase is absolutely clear in your own mind; after all you cannot accurately re-present an idea which you do not fully understand.

Step 2: Look out for any words that may carry subtle nuances which can easily get lost in the process of paraphrasing.

Step 3: Particularly if the idea is quite complex, take notes on it. Use those notes rather than the original text when rewriting the idea for this helps protect you against sticking too closely to the original; remember, you are not quoting but paraphrasing.

Step 4: Rewrite the idea, ideally using your notes so as to maintain distance between the original text and your own version of it. Bear in mind that paraphrasing is unlikely to consist merely of changing the words used to express the idea; it will almost certainly involve some restructuring and reorganising of sentences too.

Step 5: Make sure that the new text flows smoothly. Adjust it where necessary.

Step 6: Check your final text thoroughly to ensure it is an accurate reflection of the original.

 Paraphrasing does not necessarily entail shortening the length of the original text. In fact, a paraphrase of a text may, in some instances, end up being longer than the original text. Remember, the main purpose of paraphrase is not to shorten the original text but to re-present it using your own words.

 Look at the two texts below. The second is a paraphrase of the first. Notice, in particular, how the source of the idea (Wiley) is acknowledged in the paraphrase. It's as important to do this with paraphrasing as it is with quotations, the focus of our next section.

Text 1:
Whether language policies are implicit or explicit, they involve goals. On the surface these goals may be seen as either (1) language-related or (2) politically and economically motivated. Upon closer inspection, however, even goals that appear to be mostly language related are generally not without political or economic connection and impact. Among language-related goals, three broad types of policies can be identified: (1) language shift policy, (2) language maintenance policy, and (3) language enrichment policy.   (Adapted from Wiley, 2003)

Text 2:
Wiley (2003) observes that all language policies involve goals and that regardless of whether those goals are language related or politically and economically motivated, they will normally have some degree of political or economic connection or impact. He goes on to identify three broad policy types that can be found within language-related goals, namely language shift policy, language maintenance policy and language enrichment policy.

TRY IT OUT!   #13

Write a paraphrase of the following text using the '6 steps to effective paraphrasing' shown above.

Many teachers in all parts of the world claimed that having a large class prevented them from doing what they wanted to do to help learners make progress in developing their language proficiency. Yet what class size is large or too large depends to a great extent upon the individual teacher's perceptions and experiences. Teachers who have taught classes of 6–12 students in what might be described as elite contexts, such as company language programs or private language schools, complain when suddenly faced with a group of 22. Those who have coped with 40 in language learning classes cease to find that number large.   (Adapted from LoCastro, 2001)

8.4 Referencing styles

'Referencing styles' refers to the different sets of conventions that exist for citing sources in the main body of an essay, dissertation or thesis, and for listing them in the bibliography at the end of your work. Although some university departments give their students quite a bit of freedom over which style they use, provided they use it consistently throughout their work, others are much more prescriptive and require their students to conform to a particular style. Different academic disciplines tend to favour particular referencing styles, and in the case of English language and linguistics one of the most widely used is APA style – the style of the American Psychological Association and on which we will focus in this chapter. APA is one variant of the Harvard system of referencing, sometimes called the 'author-date' system and a detailed account of it can be found in the following publication: American Psychological Association. (2001). *Publication Manual of the American Psychological Association*. Washington, DC: American Psychological Association.

The Harvard system of referencing has a number of different variants the differences between which are often very minor and concerned mainly with capitalisation and punctuation; as such, many English language and linguistics departments simply ask students to use the Harvard system and are content with whichever variant a student selects. Academic journals, however, will normally specify a particular variant and are not flexible in the same way. It's important to remember this should you choose to submit some of your work for publication at some point.

Whichever referencing style you end up using, it's important always to keep in mind the purpose of accurate referencing, namely to acknowledge the ideas of other scholars whose work you have drawn on in your essay or research project, and to enable your reader to easily locate the various sources you have cited and verify the information you have provided. This is done in two ways: by in-text referencing and end-of-text referencing – called the bibliography. In-text referencing refers (a) to the method of quoting your sources directly (as opposed to paraphrasing ideas), and (b) to citing sources you've used and providing their authors' names and the dates/page numbers of those sources. The end-of-text referencing (bibliography) comprises a list of all references you have used in your essay or research report and that includes authors' names, year of publication, title of the work, place of publication and the name of the publisher. As with in-text references, bibliographic entries need to be formatted in a certain way if they are to accord with APA style.

8.5 In-text referencing: how should I quote my sources?

Quoting extended extracts

If you want to include a quotation in your writing which exceeds two or three lines in length, it's normal practice to set it off from the rest of the text in the paragraph by:

- leaving a free line before and after it;
- indenting about 1 centimetre from both left and right margins, justifying both; and
- using a slightly smaller font – for example, a size 10 instead a size 12.

 But language is more than just a container for information and, as such, it is not neutral in learning. It is the vehicle of particular cultural traditions that structure the dialogue of learning and personal engagement with reality. As Gallagher (1992) writes:

> Language like the windowpane, has a certain shape of its own which, outside the user's awareness, may magnify or diminish the objects seen through it. Like the windowpane, language can have a distorting effect. But even more than this ... language is not only an aperture to an already made world, but helps to constitute the world (p. 114).

Learning and coming to know is an act of social, cultural, and historical formation. It is incorporated in and constructed by human beings as they ascribe meaning to phenomena in their experience of engaging with the world they are interpreting through social interaction.

(From Scarino, 2010)

Notice how, in this particular example, a colon is used to introduce the quotation (see also section 2.6, Colons, Rule no. 2). An alternative approach is not to use a colon and instead include the quotation as a natural continuation of the sentence immediately preceding it.

 The theory of language on which the study skills approach is based emphasises surface features, grammar and spelling. The academic literacies model, in contrast, is less crude and insensitive and ... sees the literacy demands of the curriculum as involving a variety of communicative practices, including genres, fields and disciplines. From the student point of view a dominant feature of academic literacy practices is the requirement to switch practices between one setting and another, to deploy a repertoire of linguistic practices appropriate to each setting, and to handle the social meanings and identities that each evokes (Lea and Street, 1998: 159).

These 'settings', or disciplines, are, as Rex and McEachen (1999) note, recognised not only by specialised vocabularies, concepts and knowledges, but also by accepted and valued patterns of meaning-making activity (genres, rhetorical structures, argument formulations, narrative devices etc.) and ways of contesting meaning.

TRY IT OUT! #14

Look at the following extended quotation. Format it correctly and contextualise it by preceding and following it with an appropriate sentence or two.

Despite certain superficial similarities to human language, the communicative systems of various animal species are fundamentally different. This is true, for example, of the gestures that make up the courtship rituals of spiders, the dance of the honeybee that indicates the direction and distance of food sources, and of bird calls and songs. In all such cases, the number of messages that can be conveyed is finite, and the messages are stimulus controlled.

(Adapted from Fromkin and Rodman, 1998)

Quoting shorter extracts

Where they involve shorter extracts – that is, extracts of less than two of three sentences in length – quotations can be integrated into the main text of the paragraph and it's not necessary, therefore, to offset them and leave a free line before and after the quotation. Look at the following two examples.

 There are some limitations in a faculty survey approach, in that survey respondents may not accurately describe their practices. As Anson (1988) notes, '[teachers] may simply believe in certain principles of teaching and learning, responding to a questionnaire under the assumption that their choices accurately reflect what they do in practice' (p. 13). Horowitz (1986), agreeing with Johns (1981) and Zemelman (1978), comments that 'the use of a questionnaire or interview leaves open the question of whether the data reflect what the respondents do, what they think they do, or what they want the researchers to think they do' (p. 448).

(Adapted from Taylor, 1996)

In his studies of code switching, for example, Gumperz defines two types of switching from one language variety to another. First is *situational code switching*: People may switch in accord with 'clear changes in ... participants' definition of "each other's" rights and obligation' (1971, p. 294). Second is *metaphorical code* switching: People may switch varieties within a single situation just to convey a different view of that situation and their relationship. In such cases, the language switch 'relates to particular kinds of topics or subject matters' and is used 'in the enactment of two or more different relationships among the same set of individuals' (1971, p. 295). (From Schiffrin, 2003)

 Square Brackets – Notice how, in the first example, the word *teachers* appears in square brackets. This means it has been added by author Carol Taylor, who is quoting the source. Why has she added it? Because had she not done so, the subject of the sentence (i.e. teachers) might not be evident to the reader due to the fact that the quotation has been removed from its original context.

Ellipses (...) – In the second example, the three dots that appear in line three are used to tell the reader that a part of the original text that's being quoted has been omitted (elided) by author Deborah Schiffrin. If you ever decide to omit part of a quotation, you should always signal it in this way, otherwise you're misrepresenting the original source.

Whenever you quote a source, be sure to provide the name of its author, its year of publication and the page number (or page range, if it spans two pages or more) from which the quotation has been taken. If it's a page range, it will look something like this: (2010, pp. 178–179). Sometimes the author's name and the year of publication may be separated from the page number (as in the first of our two examples), and sometimes the author's name will be separated from the year of publication and page number (as in our second example). Obviously, if it's clear who the author of the quotation is, then it's not necessary to repeat their name with the year of publication and/or the page number. However, a writer will sometimes include a quotation without having previously introduced the author of that quotation. In this case, all the relevant information should be included in the bracketed reference, as in the following example:

 The case of globally aphasic Brother John, a Catholic monk, has been cited as offering 'striking support ... for the retention of ideation or thought processes in the absence of language, and for the separability of linguistic and cognitive competence' (Dingwall 1998, p. 72).

8.6 In-text referencing: citing without quoting

There will be many occasions when you'll want to refer to the work of other scholars without necessarily wishing to quote them. This will be the case when you paraphrase their ideas or when you simply wish to indicate to the reader that you're aware of their work and how it relates to the ideas about which you're writing. In either case, you must once again ensure that you provide accurate in-text references to their work, as in the following examples:

 1. In a two-year investigation of 13 Canadian French-English infant bilinguals with a commencing average age of 34 months, Doyle et al. (1978) also came to the conclusion that there is no evidence that the bilingual child's languages must be separated by person or location, at least as far as optimal vocabulary growth is concerned.   (From Saunders, 1988)

2. The notion of *man* as the unmarked category and *woman* as the marked category is also reflected in pairs of words that are distinguished by gender. As Graddol and Swann (1989) mention, the masculine terms *dog* and *lion* in pairs are considered the 'neutral' terms whereas the feminine counterparts, *bitch* and *lioness* are semantically marked ... However, using suffixes to mark gender seems to be declining (Graddol & Swann, 1989; Poynton, 1989).   (From Freeman and McElhinny, 2003)

3. Analyses of metaphor provide a powerful means of understanding how language use shapes experience (see Lakoff & Johnson, 1980, for further discussion). Martin (1987), for example, moves beyond an analysis of the lexicon to explore how metaphors about women's experiences can reflect gender-based ideologies.   (From Freeman and McElhinny, 2003)

4. The Cape Education Commission of 1892 collected evidence of the 'origin of bilingualism' in the early part of the century (Rose & Tunmer, 1975: 150–153) where provision was made for children to be taught in English or Dutch or both in primary school. The British did, however, attempt to force the English-only in secondary school and this generated resistance and exacerbated a distrust of the English among the Dutch, especially after 1873 (ibid.: 154).   (From Heugh, 2003)

5. At no point did PANSALB engage in an evaluation of related discussions elsewhere (for example in Peru and Nicaragua) about the vexed issue of the authenticity in linguistic description or new corpus planning activities (e.g. Hornberger & King 1998, Freeland 2002, 2003). Neither did it interrogate the process of corpus planning or the critique that corpus planning by definition, is exclusionary and often defeating of its explicit purpose (Hornberger & King op.cit.).   (From Heugh, 2003)

6. Within this development of what has been coined the cultural turn (cf. Lefevere and Bassnett 1990), the systemic reflection on the comparison of target and source texts more or less has been pushed to the background.   (From Coster, 2002)

7. Young, as early as 1978, warned of the consequences of teachers inadequately proficient in English.   (Young 1978, pp. 188–189).
                                                        (From Heugh 1999, p. 303)

8. Although it retained many of the fundamental notions of 'classical' transformational grammar, Principles and Parameters Theory (PPT) differed from earlier versions of the theory in several ways (Chomsky, 1981, 1986b; Haegeman, 1991; Napoli, 1993; Cook & Newson, 1996).
                                        (From Ratner, Gleason and Narasimhan 1998, p. 24)

A heads-up on abbreviations in referencing

et al. – In the first of the above examples, reference is made to 'Doyle et al.' 'et al.' means 'and others' and indicates that Doyle was one of a number of authors of the work to which Saunders is referring. 'Et al.' is used when the number of authors is more than two. The first time you mention a work by multiple authors, use all of their names; however, use 'et al.' on all subsequent occasions (see also section 9.17: What about Latin words and abbreviations?).

'**and**' **vs.** '**&**' – In the examples above, you will notice that both 'and' and '&' have been used. A frequently adopted convention states that 'and' is used when the authors' names are used as part of the sentence (e.g. 'As Graddol and Swann (1989) mention...') whereas '&' is used when the authors' names are used in the bracketed citation (e.g. 'However, using suffixes to mark gender seems to be declining (Graddol & Swann, 1989; Poynton, 1989)').

ibid. and **op. cit.** – In examples 4 and 5, 'ibid.' and 'op. cit.' are used respectively. These Latin abbreviations are both used to refer to a work that has already been mentioned previously and they save the writer having to repeat the full reference multiple times. This also makes it less tiresome for the reader. As a writer, however, you must make it obvious to which previous reference it refers. It would, for example, be unhelpful to refer back to a reference appearing a few pages earlier or in a previous chapter! 'Op. cit.' is used instead of 'ibid.' to cite a reference that does not immediately follow an earlier reference to the same source and/or is separated from it by references to other sources.

cf. – In example 6, the Latin abbreviation 'cf.' precedes the reference to Lefevere and Bassnett. 'Cf.' means 'compare' – or, perhaps more helpfully, 'compare the passage I've just discussed with another one; namely that of Lefevere and Bassnett'. Although it's not exactly the same, it's meaning is similar to 'see also'.

pp. – Note the use of 'pp.' in example 7, to indicate the page range that the quotation spans (188–189).

1986b – In the final example, you will notice that Ratner, Gleason and Narasimhan have used the letter 'b' after the reference year. Writers do this when they cite two or more works published by the same author in the same year and wish to distinguish between them for the benefit of the reader. The fact that Ratner et al. use the letter 'b' tells us that they've already made reference to another Chomsky work elsewhere which they will have cited as 'Chomsky, 1986a'. Were they to use a third Chomsky work also published in 1986, that would have to be cited as 'Chomsky, 1986c'. As we'll see, this 'coding' is also reflected in the bibliography.

Paraphrasing from a secondary source

You will occasionally face a situation where a source you wish to refer to is unavailable and, consequently, you have to refer to someone else's citation of that source. When you do this, you're said to be using a 'secondary source' – the source is one step removed from the original. Although using secondary sources is quite common in news reporting, where it can sometimes be difficult to 'get to' a primary source (particularly if it's somebody who doesn't wish to face the press), doing so in academic writing is strongly discouraged and primary sources should always be used if at all possible. If you absolutely have to use a secondary source then your citation should look like this:

 Pollitt and Murray (cited in Seyek 2009) claim that one useful approach to creating a more natural scale via which to judge students' performance in oral tests of language proficiency is to combine Kelly's 'Repertory Grid' procedure and Thurstone's 'Method of Paired Comparisons'.
or
One useful approach to creating a more natural scale via which to judge students' performance in oral tests of language proficiency is to combine Kelly's 'Repertory Grid' procedure and Thurstone's 'Method of Paired Comparisons' (Pollitt & Murray, cited in Seyek 2009).

Finally, if your secondary source has more than two authors, remember to use 'et al.' (see above):

 Hinckelstein et al. (cited in Taylor & Gravelle 2006) argue that ...
or
... (Hinckelstein et al., cited in Taylor & Gravelle 2006).

Citing electronic sources

When it comes to citing electronic sources in the main body of your text, the rules are essentially the same as those for in-print (hard copy) sources; that is, you're required to provide the author's name, the year of publication, and the page number(s) where relevant. This is the case whether the source is a journal article from an electronic database, an internet website, an e-book, an internet blog/forum, electronic conference proceedings or an email communication. However, if you wish to refer to a general resource, service or homepage, you need to include the URL (web address) in the body of your text. In *all* cases, the url will need to be included for all in-text references in the bibliographic listing (see section 8.7). Look at these examples:

 Flische (2004) argues that there is no pragmatics equivalent to a phonological core that helps ensure mutual intelligibility and is 'cross-culturally democratic' in the way Jenkins (2000) suggests.

Seven of the ten subjects interviewed stated that their opinions had been influenced in part by ideas they had been exposed to via the Internet-based *Phonological Issues* forum (www.phonological_issues_debated.uniund.org).

The Linguistics Society of America (www.lsadc.org/) is one such resource.

If you wish to cite a personal (email) communication, cite the initials and surname of the communicator and give as exact a date as possible: e.g. According to J. L. Souraya, (personal communication, December 5,

2008)... And remember, because emails do not provide recoverable data, they are not included in the bibliography.

8.7. The bibliography: what is it and how should I format it?

A bibliography is a complete list of works that you have cited in your writing, whether in the main body of the text or as footnotes. It should appear at the end of your work and its primary purpose is to enable your reader to locate any of the references you've cited in the main body of your text by providing full details of their publication.

Before looking at the detail of how to format a Harvard-APA style bibliography, here are a few general principles you need to bear in mind when creating your bibliography.

- List all and only those items you've cited in your text and read. Do not include sources you've included as 'cited in' other sources (see 'Paraphrasing from a secondary source', above).
- Include the author's name but do *not* include their title (e.g. 'Professor'). List references alphabetically according to authors' surnames. Where there are multiple authors, keep the names in the same order as they appear on the work being cited. Put initials after rather than before surnames.
- Where you have cited multiple works by the same author some of which are sole-authored, some joint-authored and some multiple-authored, the sole-authored works should be listed first, joint-authored second, and multiple-authored last. However, this only applies if the same author's name appears first (i.e. they are first author) in each of these three cases.
- In the case of a work that you've cited and which appeared in an edited volume, be sure to list the author of the work cited and *not* the editor(s) of the volume.
- Include the year of publication of the work you've cited.
- Include the title of the work you've cited.
- Cite the source of the work. If it's an article or review in a journal, provide the journal's name, volume and issue number, along with inclusive page numbers of the article. If the work is a book, give the city of publication and the name of the publisher. If the work is a chapter in an edited volume, provide the name(s) of the editor of the volume, the title of the volume, the city of publication, the name of the publisher, and the inclusive page numbers for the chapter.
- For Internet sites, include the author's name(s), the date of publication, the title of the page, the URL (web address), and the date that you accessed the site.
- Check the appropriate bibliographic formatting conventions, including punctuation. These are often subtle and easy to miss.

The following table lists the various different kinds of sources you're most likely draw on in your writing and provides examples of how to format these according to the Harvard-APA style of referencing.

Harvard-APA bibliographic referencing conventions	
Sole-authored book	McLaughlin, B. (1985). *Second language acquisition in childhood: Vol. 2. School-age children.* Hillsdale, NJ: Erlbaum.
Joint-authored book	Bassnett, S., & Lefevere, A. (1998). *Constructing cultures. Essays on literary translation.* Clevedon: Multilingual Matters.
Multiple-authored book (3 or more authors)	Vasquez, O. A., Pease-Alvarez, L., & Shannon, S. M. (1994). *Pushing boundaries: Language and culture in a Mexicano community.* Cambridge: Cambridge University Press.
Edited book	Singler, J. V. (Ed.). (1990). *Pidgin and creole tense-mood-aspect systems.* Amsterdam and Philadelphia: John Benjamins.
	Lundquist, L., & Jarvella, R. J. (Eds.). (2000). *Language, text, and knowledge: Mental models of expert communication.* Berlin: Mouton de Gruyter.
More than one publication by the same author in the same year	Cutler, A. (1980a). Syllable omission errors and isochrony. In H. W. Dechert & M. Raupach (Eds.), *Temporal variables in speech* (pp. 183–290). The Hague: Mouton.
	Cutler, A. (1980b). Errors of stress and intonation. In V. A. Fromkin (Ed.), *Errors in linguistic performance: Slips of the tongue, ear, pen, and hand* (pp. 67–80). New York: Academic Press.
Institution, organisation or association as author	University of Western Australia. (2005). *Academic conduct: Guidelines for faculties and other teaching and supervision sections at UWA: Ethical scholarship, academic literacy and academic misconduct.* UWA Handbook. Perth: University of Western Australia
Chapter of an edited book	Shibamoto, J. (1987). The womanly woman: Manipulation of stereotypical and nonstereotypical features of Japanese female speech. In S. Philips, S. Steele, & C. Tanz (Eds.), *Language gender and sex in comparative perspective* (pp. 26–49). Cambridge: Cambridge University Press.

129

Chapter of a non-edited book	Stephenson, D. W. (2009). The problem with apostrophes. In *English as living language* (pp. 123–152). London: Hadleigh Press.
Journal article	MacKay, D. (1979). Lexical insertion, inflection, and derivation: Creative processes in word production. *Journal of Psycholinguistic Research, 8,* 477–498.
	Zuengler, J., & Bent, B. (1991). Relative knowledge of content domain: An influence on native–non-native conversations. *Applied Linguistics, 12*(4), 397–415.
Journal article (in press)	Murray, N. (in press). Pragmatics, awareness-raising, and the Cooperative Principle. *ELT Journal.*
Foreign-language journal article	Bally, C. (1922). Copule zéro et faits connexe's [Zero copula and related issues]. *Bulletin de la Société de Linguistique de Paris, 23,* 1–6.
Abstract	Lee, J. H. (2010). A subject–object asymmetry in the comprehension of *wh*-questions by Korean learners of English [abstract]. *Applied Linguistics, 31*(1), 136–155.
An anonymous work	Anonymous. (1989, 17 February). The literacy problem in schools. *The Daily Herald,* p. 14.
A work with a foreign title	Alonso, M. (1968). *Gramática del español contemporáneo* [A grammar of contemporary Spanish]. Madrid: Guadarrama.
	Ibragimov, G.X. [Г.Х. Ибрагимов]. (1990). Цахурский язык [The Tsakhur language]. Moscow: Nauka.
A translated work	Walter, H. (1994). *French inside out: The worldwide development of the French language in the past, present and the future* (P. Fawcett, Trans.). London: Routledge. (Original work published 1988).
Second, further or revised editions	Crystal, D. (1987). *Child language, learning and linguistics: an overview for the teaching and therapeutic professions.* (2nd ed.). London: Arnold.
Date of publication unknown	Patrie, J. (n.d.). *Language attrition in Japanese returnee students.* Osaka: Beythien Press.
Conference proceedings	Lakoff, R. (1977). What you can do with words: Politeness, pragmatics and performatives. In A. Rogers, B. Wall, & J. Murphy (Eds.), *Proceedings of the Texas conference on performance, presuppositions, and implicatures* (pp. 79–105). Arlington, VA: Center for Applied Linguistics.
Unpublished manuscript submitted for publication	Khalid, F. (2000). *The Arabic tense system.* Manuscript submitted for publication.

130

Unpublished manuscript not submitted for publication	Nmebo, K. (1994). *Dying languages of sub-Saharan Africa*. Unpublished manuscript.
Published dissertation or thesis	Murata, T. (1999). *Particle use in Japanese*. Doctoral dissertation. Meyerlicht: Gudstadt University.
Unpublished dissertation or thesis	Morrisette, M. L. (2000). *Lexical influences on the process of sound change in phonological acquisition*. Unpublished doctoral dissertation, Indiana University, Bloomington.
Unpublished paper presented at a conference, special interest group, etc.	Patel, H. (2003, March). *Dealing with apologies in English*. Paper presented JLA Pragmatics Special Interest Group, Kobe, Japan.
Review	Davies, A. (2008). We are not quite sure what ELF is. [Review of the book *English as a lingua franca: Attitude and identity*, by J. Jenkins]. *Language Assessment Quarterly*, 5(4), 360–364.
Government publications	Department of Arts, Culture, Science and Technology. (1996). Towards a national language plan for South Africa. *Final report of the language plan task group (LANGTAG)*. Pretoria: DOE.
	Shuy, R. W., Wolfram, W., & Riley, W. (1967). *Linguistic correlates of social stratification in Detroit speech*. USOE Final Report No. 6–1347.
Newspaper article	Westrup, B. (2006, 15 August). Immigration and the languages education debate. *Daily Globe*, p. 9.
Encyclopaedia	Bakker, M., Koster, C., & van Leuven-Zwart, K. (1997). Shifts of translation. In M. Baker (Ed.), *Encyclopaedia of translation studies* (pp. 226–231). London: Routledge.

Harvard-APA: Dealing with electronic sources

Internet site with an author	Kasper, G. (2009). Locating politeness in interaction. Retrieved January 23, 2011 from http://sastra.um.ac.id/wp-content/uploads2010/01/PU-Gabriele-Kasper-Locating-Politeness-in-Interaction.pdf.
Electronic copy of journal article retrieved from database	Housen, A., & Kuiken, F. (2009). Complexity, accuracy, and fluency in second language acquisition. *Applied Linguistics 30*, (4), 461–573.

Journal article from an electronic journal	Garcia, P. (2004). Pragmatic comprehension of high and low level language learners. *TESL-EJ, 8*(2). Viewed 18 February 2005, http://berkeley.edu/TESL-EJ/ej30/a!.html.
Internet article based on a print source	Beck, S. (2005). There and back again: A semantic analysis [Electronic version]. Journal *of Semantics, 22*, 3–51.
Newsgroups, online forums, electronic mailing lists	Baker, N. (2009, June 30). Aspirated stops in Sanskrit. Message posted to http://www.lingforum.com/forum/viewforum.php?f=3
	If name unknown, use email address: Sefa.lv@gmail.com (2009, June 30). Aspirated stops in Sanskrit. Message posted to http://www.lingforum.com/forum/viewforum.php?f=3
Newspaper article	Perpitch, N. (2009, June). Language fund risks being lip service. *The Australian.* Retrieved November 6, 2009 from http://www.theaustralian.com.au/news/language-fund-risks-being-lip-service/story-0–1225740664711
Government publication	Department of Education, Employment and Workplace Relations. (2009). Good practice principles for English language proficiency for international students in Australian universities. http://www.deewr.gov.au/HigherEducation/Publications/ Documents/Final_Report-Good_Practice_Principles.pdf (accessed 3/6/09).

8.8 Increasing your efficiency: using bibliographic software packages

In section 4.2 we looked at how important it is to record your sources meticulously. Today, the job of keeping track of sources and, subsequently, of formatting them for the purposes of a bibliography has been made much easier thanks to the availability of software packages designed specifically for this purpose. Three of the most popular such packages are Endnote (www.endnote.com), RefWorks (www.refworks.com – a web-based service) and Reference Manager (www.refman.com). While it requires some investment of your time initially, it's certainly worthwhile familiarising yourself with at least one of these packages, for the time you spend getting to grips with it and inputting the sources that you cite in your writing will pay off handsomely in the long run. By using 'bibliographic management software' of this kind, you can create a database of references that can be input manually or imported directly from library catalogues and commercial databases. And once you've done that, the software is able to create a bibliography and format it for you, in whichever style you wish, and within whatever word processing programme you are using – thereby saving you many hours of work over the course of your studies. In fact, even as you cite references in the main text, programmes like Endnote are busy building your bibliography, adding each new source as you cite it. Recent versions of Endnote will even allow you to import *publisher-created* pdf files and identify the necessary bibliographical information before adding the source to your bibliography. If you don't already use this kind of software, it's certainly worth checking out what it can do for you.

 Most universities will have licensing agreements with the providers of bibliographic management software packages that allow you to download them free to your computer at no cost to you. Make the most of this service!

TRY IT OUT! #15

Look at the reference information below. Use it to create a bibliography correctly formatted according to Harvard-APA style. Be careful to use the correct font styles and punctuation.

AUTHOR:	D. Slobin
DATE:	1966
TITLE:	grammatical transformations and sentence comprehension in childhood and adulthood
PUBLISHER:	journal of verbal learning and verbal behaviour 5 219–227

AUTHOR:	P. Trudgill
DATE:	1990
TITLE:	the dialects of England
PUBLISHER:	Oxford: Blackwell

AUTHOR:	S. Ehrlich, R. King
DATE:	1992
TITLE:	feminist meanings and sexist speech communities
SOURCE:	K. Hall, M. Bucholtz, B. Moonwomon (editors) Locating power: proceedings of the second Berkeley women and language conference (pages 100–107)
PUBLISHER:	Berkeley: Berkeley Women and Language Group, Department of Linguistics, University of California at Berkeley

---

TRY IT OUT! (*cont.*) #15

AUTHOR:	L. Travers
DATE:	7 August 2010 p. 3
TITLE:	why is RP not good enough anymore?
PUBLISHER:	National Tribune

AUTHOR:	B. Johnstone
DATE:	1993
TITLE:	community and contest: Midwestern men and women creating their worlds in conversational storytelling
SOURCE:	D. Tannen (editor) Gender and conversational interaction (pages 62–82)
PUBLISHER:	Oxford: Oxford: Oxford University Press.

AUTHOR:	L. Bailey
DATE:	19 March 2010
TITLE:	pronoun position
SOURCE:	http://www.englishforums.com/English/PronounPosition/nrqwz/post.htm (message posted to forum)

AUTHOR:	K. Pahl
DATE:	2005
TITLE:	review: a critical discourse analysis of family literacy practices: Power in and out of print (a review)
PUBLISHER:	applied linguistics 26 131–134

AUTHOR:	A. M. El Zawawy
DATE:	2009 (viewed May 16, 2010)
TITLE:	rethinking construction grammar: contributions and outstanding questions
PUBLISHER:	Web journal of formal, computational & cognitive linguistics

http://fccl.ksu.ru/issue11/FCCL_09_Rethinking_Construction_Grammar.pdf

---

8.9 Handy language

The following phrases are widely used to cite authors and/or introduce quotations and paraphrases:

X states/has stated that …	*It has been argued/proposed that …*
X and Y have suggested that …	*X argues: …*
X et al. have made a stronger	*X explains that …*

claim, insisting that …
X puts/explains/describes it thus: …
Referring to …, X comments …
X goes on to argue that …
He claims that any theory of learning
needs to '…

As X maintains, …
X amplifies on this as follows: …
In her introduction to …, X states: …
According to X, …
In the words of X, '…
X describes this as/in terms of …

Chapter 8 Key points checklist

- Referencing your sources meticulously shows your familiarity with the literature and is one key way of avoiding accusations of plagiarism – the cardinal sin of academic writing.

- There are two ways of incorporating the ideas of other scholars into your writing: through direct quotation and through paraphrasing.

- Even when paraphrasing you need to acknowledge the source you are paraphrasing.

- Paraphrase should be brief but capture accurately the essence of the source idea.

- It's important to check the preferred referencing style of your department/ discipline.

- Be consistent in the way you reference your sources.

- Quotations longer than two or three lines should be set off from the text immediately preceding and following it by means of (i) a line space before and after the quotation, (ii) an indentation of the left and right margins (both justified), and (iii) the use of a smaller font.

- Quotations shorter than two or three lines should be integrated into the main text of the paragraph.

- Quotations should be accompanied by the author's name, the year of publication of the book/article in which it appeared, and the relevant page numbers.

- Wherever possible, use primary rather than secondary sources.

- Where necessary, include the URL (web address) for electronic sources, with the date you accessed them.

- Bibliographies should include details of all sources cited and read, listed in alphabetical order according to author surname.

- Keep a detailed record of all sources you use to avoid the frustration of having to re-identify them later on.

Stylistic issues

'I worry about how I'm expected to write at uni – you know, how formal I should be, whether there's a special style and so on. I worry that my school essays haven't prepared me.'

What's covered in this chapter:
Concision and clarity
The use of first person singular – 'I'
'All-or-nothing' language
Using present tense to refer to others' work
Emotive and biased language
Vague and empty language (see also 3.3: How to argue)
Casual language: colloquialisms and slang
Shortened forms
Using humour
Formatting your work – some dos and don'ts
Clichés
Dealing with jargon
Keeping your writing gender-neutral
Using footnotes: a reminder
Avoiding rhetorical questions
Formatting linguistic examples
What about Latin words and abbreviations?
Checking and editing your work

Much of this book has looked at basic principles of researching and structuring your writing in English language and linguistics. This chapter looks at one other key ingredient that is necessary if your work is to 'feel right' and conform to the expectations of your discipline and therefore those of your lecturers and examiners as well: good style. Your writing must consistently demonstrate an academic style that is not only engaging but appropriate. While we've considered some of the factors that can help make your writing engaging (e.g. sound and incisive critical analysis, well-articulated reasoning, original thinking, the effective use of thesis statements and examples), it's important to remember that the choices you make as you strive for a style that's also appropriate are equally if not more important, for, ultimately, they can make the difference between an exceptional piece of work and one that's mediocre, even poor.

9.1 Concision and clarity

Although we looked at concision in section 2.5, it is worth revisiting it briefly here in the light of its importance to good academic writing. Concision, you'll recall, means keeping your writing brief and to the point, and avoiding waffle and the inclusion of information that's peripheral to your main discussion and which doesn't have a direct and immediate bearing on it. Such information is likely to be seen by the reader as irrelevant and an unnecessary distraction. Writing that is concise tends to be clear and easy to understand and it can be achieved by adhering to a few key strategies highlighted in the following list:

Tips for Achieving clarity in your writing

- Make sure that the ideas you wish to express are crystal clear in your own mind (see also section 3.3). Waffly or 'woolly' writing is often the result of trying to clarify ideas *as* you are writing rather than *prior to* doing so. In other words, do not try to formulate fully your ideas *through* writing them but *before* writing them.
- Don't say in two or three sentences what you can say just as easily in one. Be concise and economical.
- Keep your language simple and straightforward. Don't try to use ostentatious language where simpler, more everyday language will do just as well. Students often struggle, unnecessarily, to make their language sound more erudite by using complex structures and sophisticated vocabulary. Remember: avoid making your expression of ideas more difficult than it needs to be.
- Avoid flowery language. It detracts from the serious, academic feel of your work as well as its clarity and therefore undermines its content, regardless of how well conceived it may be.
- Minimise your use of technical language and jargon except where absolutely necessary.

- As you proof-read your work, ask yourself whether the language is getting in the way of the meaning. Is there a way of simplifying what you want to say and making it more readable without making it feel simplistic and naïve?
- Run your writing by a friend to see whether they feel it's clearly and concisely written or whether they find it heavy-going and difficult to process.
- Check your writing for instances of ambiguity – where a reader may interpret what you've written in a way that's different from what you intend.
- Check your writing for instances of repetition or redundancy.

9.2 The use of first person singular – 'I'

The question of whether or not to use 'I' in academic writing tends to cause a lot of angst among students, and it therefore justifies a short section of its own.

The fact is that attitudes to using 'I' in written academic discourse are changing. Traditionally, it was not considered appropriate – probably because it called into question the objectivity of the writer and their right to (apparently) presume that their opinion mattered or had any authority. As such, while established scholars in certain disciplines might get away with using it, undergraduates – who were 'wet behind the ears' and had yet to 'prove' themselves – were very likely to be taken to task for doing so. This, however, has changed quite dramatically in recent years; attitudes have changed and the use of first person singular is becoming more widely accepted in the academic community, and certainly in linguistics. Yet even today, different disciplines – and even different lecturers – have different views on whether or not it's acceptable, and I would advise, therefore, that you check to see whether there are any departmental conventions or rulings on this, and also what the expectations are of individual lecturers who will be looking at your work and assigning marks to it. If you're still unclear, I would suggest playing it safe and avoiding the use of 'I' by substituting alternative forms of expression that depersonalise your language. Here are some ways that you might do this (you will notice that in many cases it involves substituting active with passive voice):

Strategies for avoiding the use of first person singular: 'I'

Instead of ...	consider using ...
I	this writer/the author
I believe/am of the opinion that ...	it can be argued that ... /there is reason to suppose/believe that ...

	there is a case for saying that ...
I don't think this argument is valid	this argument is/appears to be invalid
I disagree (with this claim)	there is reason to question (this claim)
I observed that ...	it was observed that ...
I found the results surprising because ...	the results were surprising in that ...
I noticed/observed that ...	it was discovered that ...
I was intrigued to find that ...	the finding that ... was intriguing
I think there are reasons to question this	there are reasons to question this
I take this to mean that ...	this can be taken to mean that ... /there is reason to suppose/believe that ...
I randomly selected six subjects	six subjects were randomly selected
I considered it unethical to conduct the study under such conditions	it was considered unethical to conduct the study under such conditions
I decided to use a mixed methods approach	the decision was taken to use a mixed methods approach

9.3 'All-or-nothing' language

We saw in section 3.3. (*Presenting your arguments most effectively – Step 5: Using persuasive language*) how, in an academic context in particular, it can be dangerous to use language that's not moderate or measured. Words and phrases that are absolute – what I call 'all-or-nothing language' – should only be used very sparingly and when there really is absolutely no room for doubt over the statements to which they are being applied. Such situations are, in reality, exceedingly rare in most disciplines, particularly the humanities and social sciences, and certainly in linguistics. Most linguistic rules and the way they are deployed, for example, almost always have exceptions and we are therefore almost never able to say that form X always behaves in fashion Y in environment/context Z. Similarly, we can never say that all languages exhibit a particular feature, for there are languages in the world of which we know little or nothing. You get the point ...! In cases like these, we have to tone down our language because unless the situation truly warrants it we risk appearing reckless, naive or both.

Of course, if you're describing language data, there are likely to be a considerably greater number of occasions where you're at liberty to use absolute language – after all, you'll be reporting observable phenomena based only on what is understood to be a restricted sample of language. As such, it is understood that any observations reported will be valid only so far as that particular sample is concerned – although it may be strongly suggestive of greater generalisability. Therefore, in reporting on data, statements of the following kind are fairly commonplace in linguistics:

> *Despite the count/non-count noun rule, all subjects used* less *rather than* fewer *in every instance, thus supporting the hypothesis.*

Words/phrases to be used with caution

always	*never*	*never occurs*	*absolute/absolutely*
completely	*entirely*	*definitely*	*only*
all	*everybody*	*without exception*	*universal/universally accepted*
true/truth	*undeniable*	*for sure*	*unquestionable/unquestionably*
certainly	*whatsoever*	*without doubt*	*indisputable/indisputable truth*

 Remember: while it's important to be careful when using all-or-nothing language, using language that is too tentative can also be a bad thing in that it can make you look as though you're hedging because you're uncertain and lacking conviction.

9.4 Using present tense to refer to others' work

Generally, it's considered good practice to refer to the work of other scholars by using the present tense. The reason for this is that it indicates that the work you're citing remains relevant to your own discussion, despite perhaps having been written a long time ago, possibly by someone who is no longer living. In other words, it 'brings their ideas into the present' by keying them into your current work. Compare the following:

> *In his seminal 1967 paper, Corder identified a five-stage process of error analysis.*

> *In his seminal paper 1967 paper, Corder identifies a five-stage process of error analysis.*

> *Smith conducted a study that demonstrated that …*

> *Smith (2002) demonstrates that …*

You may choose the past tense if you wish to show that a particular work or idea is specifically of historical interest.

9.5 Emotive and biased language

As its name suggests, emotive language is language used by a speaker or writer which indicates that he or she has an emotional investment in the things they're writing about. While, as a writer, it is natural to feel strongly about some of the ideas you commit to paper, it's important not to let this colour your language in such a way that it risks losing its objectivity and therefore feeling un-academic (see section 3.3: How to argue – Bias). Remember: in academic writing you must always be seen to be fair and objective in your discussion and evaluation of ideas. If your reader begins to doubt that objectivity, they'll lose faith in your arguments and the ideas that underlie them. This in turn means that the chances of your getting a good grade for your work are greatly reduced.

The table below highlights a selection of emotive words and phrases that will quickly put your reader on guard and most of which have appeared at some time or other in my students' essays. Many of these words are also unacceptable because they are overly casual (see section 9.4).

Emotive words to be treated with caution				
ridiculous	*outrageous*	*absurd*	*no idea at all*	*incredible*
hopeless	*brilliant*	*fantastic*	*idiotic*	*astonishing*
terrible	*amazing*	*awesome*	*superb*	*crazy*
pathetic	*rubbish*	*trash*	*abysmal*	*perfect*

 While it's natural to feel strongly about some of the ideas you write about, you mustn't let your own particular perspective and emotions get in the way of presenting facts and arguments in a neutral fashion. Be sure to tone down your language in order to appear emotionally distanced from what you're discussing.

Finally, beware of stereotyping – also a kind of bias, and certainly unscholarly. Sentences such as *Being Japanese, they were poor language learners and therefore struggled to learn the functions taught them* are unacceptable and seriously undermine the credibility of your work.

9.6 Vague and empty language

We saw in section 3.3 (How to argue) that when we hedge our writing tends to become vague, and that this is undesirable in academic writing. Vague writing suggests that either: (a) your ideas are themselves vague and ill-formed; (b) you don't understand the ideas of other writers that you are citing; or (c) you're deliberately manipulating or misleading your reader by being deliberately obtuse or economical with the truth. Whatever the reason, the impact on your reader is negative. Some particular words that demand caution are listed in the following table. I'm not suggesting that these should never be used, only that they be used discriminatingly.

Hedging words to be treated with caution				
may	*might*	*can*	*could*	*should*
rather	*fairly*	*perhaps*	*possibly*	*probably*
around	*about*	*seems*	*appears*	*tends (to)*
usually	*sometimes*	*quite*	*generally*	*reasonably*

Similarly, avoid the temptation to use words that sound good and which you think your reader will want to hear rather than words that accurately express what you actually mean!

9.7 Casual language: colloquialisms and slang

In the same way that you should guard against using emotive language in your writing, you should also avoid casual language (and spellings), including colloquialisms and slang. These kinds of informal language are not in keeping with the more formal, conservative style expected of academic writing. Although even spoken language requires us to conform to certain expectations (in an interview situation, for example, or a court of law), most written language differs significantly from spoken language in that, depending on who we are writing for, we generally have to think more about the stylistic conventions appropriate to particular situations and what form our writing should take. This is particularly true of the university setting, where failure to conform to academic writing conventions by using inappropriate language that is too informal will mean that your writing and the ideas it expresses will feel 'light'. It will feel less serious and therefore carry less weight. Furthermore, it will indicate that you're not familiar with the conventions and expectations of this kind of writing.

TRY IT OUT! #16

Look at the informal expressions listed in the left column below. In the right column, write one or more formal alternatives that would be acceptable in academic writing. The first word has been done as an example.

Informal	Formal
like	*such as, similar to, comparable to*
totally	
low-down	
cool	
really	

OK
the best of the lot
all right
honestly
nice
cute (as in 'a cute idea')
kind of/almost
awesome

Examples of informal language to be avoided include: *kind of*, *no way*, *really/way* (meaning *very*), *totally* and *anyway* (at the start of a sentence).

Listed in the left column in the box below are a number of other words and phrases which, although not necessarily inappropriate, can be usefully replaced by words (in the right column) that feel more eloquent without making your writing feel stilted and pompous. These words tend to feature widely in academic discourse; however, be careful not to overuse them.

Giving your language an 'academic' flavour

Instead of . . .	consider using . . .
a lot	many, widely, extensively
back up	confirm, corroborate, substantiate
big, large	considerable, substantial
but, however	nevertheless, although
checked	verified
did	conducted, carried out
different from	distinct, distinguishable from
especially	particularly
factors	variables
found, noticed, recognised	identified
got rid of	eliminated
important	significant
long	extensive, extended
looked at/into	examined, investigated
numbers	figures, statistics, data
often	frequently
people	subjects (as in a study)
relationship	correlation
saw, noticed	observed
saw, found	discovered
seems	appears

shows	illustrates, indicates, demonstrates
so	therefore, consequently
very	highly, considerably, exceptionally
give	provide

* Be careful: the words in the right column may not always serve as synonyms for those in the left column. Nor are they necessarily always more desirable.

9.8 Shortened forms

Shortened forms refer to words that contain apostrophes but which can instead be written out in full without apostrophes. They include:

Shortened form	Full form
it's	*it is*
they're	*they are*
won't/wouldn't	*will not/would not*
can't/ couldn't	*cannot/could not*
shouldn't	*should not*
mustn't	*must not*
hasn't/haven't/hadn't	*has not/have not/had not*
wasn't/weren't	*was not/were not*
I'll/he'll/she'll/we'll/they'll	*I will/he will/she will/we will/they will*
there's	*there is*

As we noted in Chapter 2, shortened forms are generally considered unacceptable in academic writing because they too are associated with casual forms of writing. Once again though, within the study of language and linguistics, you may find yourself using shortened forms when faithfully recording spoken or written data in the precise way it was originally produced. Obviously, in this particular context it's acceptable.

It's important to remember that not all words that include an apostrophe are shortened forms – for example, when the apostrophe is used to indicate possession (see section 2.6), as in the following examples:

> *The researcher's primary tool is . . .*
> *The linguist's main concern is with . . .*
> *Elsa's pronunciation of this particular dipthong consistently exhibited . . .*
> *Pienemann's 1983 study is notable in that . . .*

In these instances, the apostrophe is not only acceptable but necessary.

Finally, shortened forms can also include non-conventional spellings which reflect shortened spoken forms of words such as *gonna*, *wanna*, *cos* and *thinkin'*. Such spellings are considered unacceptable in academic writing and you can be certain that your lecturers will not approve of them!

9.9 Using humour

The use of humour in written work is a dangerous thing and I generally advise strongly against it. Academic work is by its very nature a serious business and, while there may be a rare opportunity to inject a little humour into your writing, attempts to do so can easily backfire and end up making you look naive and immature. The ability to 'pull off' humour in your writing requires the ability to know when it's appropriate and to adopt a tone and sophistication that will go some way to ensuring that it's well received by your reader. Undergraduates rarely have this ability and are therefore well advised to steer clear of humour and any attempts to adopt a 'jokey' tone in their writing.

9.10 Formatting your work – some dos and don'ts (see also section 6.4)

First impressions are always important, even in academic work, and by following a number of simple rules you can give your written work a polished and professional feel.

Do use headings and sub-headings to indicate the status of sections and make the organisation of your work more transparent and the structure easier to follow.

Do justify your text so that all the printed lines in a paragraph (except the final line) are of the same length.

Do ensure you leave adequate margins (at least 2–3 cms) on either side of the page. This improves the look of your work and allows your lecturers to write feedback in the margins, should they wish to do so.

Do leave a free line before a section heading or sub-heading.

Do be consistent in your use of font size. Try to stick with one font and one font size (normally 12) as far as possible, except for headings, where you may wish to increase the font size to 14, while keeping it at 12 for sub-headings.

Do bold your title and headings. You may also wish to bold some sub-headings depending on how you choose to tier your headings (see section 6.4: Headings – sections and sub-sections, titles and sub-titles).

Do number your pages and figures.

Don't use casual fonts. Fancy fonts *such as this one* feel too informal and playful and you are best off sticking to a more traditional font such as Times New Roman or Arial.

Don't use long or ornate titles and headings. Keep them crisp and ensure that they capture the main focus of the essay or section. If possible, try and keep them to a maximum of twelve words for titles and eight words for headings.

Don't use multiple colours, except where absolutely necessary. As with fancy fonts, a kaleidoscopic piece of work risks making your work feel less serious and academic, even childish. Try to stick with black and grey scales. Where you find you do need to use other colours – for example in pie charts or other types of charts and graphs where it can be necessary to differentiate between multiple segments, bars or lines – try to use subdued colours rather than colours that require your reader to wear sunglasses!

9.11 Clichés

Clichés are expressions which are overused and therefore tend to feel tired and lacking in creativity. As such, it's best to avoid them where possible, even though it can sometimes be difficult to think of suitable alternatives. All of the clichés listed below have appeared at some time or other in my own students' work:

Same common clichés to avoid

at loggerheads	*at the end of the day*	*at this point in time*
bone of contention	*take the bull by the horns*	*a doubting Thomas*
dyed in the wool	*it goes without saying*	*hidden agenda*
hit the nail on the head	*in the same boat*	*jump on the bandwagon*
the jury is still out	*know the score*	*labour of love*
last but not least	*leaps and bounds*	*leave no stone unturned*
movers and shakers	*needless to say*	*old meets new*
only game in town	*out on a limb*	*a red herring*
see their way clear	*stick out like a sore thumb*	*the bottom line*
tried and tested	*very real concern*	*wakeup call*

TRY IT OUT! #17

Rewrite each of the sentences below without using the underlined clichés.

1. Widdowson, Nunan and Wilson were three key *movers and shakers* of the communicative movement in the 1970s and 80s.
   *Rewrite:*_____

2. Research around a natural order of acquisition of grammatical morphemes progressed by *leaps and bounds* in the mid-1980s.
Rewrite:_____

_____

3. Publishers of language-teaching materials – and particularly English language-teaching materials – were quick to *jump on the* Communicative Language Teaching *bandwagon* in the 1980s and 90s.
Rewrite:_____

_____

4. Traditionalist grammarians, who see themselves as gatekeepers of the English language, have always been *at loggerheads* with scholars and academics who see language evolution and change as inevitable and not subject to rigid rules and standards.
Rewrite:_____

9.12 Dealing with jargon

Jargon is the terminology associated with a particular academic, professional or other area of activity – in our case language and linguistics. In fact, ours is a field that has become rather notorious for what many regard as its excessive use of jargon, and acronyms in particular (FLA, SLA, TESOL, EAL, ESP, NESB, PELA, IELTS, etc.). Paolo Cordone, in speaking of the use of jargon in professional or work contexts, says this:

> Jargon, most commonly represented by acronyms and technical terms can, in fact, be found in virtually any industry and can seem obscure to outsiders who are not familiar with conventions and peculiarities of that business [in our case, language and linguistics]. However, becoming familiar with jargon is a normal process when entering a profession and it is often only a matter of time before the nuances are mastered. It is a necessity to be able to communicate effectively with colleagues and this represents a great incentive to learning it.

> However, the role of jargon as a useful linguistic element coexists with jargon as a tool for defining social relations incorporating roles of authority and submission. This happens particularly within the private sector, where unnecessary wordiness and sentence complexity are employed to prove superiority and to influence the 'lower ranks', and in the public sector, where the extreme use of jargon can often be described as writing to impress, rather than writing to inform. (From Cordone, n.d.)

In other words, when writing in a specialised field such as linguistics it is sometimes necessary to use jargon, and it may often be assumed that your reader will understand it, especially if it's your tutor! However, do no overuse it so that it obscures meaning or your lack of understanding and clutters your text, making it dense and hard work to read. As a rule, keep it to a minimum. It's generally best to use straightforward language that doesn't assume too much specialised knowledge on the part of your reader. This idea is in keeping with the push towards 'plain English' that can currently be found in many areas of life, such as the insurance and advertising industries. The point is that while sometimes necessary, jargon, particularly if overused, can have the undesirable effect of obscuring meaning and making your writing less accessible and less pleasurable to read.

9.13 Keeping your writing gender-neutral

Nowadays, use of the words *he*, *she*, *his* and *her* are increasingly discouraged in academic writing, unless you're referring to a particular individual of whom you know the sex – for example a subject in a study, or a particular author. In any other situation it's best either to rephrase what you want to say or to use the word *they*, as a substitute. Look at this example:

 Gender-specific
Evidence suggests that, even if he receives substantial amounts of input, a person who lacks integrative and/or instrumental motivation will not be an effective second-language learner.

Gender-neutral (rephrasing)
Evidence suggests that, in the absence of integrative and/or instrumental motivation, input alone is insufficient for effective second-language learning to occur.

Gender-neutral (substituting *he* with *they*)
Evidence suggests that, even if they receive substantial amounts of input, people who lack integrative and/or instrumental motivation will not be effective second-language learners.

9.14 Using footnotes: a reminder

Finally, don't forget to check your department's rules on the use of footnotes. As we saw in section 6.4 (where we also looked at how to format footnotes), increasingly footnotes are being discouraged and you're expected, wherever possible, to include information in the main body of the text. If the information is too incidental or peripheral to be included there, you may wish to ask yourself whether it's worth including at all. If you decide that it is, then consider putting it at the end of your work either as a note or, if it's longer, as an appendix (see section 10.4).

9.15 Avoiding rhetorical questions

In our discussion of conclusions (chapter 8), we saw that it's unwise to use rhetorical questions to wrap up a conclusion. This is true of academic writing generally, where your job is normally to answer questions rather than ask them!

9.16 Formatting linguistic examples

As a general rule, when you wish to highlight a particular utterance or linguistic expression as it's said or written, you should type it using italics (e.g. 'The word *interesting* can be understood in various ways'). However, when you're analysing its composition and meaning, you'll need to provide what's known as a 'gloss' – in other words an explanation of its form and/or translation of its meaning. A gloss might therefore be a 'morpheme gloss' and/or a 'word-by-word gloss'. Look at the following examples:

Example 1

i. Faye kheli khoshkel e (the original utterance in Persian)

ii. Faye very beautiful is (word-by-word gloss of the utterance)

iii. Faye kheili khoshkel-e (morpheme gloss of the utterance)

iv. Faye very-ADJ   (morpheme-by-morpheme correspondence
    beautiful-3SG   using standard abbreviations. Here
                              ADJ = adjective, and 3SG = third
                              person singular.)

v. 'Faye is very beautiful.' (a translation of the original utterance –
                              normally placed in single inverted commas)

In a text this might be explained as follows: *The words* ziba *and* khoshkel *are most commonly used in Persian to mean 'pretty'. The final e in khoshkel is the verb 'to be'. This sentence, therefore, means 'Faye is very beautiful'.*

Example 2

The three lines in this example are equivalent to iii, iv and v in example 1.

Nous   ne   faisons   rien
We+NOM   NEG   doing-1PL   nothing
'We aren't doing anything.' or 'We are doing nothing.'

Glossing conventions such as these provide a standard way of abbreviating linguistic descriptions and therefore enable those within the linguistics community to readily understand glosses. As you'll see from the example, two common glossing conventions involve what's called 'word-by-word alignment' and 'morpheme-by-morpheme correspondence'. In the former, the equivalents of the two languages being compared are aligned, as in ii, where *very* aligns precisely with its counterpart in Persian, *kheli*, just as *beautiful* aligns with *khoshkel*. In the latter, the morphological composition of the original utterance is analysed in terms of its equivalent in the comparison language – often English. As you can see from the examples, grammatical morphemes are presented in small caps. Also notice how each morpheme is separated by a hyphen unless it's a word boundary, in which case it's separated by a space. A list of standard glossing abbreviations and their meanings can be found in the table below.

1	first person	F	feminine	PROG	progressive
2	second person	FOC	focus	PROH	prohibitive
3	third person	FUT	future	POSS	Possessive
A	agent-like argument of canonical transitive verb	GEN	genitive	PRED	Predicative
ABL	Ablative	IMP	imperative	PRF	Perfect
ABS	Absolutive	INCL	inclusive	PRS	Present
ACC	Accusative	IND	indicative	PROX	proximal/ proximate
ADJ	Adjective	INDF	indefinite	PST	Past
ADV	adverb(ial)	INF	infinitive	PTCP	Participle
AGR	Agreement	INS	instrumental	PURP	Purposive
ALL	Allative	INTR	intransitive	Q	question particle/ marker
ANTIP	Antipassive	IPFV	imperfective	QUOT	Quotative
APPL	Applicative	IRR	irrealis	RECP	Reciprocal
ART	Article	LOC	locative	REFL	Reflexive
AUX	Auxiliary	M	masculine	REL	Relative
BEN	Benefactive	N	neuter	RES	Resultative
CAUS	Causative	N-	non- (e.g. NSG nonsingular, NPST nonpast)	S	single argument of canonical intransitive verb
CLF	Classifier	NEG	negation, negative	SBJ	Subject
COM	Comitative	NMLZ	nominalizer/ nominalization	SBJV	Subjunctive
COMP	Complementizer	NOM	nominative	SG	Singular
COMPL	Completive	OBJ	object	TOP	Topic
COND	Conditional	OBL	oblique	TR	Transitive

COP	Copula	P	patient-like argument of canonical transitive verb	VOC	Vocative
CVB	Converb	PASS	passive		
DAT	Dative	PFV	perfective		
DECL	Declarative	PL	plural		

 Although it's common practice to highlight a particular utterance or linguistic expression by using italics, sometimes you may need to highlight part of an extract that is *already* italicised. In this case, you can highlight the relevant part by de-italicising it.

Other symbols used before linguistic examples include the following:

* * used before an expression that is ungrammatical or non-existent (e.g. *bestest)
* ? used before an expression of questionable grammaticality (e.g. ?There are less people applying to university in the UK.)
* # used before an utterance that is pragmatically odd or inappropriate (e.g. #I want you to go out with me on a date.)
* * used before hypothesised proto-forms (in historical linguistics) (e.g. *kord-is)

Typing foreign alphabets, accented letters and phonetic symbols: a special note

As a student of linguistics you will almost certainly have to look at languages other than English which may use different alphabets and/or accented letters. This may be in the context of having to contrast two or more languages as part of an assignment, for example, or perhaps analysing a particular syntactic structure in another language. Whatever the context, you'll need to be able to type foreign alphabets and accented letters, and this can be a slow and arduous process. The good news is that there is at least one way of making that process easier and quicker. Even better, the same process can be used to type phonetic symbols – something else you'll likely have to do during the course of your degree programme.

As you probably know already, you can obtain most accented letters and phonetic symbols in MS Word by going to the *Insert* menu and selecting *Symbol*. Depending on the font you're using, you'll be able to get most, if not all the letters and symbols you need. You can also download free phonetic fonts from: www.sil.org/computing/fonts/encore-ipa.html.

The problem with this system, however, is that each time you want to type a particular letter or symbol you have to go through this process.

151

If you're using a particular letter or symbol repetitively (which tends to happen fairly rarely), you can cut and paste to speed things up, but otherwise the process remains very laborious. A good solution is to use Word's **AutoCorrect** function. The idea here is that you 'programme' Word to recognise a code that you decide on and to convert it into another letter, symbol, word or phrase automatically. So if, for example, you decide to use the code \nt\ to represent the letter ñ (called n tilde), every time you type \nt\ Word will automatically convert it to ñ. This means that you don't have to go through a series of commands but can continue typing as normal and let Word do the work!

 It's necessary to have either a space or a non-alphanumeric character before and after the code as this tells AutoCorrect where the code starts and finishes and stops it incorrectly identifying and converting *all* instances where **n** and **t** (\nt\) appear together in words – such as in *want*.

There are two very helpful articles available online which explain in detail how this system works. They are:

The easy way to type foreign alphabets and accented letters in MS word (by Dermod Quirke and Brian Holser) www.google.co.uk/#hl=en&q=the+easy+way+to+type+foreign+alphabets&meta=&aq=f&oq=the+easy+way+to+type+foreign+alphabets&fp=a8b625c7eeb9e358

The easy way to type phonetic symbols, too, in MS Word (by John Wells) www.docstoc.com/docs/18612550/eureka-ipa-ucl-londons-global-university

The codes Quirke and Holser recommend for some of the most common European accents are as follows:

Code	Letter	Code	Letter	Code	Letter	Code	Letter
\za\	ź	\em\	ē	\c,\	ç	\l/\	ł
\ub\	ŭ	\ao\	å	\a,\	ą	\oe\	œ
\ac\	â	\nt\	ñ	\ae\	æ	\o/\	ø
\eg\	è	\au\	ä	\dh\	ð	\th\	þ
\oh\	ő	\rv\	ř	\ij\	ij	\ss\	ß

Wells suggests the following codes for the phonetic letters and symbols necessary for transcribing at least English RP, French, German, Spanish and Italian. Where there's overlap with the letters in Quirk and Holser's inventory, you can use the same code. In the interests of consistency, I have used backslashes in the codes where Wells uses vertical lines.

Vowels

Code	Letter	Code	Letter	Code	Letter	Code	Letter
\A\	ɑ	\E\	ɛ	\O\	ɔ	\U\	ʊ
\{\	æ	\@\	ǝ	\2\	ø	\}\	ʉ
\6\	ɐ	\3\	ɜ	\9\	œ	V	ʌ
\Q\	ɒ	\I\	ɪ	\&\	Œ	Y	ʏ

Consonants

Code	Letter	Code	Letter	Code	Letter	Code	Letter
\B\	β	\J\	ɲ	\S\	ʃ	\?\	ʔ
\C\	ç	\L\	ʎ	\T\	θ		
\D\	ð	\N\	ŋ	\H\	ɥ		
\G\	ɣ	\R\	ʁ	\Z\	ʒ		

Length, stress and tone marks

Code	Symbol
\:\	ː
\"\	ˈ
\%\	ˌ

Diacritics

Code	Symbol
\=\	ˌ, e.g. n̩
\~\	˜, e.g. ã

Others

Code	Symbol	Code	Symbol	Code	Symbol
\I\	ɨ	\R|\	ʀ	\K\	ɬ
\t`\	ʈ	\4\	ɾ	\5\	ɫ
\n`\	ɳ	\h|\	ɦ	\M|\	ɰ

Transcribing speech phonetically, phonemically and orthographically

If, in your writing, you're focusing on pronunciation, you'll need to be able to distinguish between phonemic and phonetic script. You do this by enclosing phonemic transcriptions in slanted brackets (e.g. /d/) and phonetic script – which represents a sound's actual realisation rather than its general sound category – in square brackets (e.g. [s]). In order to demonstrate this distinction it can be helpful to consider a well-known example: the problem Japanese and Korean learners of English have differentiating

153

the English phonemes /l/ and /r/. This difficulty is a result of the fact that in their own languages there is no such phonemic distinction, and [l] and [ʁ] are allophones of the same phoneme.

9.17 What about Latin words and abbreviations?

As you read books and articles during the course of your studies, you'll come across a number of abbreviations, some in English and some in Latin. It's important that you know what these abbreviations mean, not only for the purpose of reading more effectively but because you need to be able to use them – and use them appropriately – in your own writing. The most commonly used abbreviations are featured in the box below. Try to learn them and begin using them as soon as possible; that way they'll more quickly become a normal part of your writing practice.

Common Abbreviations

English abbreviations

ch.	chapter
ed.; eds.	editor; editors
edn; edns	edition; editions
fig.	figure
ff.	and the following pages (e.g. 'Frey 1997, p. 2 ff.' = 'page 2 and the following pages of Frey 1997')
ms.; mss.	manuscript; manuscripts
n.; nn.	note/footnote; notes/footnotes
n.d.	no date given; date unknown; no date available (e.g. Sanderson, n.d.)
n. pub.	no publisher given
n.p.	no place of publication given
no.; nos.	number; numbers
p.; pp.	page; pages (e.g. Lambert et al., 1982, pp. 34–45)
para.	paragraph
supra	in that part already dealt with above;
trans.	translator/translated/translation
vol.; vols.	volume; volumes

Latin abbreviations

cf.	compare
circa	about/around (e.g. 'circa 2009' = 'around the year 2009')
e.g.	for example; for instance
et al.	and others (e.g. 'Essler et al.' = 'Essler and others' – often referring to co-authors)

---

etc.	and so forth; and so on
et seq	and the following (e.g. 'p. 76 et seq' = 'page 76 and the following pages')
ibid.	in the same article/book (e.g. 'Thompson, ibid., p. 23' = 'Thompson, on page 23 of the article previously mentioned')
i.e.	that is/that is to say
infra	below or later on in a book, article, etc.
loc. cit.	at the place quoted; from the place cited earlier (e.g. 'Havers, loc. cit.'). The author's name must be given.
op. cit.	in the book cited earlier (e.g. 'Massini, op. cit., p. 388'). The author's name and a page number must be given.
NB	note well; take note
[sic]	thus used; as written or printed in the original (used to indicate to the reader that a mistake appearing in a quotation you have used in your writing is that of the original author and not *your* mistake)
viz.	namely; in other words; that is to say

Summary: Tips for a better writing style
In the box below is a 'quick-reference' summary of the main ideas covered in this chapter.

- Keep your writing clear, concise and to the point.
- Avoid waffle.
- Have ideas clear in your head before you put 'pen to paper'.
- Avoid flowery language.
- Check for repetition, redundancy and ambiguity.
- Check regulations around the use of first person singular 'I'.
- Normally use present tense to refer to others' work unless that work is only of historical interest.
- Be measured and moderate in your use of language – avoid extreme language.
- Avoid emotive and biased language.
- Avoid vague and empty language.
- Be careful not to stereotype.
- Avoid casual language such as colloquialisms and slang.
- Don't use shortened forms; write words out in full using traditional spellings.

- Be extremely cautious about injecting humour into your writing.
- Use headings and sub-headings, using fonts to highlight them and to indicate structure.
- Use a size 12 font except for titles and headings, where a size 14 font may be preferable.
- Avoid casual font styles. Times New Roman and Arial are good choices.
- Leave a free line before a new heading or sub-heading.
- Justify your text and leave good margins.
- Number your pages and figures.
- Try to keep your titles and headings short and simple.
- Stick to black and grey scales and only use colour when absolutely necessary – for example in some charts and graphs.
- Avoid clichés and jargon.
- Keep your writing gender-neutral.
- Avoid footnotes unless absolutely necessary and permitted.
- Avoid rhetorical questions.
- Format linguistic examples correctly.
- Limit your use of abbreviations.

9.18 Checking and editing your work

Once you've completed a piece of writing it's essential that you take the time to read through it carefully and edit it where necessary in order to make any last-minute improvements. I should emphasise that this is not simply a matter of reading through it briskly and waiting for something to jump out at you; instead it's an active process that requires great concentration and an awareness of many of the principles of good writing covered in this and previous chapters – and, in particular, good writing within the fields of English language and linguistics. The checklist below will help you with this process. It lists a number of key questions that you can use to guide the editing of your work and it categorises these according to their broader area of concern. The list does not include many of the finer details discussed in this book, but it'll help you get started. Remember: the more you edit your work, the better you'll become at it.

A template for editing your work

A. Structure/Organisation

1. Does my essay have a clear introduction, body and conclusion and do these meet the basic requirements of an introduction, body and conclusion?
2. What's the main thesis of my essay? Have I articulated it clearly?

3. What are the main points that support my thesis? Have I articulated them clearly and sequenced them logically in a way that strengthens my essay?
4. Does my conclusion follow from my arguments and relate back to the introduction and thesis statement?
5. Does my essay flow well? Are the links between sentences, paragraphs and sections smooth and transparent?

B. Content

6. Have I provided sufficient evidence for my main points and arguments? Have I made any unwarranted or unsupported assumptions?
7. Have I defined and clarified key terms and ideas?
8. Are all my arguments logically watertight or do some contain logical fallacies?
9. Are my ideas clear or might another reader find some of them difficult to understand?
10. Have I amplified general statements via further explanation and/or evidence in the form of data, examples, etc.?

C. Sources

11. Have I cited all my sources correctly in the main body of the text and in the bibliography?
12. Have I made the correct decisions about where to integrate quotes into sentences and where to separate them with a free line as 'stand-alone' quotes?
13. Does my bibliography contain all and only those sources cited in my essay?
14. Have I used multiple sources that show an adequate knowledge of the relevant literature or have I relied too heavily on a limited number of sources?
15. Are there places where it might have been better to paraphrase than to quote, or vice-versa?
16. Have I made it clear which information is my own and which is obtained from other sources (and what those sources are)?
17. Have I made it clear which sources are primary and which are secondary?

D. Style

18. Is my writing style clear, concise and engaging?
19. Is the tone of my writing appropriate for an academic audience?
20. Have I made any grammatical or punctuation errors?

E. Formatting

21. Have I formatted my titles, sub-titles, headings and sub-headings correctly and consistently?
22. Is there a clear rational behind my system of headings?
23. Have I justified my text?
24. Have I left adequate margins?
25. Have I numbered and titled figures?
26. Have I used other fonts (e.g. type [Times New Roman, Arial, Calibri etc.], bold, italics) correctly and consistently?
27. Have I formatted my quotes and bibliography correctly?
28. Have I used the correct linguistic formatting conventions?

 Even after you've checked your work it's still a good idea to have somebody else read through it as they'll read it with a fresh pair of eyes and will not make any assumptions. Once you're completely satisfied with your essay and ready to submit it, remember to staple the pages together. If your essay gets dropped or mixed up with other papers, it can be a frustrating process for the lecturer to have to figure out the correct sequence of pages.

Chapter 9 Key points checklist

- Keep your writing concise and to the point. Avoid flowery language and the unnecessary use of technical language and jargon.
- Check your department's/discipline's view on the use of the first person singular 'I' in your writing.
- Be very wary of using all-or-nothing language.
- Use the present tense to refer to the work of other scholars.
- Avoid emotive, biased, vague and empty language.
- Generally avoid colloquial language and slang unless it is the focus of your essay.
- Avoid shortened forms (i.e. use 'it is' rather than 'it's').
- Be very cautious about using humour in your writing.
- In order ensure that your writing has a polished, professional feel to it, carefully check that it has been appropriately formatted – including linguistics examples.
- Avoid using clichés in your writing.
- Keep your writing gender-neutral.
- Avoid rhetorical questions.
- Familiarise yourself with commonly used Latin words and abbreviations.
- Be sure to check and edit your work as necessary before submitting it.

Writing up small-scale research projects or dissertations

'I've never done a research project before so I just don't know where to start. How big does it need to be? How original? Where do I get a good idea from? I haven't got a clue.'

What's covered in this chapter

What's expected of me as an undergraduate student with no previous research experience?

Deciding on a project: what are the important considerations?

Tips for a stress-free project: being efficient and submitting on time

The main components of a research project

Presentation and submission

10.1 What's expected of me as an undergraduate student with no previous research experience?

It's quite likely that, as part of your degree programme, you'll be required to successfully conduct and write up a small-scale research project of some kind. Typically, this will be in the form of a dissertation that you work on in your final year of study and which is normally expected to be around 10,000 words in length, although this can vary quite a bit depending on the department and university. The subject of your dissertation is, in most cases, completely open and you're free to decide your own focus according to your particular interests. In some cases, however, the dissertation project may be allied to a particular course you've taken and, as such, will need to have a focus that reflects this. Small-scale research projects tend to be a common feature of degree programmes in English language and/or linguistics and, while these may not necessarily take the form of a fully fledged dissertation, they'll still need to be carefully thought through, conducted (in the case of an empirical study) and written up. This final chapter is designed to help you in this task by providing you with some general principles that will help ensure that your particular project is brought to a successful conclusion and meets with the approval of your tutors and examiners.

The idea of having to conduct research can be quite intimidating, particularly if you have no previous experience. Often feelings of anxiety are the result of uncertainty about what exactly is expected of you and the standards you're required to meet, as well as the sense that you are 'out on your own' and having to undertake and keep control of an activity with which you are unfamiliar but which is important to your success as an undergraduate. Such feelings are perfectly natural and as such you can be sure not only that most of your peers are experiencing them to some degree but also that your lecturers are aware of this and have in place mechanisms to help guide you through the process of bringing your project to fruition.

When the time comes to begin thinking about your research project a tutor (sometimes called a supervisor) is assigned to you; in some cases *you* may get to choose your supervisor. He or she will generally be somebody whose own research interests coincide with the focus of your project, the idea being that, where possible, you have expertise available to you that has particular relevance to what you're doing. Although their approaches will vary somewhat, most tutors will be sympathetic to your situation and will not expect you to have much knowledge of how to undertake a research project. Many will, therefore, give you advice on this as a matter of course, and most – if not all – will certainly expect and welcome any questions you may have about the process.

In addition to your supervisor, there'll be other resources available to you within the department, as well as from library services and student resources units that will also assist you with your project – in particular, researching for the project and writing it up. As we've seen (section 4.1), many central services units will provide quick-reference pamphlets on such subjects as how to locate resources and how to reference sources. While these tend to be brief, rather simplistic accounts, they can nevertheless be of real help in getting you moving in the right general direction,

 While guides produced by central services units can certainly be helpful, they are necessarily very general because they have to answer to the needs of *all* university students. You should therefore use them with some caution and ask your tutor if you are unsure whether the information in these guides reflects what you should be doing specifically as a researcher in language and linguistics.

The university's rules and regulations governing dissertations

If you're conducting research as part of a dissertation, it's important that you're familiar with your university's rules and regulations governing this process. Every university publishes a booklet annually in which these are clearly stated. Although the language used is quite official-sounding and formal, try not to be put off by this. The regulations are there to help ensure that your research is trouble-free and is not side-tracked as a result of your unwittingly having broken a rule due to ignorance. Many of the rules and regulations are procedural in nature or set parameters on such things as the length of your dissertation, how original it needs to be and the formatting conventions required. As the first stage of your research project, it's well worth your while to familiarise yourself with these.

10.2 Deciding on a project: what are the important considerations?

Selecting a suitable project is about being smart, doing your homework and mapping everything out in advance so that you have a very clear idea of how you're going to negotiate the project over the coming weeks or months. A soundly conceived and implemented study is about good planning and giving ample time to addressing a number of key issues before you embark on your research rather than just jumping straight in – a recipe for disaster. This section will highlight some of those key issues.

Offering new knowledge and insight/addressing a gap in the literature

By definition, research attempts to uncover new knowledge or a new way of thinking about existing knowledge. In universities' manuals of rules and regulations governing research (discussed in 10.1), reference is typically made to the need for research to 'add significantly to knowledge of the field' or 'to form a distinct contribution to knowledge of the subject and afford evidence of originality by the discovery of new facts and/or by the exercise of independent critical power'. This latter notion of discovering new facts by the exercise of critical power is a reference to the kind of philosophical inquiry discussed above and, briefly, in sections 1.2 and 1.3.

One question undergraduate students, in particular, frequently ask is how original their research needs to be. The first thing to say in response to this question is that, as you might expect, the expectations for an undergraduate dissertation are more modest than they are for a Master's dissertation or a PhD thesis. The main reason for this is that, generally speaking, undergraduate students are less experienced academics who will not have conducted research before. Furthermore, while a PhD thesis will normally take three or more years to complete, an undergraduate dissertation will need to be completed in a period of months – and, typically, three to six months or less. The nature of the dissertation project, therefore, and the significance of the findings it generates tend, on the whole, to be less complex and less far reaching. Nevertheless, any piece of research needs to offer something original that increases knowledge of the field in some way. This may simply amount to replicating a study in a slightly different context from that of the original, or perhaps using a reduced number of subjects or adopting a different approach or research methodology. On the other hand, it may involve an entirely unique but small-scale study which addresses a gap of some kind in the existing literature of the field – and it may generate some interesting and significant findings. When it comes to research, size certainly does *not* always matter. Some of the most profound studies have been relatively small-scale!

Empirical vs library-based research: working to your strengths

Empirical research refers to research that involves the collection and analysis of data. Library-based research, in contrast, involves philosophical inquiry and is an approach that's driven by a particular view of reality. It involves thinking critically about important issues and ideas in the field, deconstructing them, creating new knowledge, generating new avenues for research and challenging the status quo. Whether you opt for an empirical or library-based study will depend on factors such as your own personal preferences and strengths, your knowledge of research methodology and time constraints – it is often the case that empirical studies take longer to complete, due to an array of possible confounding factors, some of which we'll visit in a moment. You need to decide, then, with which of these two types of research you feel most comfortable and would enjoy engaging.

Ideas for research projects

- Replicate a previous study but conduct in it a new and different context. This could be a different physical, cultural or educational context, for example.
- Take a linguistic question previously investigated in relation to one language and investigate that same question in relation to a different language.
- Replicate a previous study but employ a different approach or research methodology.
- Conduct an original study that's small-scale and manageable within the time-frame and addresses a gap in the literature.

Choosing a topic that interests you

It's generally the case in life that people do well at what they enjoy, and this certainly applies to research. It can become difficult to muster motivation for a project and to drive it to fruition if you're bored by it and/or if you're doing it purely to meet the requirements of your degree. Try, therefore, to design your research around a topic that you find interesting and the potential findings of which genuinely excite you.

Identifying a suitable tutor to supervise your project

One of the factors that should play some part in determining the focus of your research project is whether there's an academic member of staff who's well qualified to supervise it and with whom you have, or believe you can have, a good working relationship. While this is particularly important for postgraduate research that may extend over a period of years, it's still essential that you try to match a project that interests and stimulates you with a tutor who is well qualified to help you and bring the best out in you. Having said that, it may be the case that you don't get to choose your tutor; you may be assigned one instead. However, this is sometimes negotiable, so if you're not happy with the tutor you've been assigned, it's certainly worth inquiring about the possibility of switching tutors.

Having a clear focus – generating research questions and research hypotheses

Once you've decided on a suitable topic, it's essential that the purpose of your research is very clearly defined from the outset. It you're vague about what it is you're seeking to do, how you intend to go about doing it (i.e. your methodology – see below) and what you hope to achieve, you'll end up continually finding yourself disorientated and lacking clarity and direction as your research progresses. This will not only eat away at your time as you try to reconceptualise the project and place it on a sound footing, it can also be very unnerving as you struggle to make sense of what you're trying to do and to give it direction.

In deciding on your research focus and thus giving your study a clear direction, you need to construct some possible research questions and/or research hypotheses. One way of doing this is by asking yourself broad questions such as the following:

- What would I like to know about this topic?
- What aspects of the literature on this topic are most interesting to me?
- What gaps are there in the literature in relation to this topic?
- What are some controversial issues related to this topic?
- What do theoreticians want to know about this topic?
- What do practitioners want to know about this topic?

163

You may prefer to generate research questions by thinking in terms of categories such as *definition, description, classification, comparison and contrast, cause and effect, relationship, time* and *stability*. Sometimes, research questions will involve more than one of these categories. Look at the following examples of broad research question types based on these categories and which may help you develop a focus of inquiry for your research project.

How is X defined? Is this definition adequate? If not, why not?
How can I improve on this definition? (**definition**)
How might I define X in relation to Y? (**definition**)
How might I define X in different contexts? (**definition**)
What variation is there in the literature concerning how X is defined?
What is the significance of such variation? (**definition**)
Is X system of classification sound or adequate? (**classification**)
What class does X belong to? Are there any respects in which it does not belong to that class? (**classification**)
How is X similar to Y? How is X different from Y? (**comparison and contrast**)
Is X more similar to Y or Z? (**comparison and contrast**)
What is the best mechanism for differentiating X and Y? (**comparison and contrast**)
Can a causal relationship between X and Y be established? (**cause and effect**)
What causes X? What does X cause? (**cause and effect**)
Is X a greater or more important cause of Z than Y? (**cause and effect**)
Is X a direct or indirect cause of Y? (**cause and effect**)
What is the relationship between X and Y? (**relationship**)
Is there a stronger relationship between X and Z than between Y and Z? (**relationship**)
How does X change over time? (**time**)
Is X different at different points in time? (**time**)
How stable is X across factors such as gender, culture and age? (**stability**)
Is X more stable in one context than another? (**stability**)

Some of these questions will apply more to empirical studies than to library-based research.

Look at these research questions taken from an article by Janna Fox:

> *This article reports on results of the first 2 years of a longitudinal study examining the amount of time that an L2 English student has spent in an English-medium high school (i.e., language residency) as a factor in academic performance in a university. It focuses on the following research questions:*
>
> *RQ1. Does the amount of time that L2 students spend in secondary school make a difference?*

RQ2. Do cohorts of L2 students with 3, 4 and 5 years in English-medium secondary schools in Ontario perform differently in their first years at a university? If so, which amount of time is the most useful indicator of a level of language proficiency development that is adequate for study in a university?

RQ3. How do these students compare with other groups of students, such as L2 students who receive English for Academic Purposes (EAP) support, or other students admitted without language proficiency requirements?   (From Fox, 2005)

For empirical studies, an alternative to framing your research focus in terms of research questions is to construct research hypotheses, in which case you'll need to rewrite your questions as statements because hypotheses are essentially well-informed, well-supported predictions about the findings of your research. There are two main kinds of hypotheses: null hypotheses and directional hypotheses. Null hypotheses predict no difference between two or more treatments or groups, whereas directional hypotheses predict which treatment or group will do better or bring about/manifest a greater degree of change.

 In presenting your hypotheses – whether null or directional – you must show that they've been informed by a *reasoned understanding* of the relationships between the various different variables (or factors) that are expected to impact on your study and the data it generates. This, in turn, requires that you're familiar with and have taken into account the relevant literature. Remember: hypotheses based merely on your instincts are worthless and will fatally undermine the foundations of your study and thus the validity of the findings it generates.

Below are 4 hypotheses formulated for a study investigating the effects of explicit grammar instruction on student learning. The study sought to discover whether, after being taught several grammatical structures, English as a foreign language subjects improved their knowledge of those structures and generalised that knowledge to their writing.

Hypothesis 1: *Subjects receiving the treatment (i.e. specific teaching of the target structures) will perform significantly better on a grammatical test of these items than will the subjects of the control group.*

Hypothesis 2: *The treatment subjects will receive significantly higher scores on the post-test than on the pre-test of the target grammatical structures.*

Hypothesis 3: *For the treatment group subjects, there will be no significant differences in their use of the target structures as measured by a pre-treatment writing sample and a post-treatment writing sample.*

Hypothesis 4: *The subjects of the control group (non-treatment) will show no significant improvement of their control of the target structures, either in the explicit grammar test or in the pre- and post-treatment writing samples.*

TRY IT OUT! #18

Look at the following research questions. Decide to which category they belong (definition, description, classification, comparison and contrast, cause and effect, relationship, time, or stability).

1. What differences are there in the way English speakers and Japanese speakers manage agreement and disagreement?
2. What phonological processes (substitution, assimilation, syllabic structure) characterise the mispronunciations of the words of a three-year-old child?
3. Do science students generally perform better on a linguistically complex task than humanities students?
4. Are gender differences in languages more evident in formal contexts than in informal contexts?
5. How, if at all, is politeness realised in the language of text messaging?
6. When and why did English spelling diverge from its pronunciation? What reaction did it provoke at the time and what reaction does it provoke now?
7. Which elements of punctuation exhibit greatest variability in their use? What underlies such variability?
8. What are the attitudes of secondary school teachers and students to non-standard English?

Being clear about your research approach

The research approach you decide to adopt in order to answer your research questions will depend on a number of factors such as the nature of the research questions themselves (one particular approach may seem particularly suited to addressing them), your familiarity and level of comfort with particular methodologies and associated techniques, and your particular view of reality.

In this section, we'll look at four general approaches to research: philosophical inquiry, quantitative approaches, qualitative approaches and mixed-methods approaches.

Philosophical inquiry

As we saw earlier in this chapter, philosophical inquiry is distinct from empirical research in that it doesn't involve data collection: it's essentially library-based research and as such may seek to do a number of things, including:

- critically analysing a particular practice or argument;
- identifying and articulating explicitly the assumptions underlying a certain view or perspective;
- analysing a term or concept in order to clarify its meaning;
- considering alternative methods, approaches or systems that may challenge the status quo;
- synthesising research from other fields in order to shed light on your own field (linguistics certainly has a history of drawing on research in other fields such as education, psychology and sociology to clarify itself);
- deconstructing a term or concept in order to show internal contradictions or ambiguities;
- analysing a hypothetical situation so as to understand key variables in that situation; and
- establishing rigorous grounds for a proposal for a particular course of action by a group of people or an institution.

(Adapted from Murray and Beglar, 2009)

Like any research approach, philosophical inquiry brings with it certain challenges or demands. Most obviously, the quality and significance of the insights it generates are dependent on the researcher's ability to acquire a deep and clear understanding of pertinent issues and to conceptualise and articulate their analysis of and perspective on those issues. While other research approaches will, to some extent, also depend on these skills, the success of a philosophical study is *wholly* dependent on them and the stakes are therefore particularly high.

Quantitative approaches

Unlike philosophical inquiry, quantitative approaches involve collecting, analysing and, ultimately, presenting and discussing numerical data. This will normally mean developing some familiarity with test and survey design (and associated software programmes), as well as statistical analyses, both of which are integral parts of most quantitative studies. Generally, students will familiarise themselves with these tools as and when they need them. Most universities periodically provide training sessions in their design and use for those who are interested, and your tutor/supervisor will also likely be able to give you some assistance.

Here, we'll briefly look at the three main types of quantitative research: survey research, quasi-experimental studies and true experiments.

167

Survey research

Survey research typically involves the use of questionnaires administered in paper-and-pencil format or (increasingly) electronically, one-on-one interviews or focus-group interviews involving several respondents at the same time. These data collection tools lend themselves to survey research because this kind of research tends to focus on what people believe about a particular issue, their emotional reactions to various situations or their opinions about people and events.

Questionnaires have a number of advantages:

- Large amounts of data can be collected quickly and (in the case of electronic administration) relatively easily.
- Different types of questions can be asked, such as those that use a rating scale such a Likert Scale or open-ended questions.
- Response rates are usually high.
- Visuals can be included easily.
- Data entry can be quick and easy if responses are made on computer mark sheets.
- They're very cost effective.

However, if you're to elicit good data from respondents (i.e. data that is dependable and gives you the information you desire), it's crucial that your questionnaire is carefully considered and well designed. It needs to include all necessary variables relevant to your investigation and items responses to which will give you all and only the information you require. In other words, it needs to be efficient and economical. Furthermore, prior to administering the questionnaire, you need to be absolutely clear about how you'll go about analysing the data it generates and the statistical methods you'll use.

Quasi-experiments

Quasi-experiments involve more than one group. This allows the researcher to give different groups different treatments and to compare the results of each of the treatments. It's quite common in quasi-experiments for one of the groups to be selected to function as a control group – that's to say that, unlike the other groups, it does not receive any experimental treatment. The advantage of having a control group is to ensure that any changes evident in the groups that received treatment are the result of the treatment itself and not other factors. In other words the control group has to be identical in every way to the treatment groups(s) apart from the variable of interest whose effect is being tested. For example, in the study mentioned above which sought to investigate the effects of explicit grammar instruction on student learning, the control group was identical in almost every respect to the treatment groups. The only difference was that the grammatical structures in question were presented explicitly rather than implicitly. However, had the teacher of the control group been different from that of the treatment groups, then this would have confounded the findings because it could be claimed that any difference in performance between the treatment groups and the control group was the result not of the explicit teaching itself but of teacher style, for example. In other words, it would be difficult to make any confident claims about the effects of formal instruction on the learning of grammatical structures because other factors (or variables) might have been responsible for differences in performance between the control group and the treatment groups.

Quasi-experiments sometimes include a pre-test which allows you, the researcher, to be certain that your participants don't already know, for instance, what it is you're going to teach them. As a result, you can be pretty sure that any apparent gains in performance are indeed gains in performance and not the result of pre-existing knowledge! Once again, this was the case with the 'effects of formal instruction' study described above. Prior to the treatment, subjects sat a writing 'test' designed to measure students' control of the structures to be taught as part of the treatment. In this particular case they were also given a post-treatment writing 'test' to measure any gains made as a result of the treatment.

True experiments

One of the weaknesses of quasi-experiments lies in the fact that participants are not randomised but 'intact'. This means that one group may be more intelligent, insightful or motivated than another and this fact could compromise the findings generated by the study, for it may be these qualities rather than the treatment itself that are responsible for any changes in performance/behaviour. It's this notion of randomisation that distinguishes true experiments from quasi-experiments. Randomisation is central to true experiments and its strength lies in the fact that by assigning participants randomly to different groups, for example, intergroup differences and potential researcher bias are eliminated. This, in turn, means that any conclusions made on the basis of your results are more valid and reliable.

Qualitative approaches

Unlike quantitative approaches to research, qualitative approaches do not use numerical data but data collected via one or more of the following: documents, questionnaires, interview or focus group transcripts, observations of a person or situation and the field notes they may generate, and audio and video recordings. Examples of qualitative research include case studies, ethnographies, narratives, histories, bibliographies and non-participant observation.

169

Case studies

Case studies involve collecting in-depth data about a specific individual (as opposed to groups – see 'ethnography', below), context or situation in order to shed light on a particular question or phenomenon. For example, you may wish to find out how one particular bilingual individual feels about having native-like proficiency in two languages, the advantages and disadvantages they associate with being bilingual, and possibly their views on when and why they code-switch as they do. Alternatively, you may be interested in looking in detail and over time at how a particular high school implements an immersion programme. While some case studies may comprise a single in-depth interview, others will involve other instruments and may extend over a period of years. Long-term studies of this kind are referred to as 'longitudinal studies'. You may even consider conducting two or three cases studies with a view to comparing situations or experiences: for example, how two or three different institutions go about implementing a new government language policy. Case studies, then, have the advantage of offering a detailed picture of a single individual or situation. While they can provide important insights as result, you have to be cautious about generalising those insights to a larger population.

Ethnographies

The famous anthropologist and ethnologist Claude Lévi-Strauss defined ethnography as follows:

> Ethnography consists of the observation and analysis of human groups considered as individual entities (the groups are often selected, for practical and theoretical reasons unrelated to the nature of the research involved, from those societies that differ most from our own). Ethnography thus aims at recording as accurately as possible the perspective modes of life of various groups. (From Lévi-Strauss, 1963)

Research that employs an ethnographic approach attempts to understand the cultural patterns and perspectives of participants in their natural settings, to describe, analyse and interpret their culture in order to understand its shared beliefs, culture and language. It's an approach that helps the researcher understand some of the complexity that characterises a situation and the behaviours of participants in that situation and, as such, it can be helpful in answering questions such as: 'What is happening in this situation?', 'How and why does this event happen?' and 'What does this event mean to the participants involved?' An important aspect of ethnography is that, in attempting to answer these questions, ethnographers focus *not* on their own understanding of or perspective on a situation but on the participants' understanding/perspective. This requires them to build a good rapport with their participants without fundamentally changing their behaviour in the process. Here's another definition of ethnography:

> A research method located in the practice of both sociologists and anthropologists, and which should be regarded as the product of a cocktail of methodologies that share the assumption that personal engagement with the subject is the key to understanding a particular culture or social setting.
>
> Participant observation is the most common component of this cocktail, but interviews, conversational and discourse analysis, documentary analysis, film and photography, life histories all have their place in the ethnographer's repertoire. Description resides at the core of ethnography, and however that description is constructed it is the intense meaning of social life from the everyday perspective of group members that is sought.
>
> (From Hobbs, 2006)

As Hobbs suggests, ethnographers collect their data via fieldwork through observation and interviewing. They themselves are, therefore, the major instruments of data collection and in this regard ethnography differs from experimental research that relies on tests and questionnaires.

Ethnographic studies are often – though not necessarily – longitudinal in nature because they involve detailed (or 'thick') description based on careful observation, as we've seen. As such, it is unlikely that you'll adopt an ethnographic approach for the purpose of a short-term, small-scale research project. Nevertheless, depending on the time you're allowed for your study, its nature and how focused it is, ethnography may be an option and it's important, therefore, that you have some understanding of what it involves.

Narratives

Narrative inquiry can be described as the process of gathering information for the purpose of research through storytelling, and subsequently writing a narrative of the experience. The idea underlying narrative inquiry is that people's lives consist of stories that reflect how they perceive their lives and make and reflect meaning. The types of data it typically uses include orally told stories, interviews, personal letters and journals, autobiographies, field notes, photographs and video. While it shares a good deal with case studies, it tends to be more focused on the developmental nature of a particular aspect of the subject's experience over time – of a particular story. For example, it may serve to shed light on an immigrant's language growth following their arrival in their new country.

Mixed-methods approaches

As their name suggests, mixed-methods approaches are a combination of quantitative and qualitative approaches. Their advantage is that they offer you, the researcher, the benefits of both kinds of approach. For example, you may use a qualitative approach to gain a deeper understanding of the reasons underlying results acquired through a quantitative approach. As an example, imagine that you've adopted a quantitative approach to measure the extent to which the language of a group of second-language learners exposed to a new methodology develops over a specified period of time. If the results you obtain suggest that this group of learners has developed at a rate greater than that exhibited by those learners taught by a more traditional method, you may choose to apply one or more data collection instruments associated with a qualitative approach in order to identify why the new method appears to be more effective. For example, you may decide to have focus group sessions in order to see how and why the treatment group responded well to the methodology and how they felt it promoted their learning.

Of course, not all research lends itself to a mixed-methods approach, which is why a good deal of research utilises a single approach – that most suited to its purpose – rather than a combination of the two.

Once again, the approach you ultimately adopt will be determined largely by the purpose of your research, and I recommend that you consult your supervisor/tutor to ensure that you get the best match between what you wish to achieve in your study and the approach that is most likely to ensure you achieve it. Whichever approach you settle on, you need to justify your decision. Here's how Bretag, Horrocks and Smith justify their decision to use an action research methodology for the purposes of their study on developing classroom practices to support university students of non-English-speaking background:

 Dadds (1998, 41) suggests that:

> ... practitioner research [refers] to forms of enquiry which people undertake in their own working contexts and, usually, in their professional work, in whatever sphere they practice. The main purpose of the enquiry is to shed light on aspects of that work with a view to bringing about some benevolent change.

> Using Dadds' definition as the basis for the project, the research team set out to instigate and/or adapt classroom practices and teaching strategies suggested by the literature, with the purpose of improving learning outcomes for NESB students in DD and BSA.

> Fraser (1997, p. 169) argues 'action research can be the most appropriate, most effective and least threatening strategy when evaluating curriculum innovations'. Furthermore, Moller (1998, p. 71) suggests that genuine action research breaks down the binary between research and practice, and that useful action research is documented, published and scrutinised

by peers. With this advice in mind, the research team has endeavoured to document the practice/research process, beginning with the first 'cycle' of the project in Semester 1, 2002.

As each 'cycle' (semester) is completed, further reflection, documentation and peer review will take place.

(From Bretag, Horrocks and Smith, 2002)

Keeping your project manageable and allowing for contingencies

It's pretty normal for students to have only about six months to work on their dissertation – including conducting the research and writing it up – although, in some cases, that period may be slightly longer or shorter. Either way, though, it's not a lot of time and that means you'll have to choose a project that's manageable within the specified timeframe. This requires you to think carefully about a possible topic and to anticipate what your research will involve and what your chances are of accomplishing your aims. Generally speaking, projects take longer than you expect, so try to allow more time than you think you'll need and consider the possible risks and setbacks involved. This is particularly true of empirical research, where you're likely to be dependent on data provided by (often unreliable) human subjects – a situation common in linguistics, a field of study that is fundamentally concerned with language, a human phenomenon. Once again, good planning and forethought are the keys to a smooth, trouble-free project and a good way to avoid last-minute panic.

 When designing your project, it can be good idea to build in an 'escape plan' – a fall-back position to which you can retreat in the event that you feel your project is becoming unmanageable or that you're running out of time. For example you can either have a slightly different but less ambitious project in mind but which would allow you to draw on similar data, or perhaps simply decide at the planning stage that were it necessary to reduce the quantity of data collected (or perhaps change the method of its collection) the project would still retain enough integrity to meet the requirements of a dissertation.

Checking whether or not your project requires ethics approval

As we've seen, if you're considering empirical research, chances are it'll involve human subjects (or 'participants'). Not all research involving people requires ethics approval but much of it does and the purpose of seeking that approval is to protect both you as the researcher and your participants. Most importantly, it ensures that you treat your participants ethically by recognising and protecting their rights. It protects you, the researcher, by helping ensure that participants are not able to complain at a later date that they were badly treated, unaware of what they were signing up to, and had their rights infringed.

While you can certainly take advice from your tutor on whether, based on their experience, they feel your particular project will require ethics approval, it's also advisable that you check with your university's Human Research Ethics Committee – indeed, many universities require this regardless. Most universities today have such a committee and it will have produced a set of guidelines – online and probably in hard copy as well – designed to help you determine whether or not your project requires ethics approval and, if so, how to go about obtaining it. Usually this involves completing and submitting an application form on which you'll have to explain briefly the nature of your research and how it will (or could) impact on participants. In completing your application you will need to demonstrate that:

- you have or will have obtained permission from the appropriate organisations and/or institutions to gain access to your participants/data;
- you will make it clear to participants that their involvement is voluntary, that they have a right *not* to participate, and that in choosing not to participate they will not be disadvantaged in any way;
- participants will be given the right and opportunity to ask questions, along with the contact details of yourself and your supervisor for this purpose;
- you have informed participants of the purpose of the study;
- you will avoid causing participants physical or emotional distress as a result of participating in your study;
- you will not divulge the identity of participants but will use pseudonyms or identification numbers;
- you will protect the confidentiality of the data you collect; and
- you will offer to inform participants of the results of your study.

You will need to give participants an information sheet describing, in an accessible way and in adequate detail, the study and the nature of their involvement in it. This should include:

- a summary of the objectives of the study;
- a description of the procedures you will use;
- an explanation of any physical or psychological discomfort participants may experience;
- an explanation of how you'll keep their participation confidential;
- information about what will happen to their data once the study's completed;

- an explanation of the benefits – if any – they will receive by participating (e.g. a copy of the results or final report);
- reassurance that they will in no way be disadvantaged by choosing *not* to participate;
- an opportunity to ask any question or express any concerns; and
- an indication to whom they can direct any questions or concerns that they feel have not been satisfactorily addressed by you (normally your tutor/supervisor or the university's Human Research Ethics Committee).

In addition to providing participants with an information sheet, you'll also require from each of them a signed written consent form. Often, these two things are dealt with together using a single consent form.

 Build into your research plan adequate time to apply for and obtain the approval of your university's Human Research Ethics Committee. Many such committees meet on a quarterly basis (i.e. every three months), but this can vary between universities. It can then take a few weeks to obtain approval, although most universities try to minimise the turn-around time to about two weeks so as not to hinder students' progress with their studies unnecessarily.

Deciding how you will recruit subjects and on what basis

If you're conducting a study that requires the use of human subjects, then you need to decide how you're going to go about recruiting them. Methods typically used by researchers include:

- emailing students within your department and/or further afield;
- putting notices on departmental notice boards;
- placing flyers in students' pigeonholes;
- asking tutors to bring your project to the notice of their students and seminar/tutorial groups;
- requesting the help of peers who are studying with you;
- announcing your search for subjects in departmental newsletters;
- using word of mouth; and
- where, applicable, asking authorities within institutions to bring your request for subjects to the attention of those they oversee. For example, you may wish to use a group of second-language learners for your research, in which case you might decide to approach the head of a language school and request that they inform their students about your study and need for volunteers. You may choose to follow this up with an informal presentation to those students wishing to find out more about the study before deciding whether or not they wish to volunteer.

Depending on the nature of your project, not all of these methods may be suitable. Whichever method(s) you use, though, you'll want to feel confident that it'll deliver you the number of students needed for the study to proceed and produce valid results. You'll also need to decide how, if at all, you're going to recompense them for their time assisting you – a question on which the ethics committee will also require clarification. Are you going to pay the subjects for their time or use some other means to secure their participation? Oftentimes subjects are happy to participate regardless; however, if you plan not to recompense students, you may well need to spread your recruitment net wider to allow for the possibility that many potential subjects may decline to take part.

Remember, on this and all the other issues discussed in this section, your tutor/supervisor will likely be well placed to give you advice, so don't be reticent about approaching them and asking for guidance if necessary.

Deciding on a research project: key considerations

- Does my research offer new knowledge or insight? Does it address a gap in the literature?
- Is it possible to replicate an existing study but give it a new twist?
- Is the project to be empirical or theoretical (library-based)? To which type of research am I likely to be more suited?
- If the research is library-based, can I get hold of the relevant literature fairly easily and quickly?
- Do I have a genuine interest in the topic?
- Is there a tutor in the department with a research interest in and specialist knowledge of my research topic?
- Is the staff member who is able to supervise it someone with whom I can work easily? If not, is there a different research focus I can take that would allow me to work with a tutor/supervisor whose style is more suited to my own?
- Am I crystal clear about what it is I want to do? What are my research questions/hypotheses?
- Am I clear about the kind of research approach I'm going to adopt?
- How complex and wide-ranging is the project? Can I realistically complete it within the required timeframe?
- Do I have contingency measures in place for dealing with the hiccups and unpredictability associated with dealing with human subjects in particular? Will such measures ensure that I get the data I need in a timely fashion?
- If the project threatens to become too big, is it possible to de-limit it so that it becomes manageable while still maintaining its integrity?
- Does the project require ethics approval, and if so, how long will it take to obtain this? Will any potential delay seriously undermine my ability to complete the study on time?

- How and where will I recruit subjects? Will I pay them for their time or offer some other quid pro quo arrangement? How confident can I be of finding enough human subjects?

10.3 Tips for a stress-free project: being efficient and submitting on time

Whether you're writing an essay or a dissertation, being organised and disciplined is great way of keeping your stress levels to a minimum. Map out a timeline for your project and identify waypoints by which you plan to complete particular parts of it. Those waypoints may be things such as deciding on a good idea, locating a suitable supervisor, completing your search of the literature, identifying and getting a commitment from your subjects to participate, completing your collection of data, concluding your analysis of the data, completing your written review of the literature, and so on.

Once you've decided on a 'game plan' try hard to stick to it. At times this will mean having to really sweat in order not go fall behind schedule, but it'll also result in times when you find yourself slightly ahead of the game and able to take your foot off the pedal slightly. What's important is that you keep yourself in a comfort zone and don't end up in a situation where the deadline for submission of your project is looming and you're not ready to submit. If this happens and you feel things getting out of control this can cause you to panic – and when you're in panic mode it can be even more difficult to focus on what you need to do, to think clearly and to bring your project to a successful conclusion.

 Being organised also means building in breaks. Putting in solid work time is important, but so too is down-time. And remember: when you do take breaks try to switch off completely from your project and recharge your batteries. It'll be easier to do this if you know you've put in serious study time and stuck to your schedule. It's difficult to relax fully when you feel guilty!

10.4 The main components of a research project

The title

One of the things you'll need to do at some stage is decide on a final title for your project. This will go on the front page of your submission and it's important, therefore, that you get it right. Although you'll probably already have a working title it's a good idea to decide on the final title once you've completed the project because most research projects have a tendency to transform as they progress. That transformation can be significant and mean that your original title is no longer suitable.

Coming up with a good title requires careful thought. Why? Because it needs to be concise while at the same time capturing the essence of what the project is about. It also needs to be a bit catchy in order to grab the attention of the reader. While it's not a good idea to make your title too flashy or clever, a dull title can cause the reader to switch off even before they've turned the first page.

Once you've decided on a suitable title, you need to create the title page of your dissertation. Although the format of the title page can vary according to individuals' personal preferences or the particular requirements of the institution, they all contain essentially the same key information, namely the title of your project, the name of the university where you are enrolled, the degree of which it fulfils – wholly or in part – the requirements, your name, and the date on which you submitted it. Below is an illustration of a typical title page.

**Communicative Language Teaching:
Reflections and Implications for
Language Teacher Education**

Cameron McIntyre

A dissertation submitted
in partial fulfilment
of the requirements
for the degree of

BACHELOR OF ARTS IN APPLIED LINGUISTICS

University of London

17 June, 2010

The table of contents

A table of contents is important because, along with the abstract, it gives the reader an at-a-glance view of the overall design of your dissertation, the order in which you discuss the different elements and, of course, the nature of the different elements themselves. It's also a useful reference point that makes it easier for the reader to jump backwards or forwards quickly to another part of your discussion without having to search through the pages of the dissertation in order to find the particular section in which they're interested.

There are a couple of things you need to remember when designing your table of contents. First, check carefully that it reflects accurately the structure of the book and that all of the headings and sub-headings appearing within the main text of your dissertation are reflected in the table of contents and are listed in exactly the same order. In other words, be certain that the table of contents reflects the tiering of headings used in the main text (and discussed in section 6.4). Second, make sure that you include page numbers and that these tally with the headings as they appear in the main text. It's very irritating for a reader to locate a heading and its associated page number in the table of contents only to find that the page number is incorrect and that they have to rifle back and forth to find the section they're looking for! It also looks like sloppy work on your part. It's always a good idea to create your table of contents once you've completely finished writing your dissertation; that way, the chances of slipping up with headings and page numbers is reduced. It's a surprisingly common mistake (and an easy one to make) for students to construct their table of contents and later add information to the body of the dissertation, or reposition a section, and forget to adjust the table of contents so as to reflect those changes.

The acknowledgements

The acknowledgements section is where you thank those individuals and institutions that contributed in some way to your research. Normally students thank their supervisor, any participants who volunteered to be involved in the project, personal and professional colleagues who may have assisted them in some way, organisations and individuals within them who allowed access to subjects and/or data, and their families, for their support and encouragement. 'Acknowledgements' are important because they're your way of formally recognising and recording those who played a role in bringing your research project to fruition. It's a good idea, therefore, to devote some time to thinking carefully about who those individuals were; after all, you don't want to offend anyone by accidentally overlooking them!

Although acknowledgements sections of books can sometimes run to a page and a half or so, those of dissertations are unlikely to exceed more than about two-thirds of a page, although they may run longer than this if you've drawn on the services and support of an extensive list of people and/ or institutions in some capacity or other. Below is a typical example of an acknowledgements page from a dissertation – in this case a library-based dissertation:

Acknowledgements

There are a number of people who, in various different ways, contributed to the research reported in the following pages and who deserve my sincere thanks.

Firstly, the ESOL Department's postgraduate research seminar group at London University's Institute of Education. Many of the individuals who made up this vibrant community played a key role in providing a stimulating intellectual environment in which I benefited from new perspectives on my own work and on broader issues in applied linguistics. Those same individuals also provided invaluable friendship, encouragement and support throughout the duration of my degree studies. From this group, Jenny Jenkins, Nicholas Drennan and Eva Illes deserve particular thanks.

Secondly, I should thank the ESOL faculty and staff in general, and Guy Cook and Rob Batstone in particular, both of whom always provided lively and entertaining debate and the kind of controversy that provokes inquiry and reflection – so important to the research endeavour. Their helpful, constructive suggestions were always appreciated.

Most of all, I am indebted to my supervisor, Henry Widdowson, whose guidance, wisdom, unfailing moral support, clarity of insight, unerring supply of stimulating ideas, and wonderful sense of humour were always, and continue to be, a constant source of inspiration.

Finally, I must thank my family whose love, forbearance and generosity in dealing with my mood swings and reclusive behaviour was a lesson in stoicism.

Without these people – and indeed many others too numerous to name here – I could not have brought my research to a successful conclusion.

TRY IT OUT! #19

Visit your department or library and locate half a dozen dissertations or theses. Take a few minutes to read through the acknowledgement pages. Make a simple list of the features contained in each and note down any commonalities. Notice the kind of language that is used and record any 'turns of phrase' you feel might be helpful to you when it comes to writing your own dissertation.

The abstract

During the course of your studies you will no doubt have read many abstracts, for they appear at the beginning of all journal articles. Their purpose is to give the reader a brief overview of the article and what they can expect to find in the pages that follow. An abstract will normally contain a number of elements as follows:

- Background (the contextual backdrop for the study);
- Aims ('This study seeks to …');
- Samples (if an empirical study);
- Methods used;
- Results;
- Conclusions.

Have a look at the following two examples. The first is from an article titled 'Apparent subject–object inversion in Chinese', and the second from an article titled 'Teacher and learner perceptions of language learning activity'.

Abstract – example 1

This article is concerned with the problem of argument-function mismatch observed in the (apparent) subject-object inversion in Chinese consumption verbs, e.g., chi 'eat' and he 'drink', and accommodation verbs, e.g., zhu 'live' and shui 'sleep'. These verbs seem to allow the linking of (agent-SUBJ theme-OBJ) as well as (agent-OBJ theme-SUBJ), but only when the agent is also the semantic role denoting the measure or extent of the action (B and A). The account offered is formulated within LFG's lexical mapping theory. Under the simplest and also the strictest interpretation of the argument-function mapping principle (or the θ-criterion), a composite role such as ag-ext receives syntactic assignment via one composing role only; the second composing role must be suppressed. Apparent subject-object inversion occurs when in the competition between the two composing roles, agent, the agent loses out and is suppressed. This account also facilitates a natural explanation of markedness among the competing syntactic structures (R and C).   (From Her, 2009)

Abstract – example 2

A study of the impact of a major recent language education reform project in Italy employed a combination of qualitative and quantitative data collection methods, some of which could inform other studies of language learning and teaching. Impact study findings suggested interesting differences between the perceptions of learners and teachers on some of the activities in their foreign language classes. While both sides agreed in general on the virtues of communicative approaches to language teaching, there were interesting differences in the perceptions of learners and teachers on the prominence of grammar and pair work in their classes.

These differences may indicate potential problem areas of lesson planning and implementation which could usefully be given attention on teacher support programmes.

TRY IT OUT!   #20

Look carefully at the above two sample abstracts. Which of the features of abstracts listed above as bullet points are you able to identify?

A dissertation abstract – or indeed any other abstract – in essentially no different from a journal article abstract such as illustrated above. The purpose they serve and, therefore, the information they provide are the same. However, while an article abstract is typically around 150 words long, a dissertation abstract is likely to be more extensive – perhaps around 300 words, and in some cases even longer. This is a reflection of the fact that a dissertation is normally longer than an article and there is therefore more to say in such a summary statement.

Although your abstract may be only a 'miniature version' of your dissertation, it's nevertheless extremely important. Why? Because, although your supervisor and/or examiner will certainly read your work from cover to cover, others may later judge its relevance to them on the basis solely of its title and abstract and will opt to read on (or not) accordingly. It's crucial, therefore, that your abstract is an accurate reflection of your dissertation and captures the overall thrust of your work.

Now have a look at this example of a dissertation abstract, taken from a library-based research project. The title of the dissertation is *Communicative Language Teaching and Language Teacher Education*.

Abstract

This study explores a basic paradox. On the one hand, innovations that appear in the field of language teaching – or indeed any other field of endeavour – in order to be maximally effective, need in some way to be incorporated into the contexts of their application. However, such contexts are often unfavourable to the reception of new ideas which, consequently, need to undergo some measure of adjustment prior to their implementation in the classroom. As such, those ideas are seldom realisable in their 'true colours'. Furthermore, they are at times not very clear even within their own terms, and may suffer to varying degrees from vagueness, diffusion and instances of contradiction. This is no more true than in the case of the communicative approach to language teaching, unquestionably the dominant paradigm in language teaching for the past thirty-five years.

The chapters that follow report on an investigation of Communicative Language Teaching with a view to (i) identifying the basic tenets of the approach, and (ii) identifying those factors that affect the way in which communicative principles might be made acceptable and efficacious with particular reference to the language teaching/learning situation in Japan where, in the absence of appropriate modification, they are in many respects at odds with local cultural norms.

As a necessary corollary of this investigation, consideration is given to the implications for language teacher education where, it is argued, teachers-to-be need to be provided with the means via which to most effectively evaluate innovative ideas and reconcile those incongruities that arise from attempts to apply general principles to particular circumstances.

TRY IT OUT! #21

Locate three language-related dissertations (if you can't locate dissertations, use language-related articles). Analyse them carefully and, for each, write brief answers to the following questions:

A. How is the abstract structured?

1. _____

2. _____

3. _____

B. What key content appears in the abstract?

1. _____

2. _____

3. _____

C. What stylistic features do they exhibit?

1. _____

2. _____

3. _____

D. Do you have a clear sense of what you will find in the following pages?

1. Yes/No   2. Yes/No   3. Yes/No

Note: Because all abstracts are fundamentally the same, your descriptions of the three abstracts should be very similar. Those similarities are what you should aim to achieve when you come to write your own abstract.

The introduction

Like any introduction to a piece of academic work (see Chapter 5), the purpose of an introduction to a dissertation is to contextualise or 'set the scene' for the study that follows; to describe the general area in which your study is situated, how your study 'fits in' and what motivated it. You should use the introduction to target and create interest in your audience, make clear the relevance of your study for them, define key concepts and terminology and present a clear statement of the problem or issue you're investigating, why it's worth investigating, and the theoretical and/ or practical significance of such investigation. Finally, particularly if yours is an empirical study, the introduction is where you may wish to indicate your awareness of the scope of your study. You do this by stating its delimitations – that is the extent to which your results can or cannot be generalised to populations other than those that were the focus of your particular study.

Below is a sample introduction from an article on academic discourse by Karen Bennett.

Introduction

Since Robert B. Kaplan (1980 [1966]) first suggested that there might be cultural differences in discursive or expository writing patterns, many contrastive studies have appeared that have drawn attention to academic discourse practices in other cultures. As a result, English academic prose has been compared to 'teutonic, gallic and nipponic' styles (Galtung, 1981), German (Clyne, 1987a, 1987b, 1988), Indian languages (Kachru, 1987), Czech (Cmejrkova, 1996), Finnish (Mauranen, 1993), Polish (Duszak, 1994), Norwegian (Dahl, 2004), Russian/Ukrainian (Yakhontova, 2006), and – most relevantly for this paper – Spanish (Martín Martín, 2003; Moreno, 1997; Mur Dueñas, 2007a, 2007b), to name but a few.

However, the formal constitution of the discipline known as Contrastive Rhetoric (defined by Connor [1996: ix] as 'the study of how a person's first language and culture influences his or her writing in a second language') has emphasised the fact that most of this comparative activity has ultimately served to reinforce the hegemony of English Academic Discourse (EAD). That is to say, by focusing upon the technical question of how to reduce L1 interference in learners' English texts, teachers and researchers are actively discouraged from considering the broader ideological issue of how knowledge is construed elsewhere. Indeed, the EAP industry is largely sustained by a legitimizing discourse that portrays EAD as the only valid vehicle for academic inquiry (Lyotard, 1984 [1979]; Phillipson, 1992; Pennycook, 1994).

Yet other 'academic discourses' do exist, sometimes so different from EAD in their structure and epistemological framework that they are scarcely recognisable as such to English-speaking practitioners. In Portugal, for example, much academic production in the humanities is couched in a style that would seem to have more in common with literary discourse than scientific. Typical features include a taste for 'copiousness', manifested by a general wordiness and much redundancy; a preference for a high-flown erudite register (including complex syntax, lexical abstraction, etc.); a propensity for indirectness, meaning that the main idea is often embedded, deferred or adorned at all ranks; and the extensive use of figurative language and other forms of subjectivity.

This paper describes a survey into academic writing practices in Portugal designed, amongst other things, to explore the prevalence of such features and dispel the belief (widespread amongst English teachers, translators and editors) that such texts are simply badly written. Hence, it contributes to the debate on linguistic imperialism (Canagarajah, 1999, 2002; Pennycook, 1994; Phillipson, 1992; Swales, 1997; Tardy, 2004) by providing concrete evidence of the existence of alternative ways of construing knowledge.

(From Bennett, 2010)

The literature review

The literature review is an essential part of most research for it serves at least four purposes:

- It exposes you to a broad range of ideas and perspectives and in doing so enriches you as a researcher, even though many of those ideas will not necessarily directly feed into your project.
- It gives you the opportunity to learn from the successes and failures of previous researchers and, as a result, to design and conduct a study that has more veracity and the results of which are, therefore, more likely to be valid.
- It serves as the basis of your own study, for as we have seen, your own study has to be positioned or 'located' within the literature. Con-textualising it in this way gives it meaning and makes its potential significance clear to the reader. Part of this process of 'locating your study' involves identifying consistency, conflict, partiality and gaps in the literature, as well as studies that might be profitably extended.

It is one or more of these things that should ultimately inform or 'frame' your study.

- It provides you with an opportunity to demonstrate your familiarity with and understanding of the current literature relevant to your study and to show your scholarly competence through insightfully critically appraising the ideas present in that literature. This is important because a comprehensive, well-organised and incisive literature review will give the reader confidence in your study and they will, therefore, approach it with a positive mindset.

Although the importance of taking a critical stance when approaching ideas was discussed briefly in section 1.2, it's helpful to consider here what this really means. First and foremost, reading critically means reading carefully – and, where necessary, rereading – to ensure understanding, comparing the views and findings of different researchers and writers, and evaluating the strengths and weaknesses of different studies or theoretical positions. Below is a model for organising your literature review and critically appraising the sources that you read and report on in that review.

Model for organising your literature review
- State the purpose(s) of the study and/or the research question(s) or hypotheses.
- Provide information about the participants (how many, nationality, sex, etc.).
- Present and comment on any key information concerning the methodology.
- Summarise the author's analysis, interpretation and discussion of the results.
- Point out any limitations or significant flaws in the study and/or how the study supports or does not support the results of other studies. Questions you might ask yourself as you read others' work include:
  - How well has the author represented and/or summarised the current knowledge of the area?
  - How well have they understood key variables, theoretical positions or models, and how accurately and objectively have they described them?
  - Have they selected an appropriate methodology for studying the problem?
  - How well have they analysed and interpreted their data?

> **TRY IT OUT!**   #22
>
> *Find two language journal articles that each report on a study.*
> *Identify and highlight in each article the different elements of the*
> *report listed in the organisational model above. Then write a brief*
> *summary and critical appraisal of each study as this might appear in*
> *a literature review.*

As you write your literature review you'll inevitably summarise and evaluate the work of numerous researchers and writers. It can be helpful, therefore, to package your analysis into categories or themes so as to give it a more organised feel and make it more manageable for both you and your reader. You'll probably also want to synthesise and summarise information periodically for the same reason (see sections 7.1–7.4).

Although you should have identified and described, in the abstract and introduction, the problem you're researching and the major purposes of the study, it's important to do so in greater detail as part of your literature review. This is because these things will assume greater meaning and significance for your reader, appearing as they do within the context of a comprehensive literature review. In other words, if done well, the literature review will make it very apparent how the problem you're addressing in your study emerges from broader themes and issues and why it needs researching. Having highlighted the problem in relation to the literature, you'll then need to articulate that problem in terms of your particular set of research questions and the associated research hypotheses that you construct (see section 10.2).

The methodology

The methodology section is where you describe your research participants, the data collection instruments you used in your study and the procedures you employed. It's important to describe these things because it gives your reader the opportunity to fully evaluate your research – after all, if your methodology is flawed it's likely to undermine the validity of your findings. Equally, if your methodology is sound, it'll give the reader confidence in your findings and any conclusions you draw based on those findings.

Research participants

Research *subjects* are increasingly referred to as research *participants*, although they may sometimes be referred to as *individuals*, or, for persons who have responded to a survey or questionnaire, as *respondents*. Describing

187

them in detail is important because it allows the reader to more confidently interpret your results and determine their generalisability. For example, if your participants are unique in certain respects or embody very particular characteristics, then this is likely to mean that your results are less generalisable to other groups or populations who do not share those characteristics. Although the kind of information you provide about your participants will vary according to the nature of your study and what is most relevant to its purposes, information that typically features in descriptions of participants includes:

- sex;
- age;
- marital status;
- educational level;
- ethnicity;
- how they were assigned to groups for the purpose of the research.

As a student of English language/linguistics, you may well need to include other kinds of information such as:

- number of years teaching language;
- length of time studying a language;
- previous language-learning experience;
- language background/first language;
- time spent in the L2 country;
- language competence in the L2 according to scores on tests such as IELTS, TOEFL and Cambridge Proficiency.

In addition to describing your participants you'll need to explain the reasons why they were selected to take part in your study and how you recruited them. Again, this will depend on the problem your research seeks to address and on your hypotheses.

Below is a sample description of research participants taken from a study by Gass, Svetics and Lamelin:

 Participants for this study were 34 English speakers (1 was a native speaker of Romanian) enrolled in an Italian as a foreign language course at a large mid-western university in the United States. Some had spent some time in Italy; others were heritage learners. They were scattered across all proficiency levels and both attention conditions. Only one indicated prior language study (Spanish, French, and Portuguese). Twenty-six participants were female and 8 were male. They were enrolled in the 2nd semester of first-, second-, or third-year Italian classes. Table 2 breaks down participant characteristics according to level and gender.

(From Gass, Svetics and Lemelin, 2003)

TRY IT OUT! #23

Look at the following example from Barkaoui (2010). Make a list of any characteristics of participants described by the authors. Then locate another article from one of your course reading lists and do the same.

The study included 31 novice and 29 experienced raters. Participants were assigned to groups based on their response to a background questionnaire. Experienced raters were graduate students and/or ESL instructors who had been teaching and rating ESL writing for at least 5 years, had a Master of Arts or Master of Education degree, had received specific training in assessment and essay rating, and rated themselves as competent or expert raters. Novice raters were mainly students who were enrolled in or had just completed a pre-service or teacher-training program in ESL, had no ESL teaching and rating experience at all at the time of data collection, and rated themselves as novices. The participants were recruited from various universities in southern Ontario, Canada. They varied in terms of their gender, age, and L1 backgrounds, but all were native or highly proficient NNES. Table 1 describes the profile of a typical participant in each group.

(From Barkaoui, 2010)

Data collection instruments

Data collection instruments are just what they sound like. They're the tools you'll use to elicit the data you need from your participants and they will, therefore, be selected according to how effectively they promise to help you address your research questions. They'll also reflect the research approach you've adopted (see section 10.2). Data collection instruments include such things as tests, questionnaires, audio-video recorders, and interview prompts. Whichever instrument(s) you select for your study, you'll need to provide a clear rationale for why you opted for those particular instruments and not for others – in much the same way as you have to justify your choice of participants. This is important because it allows others to understand your study more fully – to acquire a sense of how you operationalised the variables involved and of how to go about replicating the study, should they choose to do so.

Look at how the following researcher describes some of the instruments used in his study, which considered whether essay raters' evaluation criteria change with experience.

 To examine the relationships between the analytic and holistic scores and the effects of rater experience on these relationships, multilevel modeling (MLM) was used. MLM is an advanced form of multiple

189

regression analysis that takes into account the hierarchical structure of data (Hox, 2002; Luke, 2004). Hierarchical data means that observations at lower levels are nested within units at higher levels. In this study, ratings are nested within raters. With nested data, there may be more variation between raters than within raters, a violation of the independence of observations assumption that underlies traditional multiple-regression analysis. MLM addresses this problem, because it assumes independence of observations between raters, but not between ratings within a rater (Hox, 2002; Luke, 2004). MLM also allows the examination of the effects of rater variables (e.g., experience) on holistic scores (main effects) and on the relationships between the analytic and holistic scores (called cross- level interaction effects in MLM; Hox, 2002).

The software program HLM 6.0 for Windows (Raudenbush, Bryk, Cheong, & Congdon, 2004) was used to build and test various MLM models, following procedures suggested by Hox (2002), before identifying the final model that fit the data. In addition to the outcome variable, holistic scores, the study included one rater-level (called Level-2 in MLM) predictor, rater experience (coded 0 for novice and 1 for experienced), and seven measures of essay features that constitute the Level-1 predictors. These measures were the five categories in the analytic scale as well as essay length (number of words per essay measured using the word count function in Microsoft Word) and essay topic. The prompt was used as a measure of essay topic (what the essay is about), with the study prompt coded 0 and the sports prompt coded 1.   (From Barkaoui, 2010)

 If you use a test, questionnaire or interview prompts to collect your data, include a copy of these as an appendix at the back of your work.

Procedures

Having described your participants and data collection instruments, you now need to describe the procedures you followed; that is, what you did and the order in which you did it. As with the instruments used, your description of the procedures needs to be detailed enough to allow other researchers to replicate your study, should they wish to do so. Often, the procedures and the instruments employed as part of them are reported together. This is illustrated nicely in the Barkaoui example above.

Here's another description of procedure from an article by Silvia Gennari:

 Participants were 37 undergraduate psychology students at the University of Wisconsin–Madison who logged into a Web site to participate in the experiment. The instructions indicated that they would read a series of illustrated stories and that, after reading each story, they would provide a summary description of what happened in it. They were explicitly told to use one sentence to describe the story, rather than a sequence of them, and to use the pictures as memory aids. Accompanying pictures helped them to keep in mind the main events of the stories. Full instructions are reproduced in the Appendix. Each participant saw only one version of each story, and story versions were counterbalanced across participants, such that each participant saw two cardinal quantifier stories with the intended *two-not* interpretation, two cardinal quantifier stories with the *not-two* isomorphic interpretation, two universal quantifier stories with the *not-every* interpretation, and two with the intended *every-not* isomorphic interpretation. The order of stories was random.   (From Gennari, 2005)

The results

The results section is where you report on the data obtained from your methodology. The results that you record here essentially serve to answer your research questions or, in the case of hypotheses, to support (confirm), partially support or not support (disconfirm) those hypotheses.

Although scholars sometimes conflate the 'results' and 'discussion' sections when writing up their research, it's generally best to keep the two separate as it can help maintain clarity for both writer and reader. However, if you do choose to separate them, be sure to keep the results section brief: report only on the data itself and minimise any analysis of/ commentary on it; this should be reserved for the discussion section.

How you organise the presentation of your results is largely up to you; what's important is that, however you decide to approach this task, the data should be presented succinctly, logically, clearly and in a way that is most easily accessible to your reader. There are two key considerations to bear in mind here. Firstly, using your research questions or hypotheses can be a useful basis on which to present your results: remind the reader of your research questions/hypotheses (see section 10.2) and present your results in relation to each of those questions/hypotheses, dealing with each question or hypothesis in turn. Secondly, some kind of visual (for example, a graph or chart) can be an excellent way to present results as it will often allow you to be succinct and to give an at-a-glance picture of the results (see also section 6.4, Figures). Although quantitative studies often lend themselves particularly well to graphic representations, qualitative studies frequently also make use of them.

 In reporting your results, be careful not to emphasise those that confirmed your hypotheses and downplay those that turned out contrary to your expectations. Remember: results that disconfirm hypotheses can often be as interesting and informative as those that confirm them and you need to be seen to be objective.

Have a look at this example from an article that discusses the implementation of a university policy of post-enrolment English language assessment:

 Results and discussion

A total of 86 students (67 undergraduate and 19 graduate), or 13%, achieved a score in the lower or 'support required' band (3.3 or less out of 6). All of these students were EAL. Another 192, or 29%, scored in the middle 'support recommended' band (3.4–4). This means that 42% of assessed students achieved a score in the lower two bands. The remaining 387 students or 58% received a score in the upper band (greater than 4) at which level their language skills were diagnosed as 'sufficient'.

One hundred and fifty-one ESB undergraduate students and one ESB graduate student, self identified through a questionnaire at the commencement of DELA, participated in the assessment. Of the undergraduate cohort, none achieved a score in the 'required' band and only eight scored in the 'recommended band', or 5% of this cohort. All students who sat DELA were informed via a database-generated email of their results and recommendations for language enrichment programs. They were also advised to seek further information from their respective faculties, although not all did so. Faculties also followed up with students in the 'support required' band – and some in the 'support recommended' band. This took the form of face-to-face consultations, group presentations, and email correspondence. (From Ransom, 2009)

In the following example the author has conflated the results and discussion:

In this section, we describe and present the results from the t-test analysis of the performance of everyone (all students together) and children and adults (separately) on related and unrelated vocabulary, both on SHT and LT tests. Figure 1 presents the results of the most important pairs for discussion. It is clear from the table above that adult beginners performed significantly better on the unrelated vocabulary test than on the related vocabulary test. Children (intermediate level) showed no significant difference in test scores between related and unrelated vocabulary. This suggests tentatively that the presentation of unrelated vocabulary may assist learning of new L2 words more than related vocabulary only at beginners' level (adults). The result above is compatible with the results of previous research (Tinkham 1997; Waring 1997; Schneider, Healy, and Bourne 1998; Finkbeiner and Nicol 2003) illustrating that presenting L2 students (beginners) with their new vocabulary grouped together in sets of syntactically and semantically similar words impedes rather than facilitates the learning of those words. It is crucial to mention that these results reinforce the positions stated by the researchers mentioned above since they were extracted from natural language in an EFL classroom through a teaching procedure. Extensive research into 'interference theory' (Baddeley 1990) suggests that as similarity increases between targeted information and other information learnt either before or after the targeted information, the difficulty of learning and remembering the targeted information also increases (Tinkham 1997). Similarly the 'distinctiveness hypothesis' (see Hunt and Mitchell 1982), which relates ease of learning to the distinctiveness (non similarity) of the information to be learnt, also validates the above argument. It is important to point out that these results apply to beginner-level EFL adults and not to intermediate EFL children where there is no significant difference between related versus unrelated vocabulary test scores. Based on the high mean scores for the adults, especially in unrelated vocabulary, we made the following assumptions:

One probable reason for the adults achieving higher scores was motivation. It seemed that adults were highly motivated and more conscientious learners for personal and professional reasons. Motivation has to do with the emotional dimension of L2 learning. The main reason they joined the English seminars was to acquire a certificate in English in order to use it professionally and for personal interest. Children on the other hand provided quite low scores both in related and unrelated vocabulary, possibly due to lack of motivation. Another possible reason for the adults' higher scores was that adults, in general, can master certain aspects of a foreign language even well into adulthood. Adult L2 learners routinely achieve high levels of proficiency in these aspects of a foreign language. Lexical and syntactical competence becomes easier for them in contrast to phonology, which becomes very difficult to acquire.

(From Papathanasiou, 2009)

The discussion

Having reported your results, you will then need to discuss them. This essentially means commenting on and interpreting them. As with the results section, a good way of organising your discussion is according to your research questions or hypotheses, taking each question or hypothesis in turn and reflecting on it in the light of the results generated by your study. In commenting on and interpreting the results of your study you should strive to do a number of things:

- *Relate your results to previous research* – comparing and contrasting, and where possible, explaining the reasons for any divergence.
- *Consider the theoretical implications of your results* – if your study uses a particular theory or model and/or has been designed to test that theory/ model, look at whether or not your results support it. Try to explain why they turned out as they did and, where appropriate, offer possible alternative reasons for the results you obtained.

193

- *Consider the practical implications of your results* – for example, your study may have consequences for the way in which language teachers are trained or for the way students are taught a second language or a particular aspect of language.
- *Reflect on the way(s) in which your study has contributed to the field* – how it has advanced our understanding of it. Provided that you have employed a sound methodology, and where your results warrant it, you can and should claim such a contribution strongly, clearly and confidently while also qualifying your findings and interpretations, where necessary, on the understanding that they may not necessarily apply equally in all contexts. As we've seen, it's important to acknowledge the limitations of your work for this shows that you have the capacity to critically analyse it in an objective, unbiased manner. While this *may* appear to limit the impact of your research, it certainly does not undermine you as a researcher – quite the contrary in fact!

The conclusion

The conclusion section of your research project is where you bring everything together, tie up any loose ends and give your report a sense of closure. Generally, a conclusion to a research report is the same as any other conclusion (see Chapter 7) although it's likely to be longer. Most conclusions to a study will contain a number of components as follows:

A summary of the main findings – Although you may have included brief summaries elsewhere in your report – at the end of each chapter for example – it's a good idea to include a summary as part of or just prior to your conclusion; after all, as we've seen, your conclusion has to be a brief commentary on the main points you've made in your discussion and it can, therefore, be helpful just to recap those main points for the reader before commenting on them.

A statement of the limitations of your study – As we've seen, as a researcher it's important that you're seen to be fair and objective. This, in part, means acknowledging any shortcomings with your study. This is important because it enables your reader to evaluate what you have done and, where possible, address those shortcomings should they choose to replicate the study. In addressing the limitations of their study, researchers frequently make reference to such things as flawed research design, inappropriate instruments, problems with participants, and variables that were not accounted for but which appeared important in hindsight.

Suggestions for future research – Based on your understanding of the literature relevant to your study and the results obtained, it's normal practice to make a series of recommendations for future research. Those recommendations may involve addressing some of the shortcomings you've identified in your own study and/or they may simply look at ways of extending your study in some respect or investigating a related area in a way that builds upon the findings of your own study.

A final statement concerning the contribution of your study – Often researchers wrap up their conclusion with a brief statement of the way(s) in which their study has contributed to our understanding of the field; of its implications or significance.

The bibliography

As we saw in section 8.7, a bibliography is a complete list of those works you've cited in your research report. Regardless of whether you've cited them in the main body of the text or as footnotes, they should all be listed alphabetically in the bibliography in the manner described in Chapter 8. The bibliography is an essential part of any research report and it needs to be put together carefully: it's all too easy to forget to list a book or article that you've used – a fact which emphasises the importance of keeping a very careful record of your sources and of noting them down systematically as and when you draw on them.

The appendices

The appendices are where you put documentation that supports your research report and which would have been too peripheral or (more likely) too large to appear in the main body of the text. Typically, it will include materials such as tables and charts, questionnaires and other such research instruments (see also section 1.9).

10.5 Presentation and submission

Having completed your essay or research project the final stage is to ensure that you present it well. Here's a checklist that you can use to help ensure that the final product you submit is something of which you feel proud and is not let down by careless presentation:

A pre-submission checklist
- Are all pages correctly numbered?
- Are all figures correctly numbered and titled?
- Is the system of headings/numbering consistent and comprehensive?
- Are quotations correctly formatted?
- Have all quotations and other source materials been correctly acknowledged?
- Have footnotes (if permitted and used) been correctly formatted?
- Is the bibliography correctly formatted and comprehensive?

- Does each page contain your name/essay title in the header (if required)?
- Does the title page have all necessary information?
- Does the table of contents (where required) reflect the order and page numbers of chapters, sections and sub-headings as they appear in the main text?
- Does the text paginate well?
- Have you edited the work for typos, spelling and punctuation errors?
- Have you eliminated all colour typeface and non-traditional fonts, except where absolutely necessary?
- Has a friend or colleague proof-read it?
- Is the length of your work within the required word count?
- Have all appendices been included?
- If the work is an essay, have you collated all the pages in the correct order? Have they been stapled or paper-clipped together (if required)? Have you put it in a plastic sleeve with your name clearly visible?
- If the work is a research report such as a dissertation, have you had it correctly bound?

The very best of luck with your submission!

Chapter 10 Key points checklist

- Before beginning your research project, make sure you're familiar with your university's rules and regulations.
- Choose a research question that addresses a gap in the literature or a project that provides a useful and original synthesis of existing literature.
- Choose a project that interests you and for which you can find a supervisor with whom you are able to work well and who has the expertise needed to supervise you.
- Clarify your focus by constructing a set of research questions or hypotheses.
- Familiarise yourself with the various research approaches and choose the one(s) most suitable given your research questions – i.e. most likely to answer those questions.
- Be sure you obtain ethics approval if your research involves human subjects.
- Try and anticipate potential problems and have measures in place to deal with them.
- Your research report should contain the following key components: a title page, an introduction, an abstract, an 'acknowledgements' page, a table of contents,

a literature review, a methodology section, a results section, a discussion section, a conclusion, a bibliography and, where necessary, appendices.

- Choose a title that accurately reflects the nature of your project but which is concise.

- Make sure your table of contents accurately reflects the structure of your dissertation and that the headings and page numbers tally and are correct.

- Remember to mention all individuals and institutions that helped make your project possible.

- Your abstract should be a very concise overview of your project, typically not exceeding around 500 words and including background, aims, samples (if an empirical study), methods, results and conclusions.

- Use your introduction to create interest in your audience, make clear the relevance of your study, define key concepts and terminology, and present a clear statement of the problem or issue you're investigating and its theoretical and/or practical significance.

- Your literature review should give you and your reader a thorough overview of that body of literature potentially relevant to your study and which helps contextualise or 'frame' your study.

- Your methodology should include a description of participants (where relevant), your data collection instruments and procedures.

- Relate your results to your research questions or hypotheses and remain objective in reporting them.

- Your discussion should: be critical and insightful; relate your results to previous research; consider the theoretical implications of your results and, where possible, explain why they turned out as they did; consider the practical implications of your results; and reflect on the way(s) in which your study has contributed to the field.

- Your conclusion should normally include a summary of your main findings, a statement of any limitations of your study, suggestions for future research, and a statement about the contribution of your study.

- Your bibliography should comprise a list of *all* works cited in your report, listed in alphabetical order.

- Remember to give your report a thorough editing before submitting it.

Frequently asked questions

Introduction

Below you will find some of the questions students commonly ask about writing essays and which they find particularly confusing. The questions (and my responses to them) are organised according to broad topic and at the end of each question is an indication of the chapter(s) in the book to which it relates.

Developing your own voice

'How critical can I be? Can I really challenge authority?'

The answer to this question is a big 'yes'. Remember, universities exists to develop the mind of the individual and to push the boundaries of knowledge. This can only happen if students are able to question the established wisdom. Paradigm shifts, sea changes in the way in which we look at the world or some aspect of it don't come about from being timid and from assuming that everything you hear and read is unquestionable fact; they come about because great thinkers are courageous enough to question what's often taken as fact and to prove it wrong! As an undergraduate student you have as much right to do this as a Nobel Prize winner. However, there are some *very* important caveats you must bear in mind before you opt to criticise the ideas of respected scholars – or indeed your fellow students, in a seminar or tutorial say.

- If you feel you have good reason to question the views of published writers, whoever they are, be absolutely sure you can support your case with solid evidence and a well-thought-through argument. Where possible you'll need to quote the relevant literature, although on rare occasions your criticisms may be based solely on logic or notions of a priori truth, for example, and as such require little or no reference to the literature. However, these are precisely that: *rare*, so be careful!
- Give the views you are criticising their due, where appropriate. The very fact that they are published suggests strongly that they have merit, and in acknowledging this, you not only make your own views appear less

blinkered and therefore more credible, you also indicate a depth of understanding while also appearing less arrogant.

- Keep your criticism strictly objective by basing it only on the evidence and on watertight reasoning, and avoiding language that's personal and emotive (i.e. angry-sounding or condescending). Failure to do so will very likely result in your reader questioning your motives, which in turn will detract from the force of your own argument. (Chapter 1)

'If I know that the person marking my essay has an opinion which falls clearly on one side of an argument (and may be different from my own), should I tailor my own argument so that it fits with their views?'

Students often worry that, if they take a position that's contrary to that of the lecturer who'll be marking their work, then they'll be penalised. In other words, they're often torn between writing what they really believe and writing what they think their lecturer wants to hear. There's always a niggling suspicion that by doing the latter they'll provoke a more sympathetic response ... and therefore secure a higher mark.

Although most university lecturers are big-minded enough not to let their own theoretical allegiances colour their objectivity when marking students' work, it would be unreasonable and naive of me to say that this never happens; it does. However, it basically comes down to your personal judgement about (a) each individual lecturer and how you think they're likely to respond to what you write, and (b) whether you're prepared to 'fall into line' with whatever they believe and, in doing so, suppress your own voice and academic integrity. I'm afraid it's your call! However, in making that call, it's worth remembering that lecturers are normally less interested in your particular perspective than in your ability to demonstrate knowledge of the subject you are writing about and to make a good and coherent case in support of whatever line of argument you choose to take. (Chapters 1 and 8)

Answering the question

'If I get an essay question that contains two statements and asks me to argue why one is correct and the other isn't, is it possible to argue that both are, in fact, incorrect and to present an alternative statement and supporting argument?'

This is really something you need to ask the lecturer who sets the question, for different lecturers may have different purposes in presenting you with a question of this kind. While there may be occasions when a lecturer will require you to focus only on the two statements provided (perhaps because they wish to raise your awareness of certain issues that naturally emerge from a consideration of these particular statements and which has the greater veracity), equally there may be others where they welcome a completely different angle. It makes things interesting and can be a good way for you the student to demonstrate your academic maturity and the fact that you're developing your own voice (see sections 1.3 and 8.1).

'Is it ok to begin statements with "I believe", "I think" when the essay is asking you to describe/offer your own personal opinion on a topic?'

As I mentioned in section 9.2, although it's becoming increasingly acceptable to use 'I' in academic writing, departments and faculty still have mixed feelings towards it and so it's always best to check with your department – and even with the particular tutor who set your assignment – about how they feel about your using 'I'. When a question requires you to give a personal response or perspective, it can be difficult to imagine how you might do this without using the first person singular. However, if this is what you're required to do, there are various strategies you can employ for that purpose and these are listed in section 9.2. Giving your own views is fine, provided you also show an awareness of the relevant literature. Most importantly, presenting your own views is one way of demonstrating that you're developing your own voice (see sections 1.3 and 8.1) – an important part of your academic development, as we have seen.

'In an essay, is it better to cover a small number of ideas or theories in depth, or to cover a large number in less depth?'

This is a tricky question to answer because it largely depends on the nature of the essay question. If the essay question seeks to find out whether you have a broad understanding of a particular aspect or issue in English language or linguistics, then the best way to answer it may well be to cover more ground in less depth. This should show your tutor that you know what the relevant ideas or theories are and that you have at least a reasonable understanding of them and how they relate to one another. Of course, there is always the 'word-count factor': in other words, if you only have 2,000 words to cover a lot of theoretical ground, provided the question does not require a broad overview it may be best to focus only one or two key ideas and cover these in depth. If you choose this route, however, it's always a good idea to state explicitly early on in your essay that you have opted to do this. That way your tutor won't assume that you're unaware of the ideas you haven't covered or that you've overlooked them. Once again though, if in doubt ask your tutor. (Chapter 3)

Writing to time and word limits

'During examinations, how can I make sure I finish within the time limit?'

Although each individual has their own way of dealing with this problem, students often find the following tips helpful:

- Be decisive. Once you've decided on a question, commit to it and stick with it. Often students choose a question and begin writing immediately, only to find that, within a few sentences, they dry up and don't know what to say or in which direction to go. They then panic and dither as they wonder whether or not they should change question. Generally speaking, unless it really is looking like a complete disaster, it's best to stick with your initial instincts; instead of spending time on dithering in this way and selecting and preparing an alternative question, devote it to working through the problem(s) you've encountered. Most importantly, though, try to avoid such a situation altogether by spending a few minutes thinking about the question and sketching out a simple plan. This is time well spent, as we shall see in a moment, and will indicate early on and before you've invested too much time in the question, whether or not you have what's needed to answer it well.
- Be disciplined in your allocation of time. Unless different essay questions are worth different marks – rarely the case – make sure you devote an equal amount of time to each question. Take a strict line and, if at all possible, don't allow yourself to exceed the time limit allocated to any one question. If you do, one or all of the other questions are likely to suffer. By the same token, be sure to use the full amount of time allocated to any particular question.
- Always plan. Planning doesn't just help in confirming your selection of question, in organising your ideas before you put pen to paper, and in giving you a sense of direction, it also plays a crucial time-management role. By being able to refer to a plan whilst writing your answer to a question, you can at any time locate your current position in relation to the whole essay as outlined in that plan. This gives you a rough indication of how much time you have left for the remainder of the essay. If you've allocated forty minutes to an essay, it is not unreasonable to spend five to ten minutes of that time planning.
- Obviously, keep a regular eye on the clock! (Chapter 2)

'How can I make sure I don't exceed the word limit for essays?'

Writing within a word limit takes practice and familiarity with your own approach to writing. It's also an important skill for at least two reasons.

201

Firstly, if you exceed the word limit and fail to address the problem before handing in your assignment, you risk being penalised and having marks deducted from your work. It's now common practice to require students to hand in with their assignments a signed cover sheet specifying the word count and confirming that they haven't plagiarised. Secondly, if you exceed the word limit, it can be very difficult to pare down what you've written. Why? Because not only do you have to decide what to omit (often a challenging task in itself) but, having taken that decision, you may well find that by omitting parts of your text you've lost some of the natural flow of your discussion (see section 2.2). Re-creating that flow by restitching the text together can be tricky and time-consuming, and require real dexterity with the language.

Now, even the finest writers face this problem from time to time; however, heeding a few simple tips can help avoid it.

- Careful planning (yes, that one again!). In precisely the same way that planning can help you allocate your time evenly when writing under examination conditions by helping you 'locate your current position in relation to the whole essay as outlined in that plan', it can also give you an indication of whether or not you're on target in respect of your word limit. So, for example, if, according to your plan, you are approximately halfway through a 3,000-word assignment, then you should have written around 1,500 words. If indeed you have, then you're probably on target. Of course, this is only a rough guide and it may be that the second half of your assignment requires more discussion than the first – something which might not necessarily be immediately obvious from a cursory glance at your plan.
- Some students aim for a slightly lower word limit than that specified in the assignment. So, if the assignment is a 3,000-word essay, the student will write to, say, a 2,700-word limit. The thinking here is that essays almost always run over the limit by some margin; therefore, by artificially reducing the word limit, you'll probably then end up pretty close to the *actual* word limit.
- Write concisely (see section 9.1) and avoid being unnecessarily wordy. Don't say in fifty words what you can say more elegantly in thirty. Contrary to expectation, writing economically often forces you to be more stylish and elegant in your expression; as such it can indicate greater mastery of the language.
- Use the 'word count' tool that now features in all word processing programmes. And don't just use it once you have completed the assignment; use it periodically during the writing of it in order to get a feel for whether or not you're on target with the word limit. (Chapter 3)

Citing sources/referencing

'How can I be sure my ideas are really original and I won't be accused of plagiarism?'

There's only one way to feel confident that the ideas you express in your writing are truly your own, and that's by being as thorough as possible in your review of the relevant literature. Through your reading and your discussions with lecturers and other students in seminars, tutorials and elsewhere, you become familiar with the debates that exist around the subject about which you're writing and the various ideas and theoretical positions taken by different scholars. This puts you in a position to identify gaps in the literature, inject originality into your analysis and take a unique stance on issues in the near knowledge that you aren't inadvertently plagiarising the work of others. (Chapters 1 & 8)

'If I've discussed a theory, say, with one of my tutors, can I include any opinions they expressed in my essay? Do I have to reference them – and if yes, how?'

Generally speaking, you don't need to acknowledge and reference ideas that you've heard during the course of discussions with others, whether your lecturers or anyone else. In fact, if you do make reference to an informal discussion, it can seem a little bit weak and amateurish in comparison to more 'solid' references sourced from articles and books. There's one important caveat, however: you need to be sure that the ideas you heard are not simply a reiteration of ideas that have already been reported in the literature. If you mistakenly assume that they're original and therefore don't appear in the literature (and, consequently, you fail to acknowledge and cite them), then you risk being accused of plagiarism (see section 8.2). So, once again, it comes down to your familiarity with the literature. It's difficult to over-estimate the importance to your success as a student, academic and writer of having a good knowledge of the literature of the fields of English language and linguistics and, where relevant, of associated disciplines. (Chapters 1, 2 and 8)

The introduction, body and conclusion

'What should be the relative proportions of the introduction, body and conclusion of my essay?'

There's no absolute rule here; however, a good rule of thumb is that the introduction should account for around 15–20 per cent of your essay, the body around 60–70 per cent, and the conclusion around 15–20 per cent. (Chapters 5, 6 and 7)

Using figures/illustrations

'How do I decide whether it's better to use a figure/illustration or text when describing, summarising or illustrating an idea or process? Does using one method over the other make any real difference?'

As we saw in section 6.4, visual representations of data or ideas can be an excellent and efficient way of presenting information clearly and concisely, often allowing the reader to get an at-a-glance 'picture' or sense of data or of an idea. When deciding whether or not to use some kind of visual, simply ask yourself: 'Would a visual make things clearer or more meaningful for my reader? Would it convey the sense of those ideas I wish to share more effectively than if I were to use words?' If yes, then by all means use a visual.

Linguistics glossary

Some terms used in linguistics, language studies, language teaching and SLA research. The aim is to present quick glosses, not watertight definitions.

  Based on V. J. Cook (1997), *Inside Language* (Hodder Arnold) and V. J. Cook (2004) *The English Writing System* (Hodder Arnold).

With thanks to Professor Vivian Cook for permission to use his glossary of terms; see: http://homepage.ntlworld.com/vivian.c/Linguistics/Linguistics-Glossary.htm.

additive bilingualism: L2 learning that adds to the learner's capabilities. See SUBTRACTIVE

adjacency pair: a pair of discourse moves that often go together, e.g. question and answer

agreement: Agreement consists of a change of form in one element of a *sentence* caused by a second element, to show their common NUMBER, GENDER, etc., for example Subject Verb Agreement of number in English- *One swallow DOESN'T make a summer/Two swallows DON'T make a summer.*

allophone: Allophones are alternative pronunciations of *phonemes* in a particular language that never affect the meaning. For example RP English has clear /l/ at the beginning of words such as *lick*, dark /l/ at the end of words such as *kill*, but these do not change the words if the wrong one is used; in Polish the two /l/s are different phonemes.

alphabetic principle: the writing system in which written symbols correspond to spoken sounds, contrasted with the LOGOGRAPHIC and ORTHOGRAPHIC PRINCIPLES

aphasia: Aphasia is in general the impairment of the ability to use language, particularly GRAMMAR and vocabulary, usually caused by some form of damage to the brain, sometimes accompanied by other forms of impairment, consisting of types such as BROCA'S and WERNICKE'S APHASIAS.

articulatory loop: in WORKING MEMORY theory the means by which information is kept in working memory by being audibly or silently articulated

assimilationist teaching: teaching that expects people to give up their native languages and to become speakers of the majority language of the country. See TRANSITIONAL TEACHING, SUBMERSION TEACHING.

authentic speech: 'an authentic text is a text that was created to fulfil some social purpose in the language community in which it was produced'

bilingualism: varying definitions going from perfect command of two languages to the ability to use another language for practical purposes, however trivial the use. See SECOND LANGUAGE, ADDITIVE / SUBTRACTIVE, ELITE BILINGUALISM

binding: the relationship between a *pronoun* such as *she* and its antecedent *noun* such as *Jane* as in *Jane helped herself, Helen said Jane helped her,* etc., is called binding – a complex area of the UNIVERSAL GRAMMAR theory

Broca's aphasia: a type of APHASIA characterised by loss of ability to produce but not to comprehend speech, associated with injury to Broca's area in the front left hemisphere of the brain (left frontal lobe)

canonical order: The canonical order of the *sentence* is the most usual order of the main sentence elements, SUBJECT (S), VERB (V) and OBJECT (O), in a language, for example VSO in Arabic or SVO in English. See also WORD ORDER.

case: Case is variation in the form of NOUNS and PRONOUNS to show their role in the structure of the SENTENCE, in English limited visibly to pronouns, SUBJECT case *he*, OBJECT case *him*, possessive case *his*, in Latin extending to nouns with six cases, in Finnish to fifteen, used nowadays for a more powerful abstract relationship not necessarily visible in the sentence itself.

character: the name for a single symbol of a writing system such as Chinese, i.e. 人 ('person') is a character. The term is also used in computing for any distinct symbol such as the letter <a>, number <6> or other form <@>.

clause: A clause has the attributes of a SENTENCE but may occur within a sentence, for example a relative clause *who played the alto* within the sentence *The man who played the alto was Charlie Parker.*

cognitive deficit: the limitations on processing information in a second language compared to in a first language

cognitive strategies: these involve specific conscious ways of tackling L2 learning. See LEARNING STRATEGIES.

cognitive style: a person's typical ways of thinking, seen as a continuum between field-dependent (FD) cognitive style, in which thinking relates to context, and field-independent (FI) style, in which it is independent of context

communication strategies in SLA: (1) individual solutions to psychological problems of L2 processing; (2) mutual attempts to solve L2 communication problems by participants; (3) ways of filling vocabulary gaps in L1 or L2.

communicative competence: the speaker's ability to put language to communicative use, usually traced back to Hymes. See PRAGMATIC COMPETENCE.

components of meaning: One way of describing the meaning of words is to split it up into separate components so that for example the noun *boy* can be seen as having the components [non-adult] [male], *girl* the components [non-adult] [female], *woman,* the components [adult] [female], and so on.

consciousness-raising: helping the student by drawing attention to features of the second language

consonant: Typically, in terms of sound production, a consonant is a sound which is obstructed in some way by tongue or lip contact as in /k/ *keep* or /b/ *beep*, as opposed to the unobstructed sound of a VOWEL. In terms of the sound system, a consonant is a sound that typically occurs at the beginning or end of the SYLLABLE rather than the middle, thus contrasting with vowel.

content words: Content words such as *table* or *truth* are best explained in the dictionary (lexicon). Content words form four types of LEXICAL PHRASE around lexical *heads*: NOUNS *drum*, VERBS *play,* adjectives *pretty,* and PREPOSITIONS *to*. They contrast with *grammatical words*.

creole: A creole language is a new language created when children acquire their parents' PIDGIN language as their first language, for example Hawaiian creole and Guyanese creole.

critical period hypothesis (CPH): the claim that human beings are only capable of learning language between the age of two years and the early teens

decoding versus codebreaking: processing language to get the 'message' versus processing language to get the 'rules'

derivation: Derivation is how new words are created by processes such as inflections, *trumpet + er = trumpeter*, or compounding, *wind + mill = windmill*. It contrasts with GRAMMATICAL INFLECTIONS.

dialect: A dialect is a particular variety of a language spoken by a group united by region, class, etc. It is usually seen nowadays as a matter of different vocabulary or grammar rather than of accent.

diglossia: Diglossia is a situation where there are two versions of a language with very different uses, a High form for official occasions and a Low form for everyday life, as in the difference between High German and Swiss German in German-speaking areas of Switzerland.

diphthong: A diphthong is a type of VOWEL produced by moving the tongue as it is produced from one position towards another, for example in English /fɪə/*fear* and /ləʊ/*low*. It may correspond to one or two written letters.

discourse move: the speaker's choice of what to do in the conversation, e.g. opening moves such as 'greeting'

distinctive feature: Distinctive features are a way of analysing speech sounds in terms of a certain number of on/off elements. So the /b/ in English *bass* has the feature +voice, the /p/ of *piano* has the feature-voice, and so on.

dual route model: a dual-route model of reading aloud has two processes or 'routes': the *phonological route*, which converts letters into sounds through rules, and the *lexical route*, which matches words as wholes in the mental lexicon.

dyslexia: Children with developmental dyslexia have problems with reading but not usually with other areas of development. See SPECIFIC LANGUAGE IMPAIRMENT.

elite bilingualism: either the choice by parents of bringing up children through two languages, or societies in which members of a ruling group speak a second language

epenthesis: Epenthesis is the process of adding VOWELS to make possible SYLLABLES out of impossible consonant sequences, for example *Rawanda* for *Ruanda*.

Estuary English: This is some people's name for a recent accent of British English allegedly originating from the Thames estuary, known for its use of the GLOTTAL STOP [ʔ] /beʔ/ for *bet* /bet/ and of /w/ for /l/ as in /fuw/ for *full* /ful/.

focus on form (FonF): incidental discussion of grammar arising from meaningful language in the classroom

focus on forms: deliberate discussion of grammar in the classroom without reference to meaning

font: strictly a complete set of type for printing; nowadays mostly it refers to a particular design for the whole set of characters available through a computer keyboard.

frequency: either how many times a word occurs in speech or how often it is practised by a student

fricatives: A type of CONSONANT in which the air escapes through a narrow gap created between lips, teeth and tongue, as in English /f/ *fine*, /s/ *sign*, /v/ *vine*, etc.

front/back: In PHONETICS the dimension in the position of the tongue for VOWELS from the front to the back of the mouth is called front/back

functional phrases: In syntactic theory, a functional phrase is built round a HEAD consisting of a GRAMMATICAL WORD such as the (Determiner Phrase), for example *the book*, or a grammatical inflection such as present tense '-s', as in *lives*. According to some theories, these are not available to young children.

gender: Gender is a system for allocating different elements in the *sentence* to the categories of masculine, feminine and neuter. In English gender is seen only in the link between PRONOUNS such as *she* and NOUNS such as *Susan*, in other languages it affects AGREEMENT of adjectives and VERBS with nouns. Gender is called 'natural' when it correlates with sex, 'arbitrary' when it does not, as in French *la table* (feminine, 'table') and German *das Mädchen* (neuter, 'girl').

glottal stop: A speech sound made by closing the VOCAL CORDS and then releasing them, as in a cough, symbolised by /ʔ/.

good language learner (GLL) strategies: the strategies employed by people known to be good at L2 learning

grammar: Grammar is the system of relationships between elements of the SENTENCE that links the 'sounds' to the 'meanings'. It is used to refer both to the knowledge of language in the speaker's mind and to the system as written down in rules, grammar-books and other descriptions. The type of grammar derived from classical languages that is often taught in schools is called *traditional* grammar and is more concerned with prescribing how native speakers should use language than with describing it. Main areas of grammar are WORD ORDER, GRAMMATICAL MORPHEMES, GRAMMATICAL INFLECTIONS and PHRASE STRUCTURE. See also PRESCRIPTIVE GRAMMAR, TRADITIONAL GRAMMAR.

grammatical (linguistic) competence: the native speaker's knowledge of language

grammatical inflections: Grammatical inflections are a system of showing meaning by changing word endings, as in the English '-ed' inflection meaning past tense, *I looked,* absent from some languages like Vietnamese.

grammatical morphemes: Grammatical morphemes is a collective term for MORPHEMES that primarily play a role in the grammar of the sentence, consisting in English of either GRAMMATICAL WORDS such as the articles *the/a* or PREPOSITIONS *to/in* or GRAMMATICAL INFLECTIONS such as the past tense '-ed', *liked,* or the possessive 's', *Albert's.* In recent UG these are the heads of *functional phrases.*

grammatical words: Grammatical words (also known as 'function' or 'structure' words such as PREPOSITION, *by/for,* or determiners, *a/an,* express the grammatical relationships in the sentence rather than meanings that can be captured in the lexicon.

head: The head of a LEXICAL PHRASE is a lexical head around which the phrase is built, i.e. Noun Phrases like *a good CD* have a head NOUN such as *CD.* The head of a FUNCTIONAL PHRASE may be an inflection such as '-s' or a GRAMMATICAL WORD such as *the.*

head parameter: The head parameter captures the difference between languages in which the HEAD of the phrase comes first, i.e. the PREPOSITION head comes before its 'complement' in English, *on Tuesday,* and those in which it comes last, as the postposition head comes last in Japanese, *Nihon ni* (in Japan).

h-dropping: H-dropping refers to the presence or absence of /h/ in the pronunciation of certain words where the letter 'h' is present in the spelling, as in *Harry* versus *'Arry.* In French h-dropping is part of the standard language; in English English, but not American, h-dropping is a strong social marker of low status in words like *high, hat* or *hit.*

hyper-correction: Hyper-correction is the phenomenon whereby a speaker exaggerates the prestige pronunciation beyond that used by high-status speakers, for example /hɔnest/ for *honest*.

immersion teaching: teaching the whole curriculum through the second language, best known from experiments in Canada

independent language assumption: the language of the L2 learner considered as a system of language in its own right rather than as a defective version of the target language (sometimes called 'interlanguage'. See MULTI-COMPETENCE.

infix: An infix is a MORPHEME that is added inside a word to get a new meaning, often by changing the *vowel*, as in *blow* versus *blew*. Infixes are rare in English but common in Arabic.

instrumental motivation: learning the language for a career goal or other practical reason

integrative motivation: learning the language in order to take part in the culture of its people

intonation: Intonation is the change of pitch used in the sound system of language, i.e. *John?* versus *John!* Sometimes intonation refers specifically to the use of change of pitch to show attitude or GRAMMAR in a language rather than vocabulary differences, in which case it is opposed to TONE.

IPA (International Phonetic Alphabet): Internationally agreed phonetic alphabet for writing down the sounds of languages in a consistent fashion.

laterals: Laterals are speech sounds produced asymmetrically in the mouth, typically /l/ in which one side of the tongue makes contact with the roof of the mouth but not the other.

language awareness: helping the student by raising awareness of language itself

language function: the reason why someone says something, e.g. apologizing, arguing, greeting, etc.

language maintenance and bilingual language teaching: These teach or maintain the minority language within its group. See ASSIMILATIONIST TEACHING.

learning strategy: a choice that the learner makes while learning or using the second language that affects learning, whether COGNITIVE or METACOGNITIVE. See *GLL*

length: Length usually distinguishes pairs of *vowels* in a language, such as short /ɪ/ in /pɪt/ *pit* versus long /iː/ in /piːt/ *Pete*.

lexical entry: A word has a lexical entry in the mind that gives all the information about it such as its pronunciation, meaning, and how it may be used in the structure of the *sentence*.

lexical phrase: A lexical phrase is built around a lexical HEAD such as a NOUN, *the house on the hill*, a VERB, *cross the road*, an Adjective, *quick to anger*, or a PREPOSITION, *in the spring*. It contrasts with a FUNCTIONAL PHRASE.

linguistic imperialism: means by which a 'Centre' country dominates 'Periphery' countries by making them use its language

linguistics: The academic discipline that focuses on language is called linguistics and is carried out by LINGUISTS.

linguist: In the study of language, a linguist is usually someone who studies LINGUISTICS rather than someone who speaks several languages.

logographic principle: The writing system in which written symbols correspond to meanings, as in Chinese characters. See ALPHABETIC PRINCIPLE.

mental lexicon: speakers of a language store all the words they know in a mental dictionary or 'lexicon' containing many thousands of items.

metacognitive strategies: LEARNING STRATEGIES that involve planning and directing learning at a general level

Minimalist Program(me): The Minimalist Programme is the current version of Chomsky's UNIVERSAL GRAMMAR theory, as yet only partially developed, which tries to reduce grammar to the minimum possible *principles*.

MLU (Mean Length of Utterance): MLU measures the complexity of a child's speech by averaging the number of MORPHEMES or words per utterance, useful as an L1 measure up to about the age of four years.

morpheme: A morpheme is the smallest unit in the GRAMMAR that is either a word in its own right (free morpheme), *cook*, or part of a word, *cooks* (bound morpheme '-s'). GRAMMATICAL MORPHEMES that form part of the grammar, such as the plural inflection '-s' in *books* are one type. Morphemes that change one word to another, for example *cooker, cookery, cookbook*, are part of *derivation*. See INFIX, SUFFIX.

movement: Movement is a way of describing the structure of the SENTENCE as if elements in it moved around, typically in English in questions and passive constructions. Thus the question *Will John go?* comes from a similar structure to that underlying the statement *John will come* by movement of *will*. See SUBJACENCY and STRUCTURE-DEPENDENCY.

multi-competence: the knowledge of more than one language in the same mind

multilingualism: countries where more than one language is used for everyday purposes

nasals: nasals are *consonants* created by blocking the mouth with the tongue or lips, lowering the soft palate (velum), and allowing the air to come out through the nose, as in English /m/ *mouse* and /n/ *nous*. *Vowels* may be nasalised by allowing some air to come out through the nose and mouth at the same time, as in French /sɔ̃/ *son* (sound).

native speaker: a person, usually monolingual, speaking the first language they learnt as a child

noun: The lexical category of Noun (N) consists of words such as *John, truth* and *electron*. In UNIVERSAL GRAMMAR theory, a noun is the *head* of a lexical phrase, the Noun Phrase. It can also be thought of as a potential SUBJECT of the sentence, *The truth hurts*.

number: Number is a way of signalling how many entities are involved, for example through the forms of NOUNS, PRONOUNS and VERBS. English, French, and German have two numbers, singular (*he*) and plural (*they*). Number is often used to signal other things than sheer quantity, for instance social relationship through pronouns.

object: The object of the SENTENCE is usually a Noun Phrase in a particular relationship to the VERB of the sentence acting as 'receiver of the action'; for instance the verb *see* requires an object *see something*; the verb *give* two objects *give someone* (indirect) *something* (direct).

official language: language(s) recognized by a country for official purposes

open/close: In PHONETICS the dimension in which the tongue position of VOWELS varies from the top to the bottom of the mouth is called open/close.

orthographic depth: the scale for alphabetic languages going from 'shallow' writing systems with close links between letters and sounds such as Finnish to 'deep' writing systems with more complex links such as English.

orthographic principle: A writing system in which written symbols have a system of their own, corresponding neither to sounds nor to meanings. Cf. ALPHABETIC PRINCIPLE.

parameter: In UNIVERSAL GRAMMAR theory the variation between languages is seen as a question of setting values for a small number of parameters; for example, Italian sets the PRO-DROP parameter to have a value of pro-drop and thus allows sentences without SUBJECTS, *vende* (he sells), while German sets the value to non-pro-drop and thus has subjects in all sentences *Er spricht* (he speaks). Cf. HEAD PARAMETER.

parsing: the process through which the mind works out the grammatical structure and meaning of the sentence. whether TOP-DOWN OR BOTTOM-UP

person: Person is a way of linking the *sentence* to the speech situation through the choice of PRONOUN or VERB form, often in terms of the person speaking (first person, *I/je/ich*, etc.), the person(s) spoken to (second person, *you/tu/vous/du/Sie*, etc.), and other people involved (third person), *he/she/it/ they il/elle/ils/elles er/sie/es/Sie*, etc.). Sometimes person is extended to people not previously mentioned (fourth person), as in Navaho, and to listener-included 'we' versus listener-excluded 'we', as in Melanesian Pidgin English *yumi* and *mipela*. Often linked to *number*.

phoneme: The distinctive sounds of a particular language system are its phonemes, studied in PHONOLOGY. Thus in English the sounds /p/ and /b/ are different phonemes because they distinguish /piːk/ *peak* from /biːk/ *beak*; the sounds [p] and [ph] are different phonemes in Hindi because they distinguish two words, but do not in English as they simply form two variant ALLOPHONES of the same phoneme without ever distinguishing two words.

phonetics: The sub-discipline of LINGUISTICS that studies the production and perception of the speech sounds themselves is called phonetics and contrasts with PHONOLOGY.

phonology: The area of *linguistics* that studies the sound systems of particular languages is phonology, and is contrasted with PHONETICS.

phrase structure: The phrase structure of the sentence links all the parts together in a structure like that of a family tree. So the Noun Phrase *the soprano* combines with a VERB to get the Verb Phrase *played the soprano*, which in turn combines with the Noun Phrase *Sidney Bechet* to get the SENTENCE *Sidney Bechet played the soprano*.

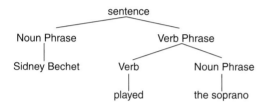

pidgin: A pidgin language is created by speakers of two different languages for communicating with each other. Pidgins share similar characteristics wherever they arise such as CV SYLLABLE structure. Examples are: Tok Pisin (Papua New Guinea), Cameroon Pidgin English, Ivory Coast Pidgin, etc. See also CREOLE.

plosive: A speech sound made by blocking the air-stream completely with the tongue or lips, allowing the air to burst out after a brief moment, as in English /t/ *tea* or /b/ *bee*. See VOICE ONSET TIME.

pragmatic competence: Chomsky's term for the speaker's ability to use language for a range of public and private functions, including communication. See GRAMMMATICAL COMPETENCE.

prefix: A prefix is a MORPHEME that is added to the beginning of a word to create another word by DERIVATION as 'Brit' is added to 'pop' to get *Britpop*.

preposition: The category of grammar called preposition (P) consists of words like *to*, *by* and *with*. In UNIVERSAL GRAMMAR theory the Preposition is the HEAD of a LEXICAL PHRASE, the Preposition Phrase. When coming before a NOUN, the category is called 'preposition', as in *in Basin Street*, when after a Noun a 'postposition', *Nippon ni* (Japan in).

prescriptive grammar: grammar that 'prescribes' what people should say rather than 'describes' what they do say

principle: In the UNIVERSAL GRAMMAR theory, principles of language are built-in to the human mind and are thus never broken in human languages. Examples are STRUCTURE-DEPENDENCY and SUBJACENCY.

pro-drop: The pro-drop *parameter* (null subject parameter) divides languages into pro-drop languages, in which the SUBJECT of the SENTENCE may be left

213

out, as in Italian *Sono di Torino* (am from Turin) and Chinese *Shuo* (speak), and non-pro-drop languages, in which the subject must be present in the actual sentence as in English, German and French.

pronoun: Pronouns such as *he* and *them* differ from NOUNS in that they refer to different things on different occasions: *She likes it* can refer to any female being liking anything; *Helen likes Coltrane* only to a specific person liking a specific object. English pronouns have CASE *(she* versus *her)* and NUMBER *(she* versus *they)*.

prototype theory: in Rosch's theory, words have whole meanings divided into basic level ('table'), superordinate level ('furniture'), and subordinate level ('coffee table')

punctuation: 'the rules for graphically structuring written language by means of a set of conventional marks'

r-dropping: Some standard accents of English such as American are 'rhotic' in that they have /r/ before CONSONANTS *bard* is /baːrd/ or before silence *fur* / fəːr /. Other accents of English such as British RP are 'non-rhotic', in that they do not have /r/ in these two positions, i.e. *bard* /baːd/, *fur* /fɜː/. R-dropping is a marker of low status in the USA and lack of r-dropping is a marker of rural accents in England.

RP: The prestige accent of British English is known by the two letters RP, originally standing for 'Received Pronunciation'. It is spoken in all regions of the UK, even if by a small minority of speakers.

sans-serif letters: letters which have no cross-strokes and usually constant line width. Fred specialized in the job of making very quaint wax toys.

schema (pl. schemas or schemata): the background knowledge on which the interpretation of a text depends

script: 'a predetermined stereotyped sequence of actions that defines a well-known situation'

second language: 'A language acquired by a person in addition to his mother tongue' UNESCO. See BILINGUALISM.

sentence: A sentence is the largest independent unit in the GRAMMAR of the language. It may include other CLAUSES within it. Sometimes it is necessary to distinguish the lexical sentences of spoken language, distinguished by their 'completeness' of structure, etc., from the textual sentences of written language, distinguished by punctuation.

serif letters: letters which have small cross-strokes (serifs) and variable line width. <Fred specialized in the job of making very quaint wax toys.>

short-term memory (STM): the memory used for keeping information for periods of time up to a few seconds. See WORKING MEMORY.

sign language: A sign language differs from other human languages only in using a gesture system rather than a sound system.

Specific Language Impairment (SLI): Specific Language Impairment (SLI) is one term for difficulties with language development in children unaccompanied by non-linguistic disabilities, possibly genetic in origin and characterised inter alia by missing *grammatical morphemes*.

structural grammar: teaching term for GRAMMAR concerned with how words go into PHRASES, phrases into sentences

structure-dependency: Structure-dependency is a restriction on MOVEMENT in human languages that makes it depend on the structure of the *sentence*, rather than on its linear order. A PRINCIPLE of UNIVERSAL GRAMMAR.

style: Style is used by Labov and others to refer to the dimension of formal to informal in language use.

subjacency: Subjacency is a restriction on grammatical MOVEMENT in the SENTENCE that prevents elements moving over more than one boundary, the definition of boundary varying as a PARAMETER from one language to another.

subject: The Subject (S) is the Noun Phrase of the *sentence* alongside the Verb Phrase in its structure, *John likes biscuits*, compulsory in non-pro-drop languages in the actual sentence but may be omitted in PRO-DROP languages; it often acts as the 'agent of the action'.

submersion teaching: extreme sink-or-swim form of ASSIMILATIONIST teaching in which minority-language children are simply put in majority-language classes

subtractive bilingualism: L2 learning that takes away from the learner's capabilities (Lambert). See ADDITIVE BILINGUALISM.

suffix: A suffix is a MORPHEME that is added to a word to create another word by DERIVATION. *Felon* thus becomes a second noun by adding '-y' *felony*, and an adjective by adding '-ous' *felonious*.

syllable: A sound structure usually consisting of a central VOWEL (V) such as /a:/, with one or more CONSONANTS (C) preceding or following it, such as /b/ or /k/ CV /ba:/ *bar* and VC /a:k/ *ark*. Languages vary in whether they permit only CV syllables or allow CVC syllables as well and in the combinations of C that may be used. See EPENTHESIS.

teachability hypothesis: 'an L2 structure can be learnt from instruction only if the learner's interlanguage is close to the point when this structure is acquired in the natural setting' (Pienemann)

tone: Usually tone means a unit of pitch change for a given language, English having about seven tones. Sometimes tone is used to contrast a tone language where tones are used to show vocabulary differences such as Chinese and an *intonation* language where tones show attitudes, *grammar*, etc., such as English.

top-down and bottom-up: starting from the *sentence* as a whole and working down to the smallest parts of it, versus starting from the smallest parts and working up

traditional grammar: 'school' GRAMMAR concerned with labelling sentences with parts of speech

transitional teaching: teaching that allows people to function in a majority language, without necessarily losing or devaluing the first language. See ASSIMILATIONIST TEACHING.

typography: 'the structuring and arranging of visual language' (Baines and Haslam, 2002, 1)

Universal Grammar: Sometimes Universal Grammar refers simply to the aspects of language that all languages have in common. In the Chomskyan sense, Universal Grammar refers to the language faculty built in to the human mind, seen as consisting of PRINCIPLES such as STRUCTURE-DEPENDENCY and PARAMETERS such as PRO-DROP.

uvular /r/: An /r/ pronounced with tongue contact at the uvula at the back of the mouth – the usual French /r/

verb: A Verb (V) is a lexical category in the GRAMMAR made up of words such as *like* and *listen*. In UG theory it is the head of the lexical Verb Phrase (VP). Different types of verbs specify whether there is a need for: no OBJECT, *Eric fainted*, one object, *Billie sang the blues*, two objects, *Mary gave the money to her brother*, an animate SUBJECT, *the man fainted* not *the rock fainted*, and so on.

vocal cords: 'Vocal cords' are flaps in the larynx which may open and close rapidly during speech to let out puffs of air, producing a basic vibrating noise called VOICE.

voice: Voice in PHONETICS is technically the vibration contributed to speech by allowing flaps in the larynx known as VOCAL CORDS to rapidly open and shut as air passes through them. Presence or absence of voice is then a DISTINCTIVE FEATURE that separates voiced sounds like the /d/ of *dime* from unvoiced sounds like the /t/ of *time*.

Voice Onset Time (VOT): When a PLOSIVE sound is created by blocking the airway through the mouth, the moment when VOICE starts is called the Voice Onset Time. Voicing may start before release (minus VOT) or after release (plus VOT). For example English /p/ is distinguished from /b/ by its longer VOT inter alia. VOTs vary from one language to another.

vowel: In terms of sound production, a vowel is a single speech sound produced by vibrating the VOCAL CORDS and not obstructing the mouth in any way, as in the /æ/ of *bank*, shaped by the position of the lips into rounded and unrounded sounds as in English /i:/ *bee* and /u:/ *boo*, and by the position of the tongue into *open/close* as in English /u:/ *loot* vs /ɔ/ *lot* and front/back as in English /e/ *bet* versus /u/ *foot*. In terms of sound structure, a vowel typically occurs as the core of the SYLLABLE rather than at the beginning or the end, thus contrasting with CONSONANT.

Wernicke's aphasia: Wernicke's aphasia is the name of a type of APHASIA involving difficulty with comprehension rather than speaking, associated with injury to Wernicke's area in the back left area of the brain (posterior upper temporal lobe).

word order: A crucial aspect of the grammar of many languages is the order of the elements in the SENTENCE, called word order in general. One variation is the order of SUBJECT, VERB and OBJECT, whether SVO, SOV, or whatever, the main order for a language sometimes being called its CANONICAL ORDER. Another word order variation is whether the language has PREPOSITIONS before NOUNS, *in New Orleans*, or postpositions after Nouns, *Nippon ni* (Japan in). See HEAD PARAMETER.

working memory: the memory system used for holding and manipulating information while various mental tasks are carried out. See ARTICULATORY LOOP.

writing system: 'a set of visible or tactile signs used to represent units of language in a systematic way': (1) 'the basic types of graphic systems designed to represent language'; (2) 'spelling, i.e. a system of rules underlying the use of the graphemes of the language' (Coulmas, 1996, 560); see *Writing System Topics website*.

Task key

Dialect is defined as a regional or socially conditioned variant of a language. Dialects may vary in their phonological, lexical, grammatical, and pragmatic conventions, but are generally mutually intelligible and often spoken by people who live in the same general geographical region. The difference between a dialect and a language is not clear, however. For example, Italian and Spanish are two different languages that are nonetheless mutually intelligible. Mandarin and Cantonese are not, although they are both considered dialects of Chinese. One whimsical linguist argued that a dialect becomes a language when its speakers get their own army (Foss and Hakes, 1978, p. 5).

From a linguistic point of view, every dialect – like every language – is a highly structured system, not an accumulation of errors caused by the failure of speakers to master the standard dialect. To prefer one dialect over another would be to display 'dialectical chauvinism', just as to prefer your own native language to any other would be to display 'linguistic chauvinism'.

As linguists such as Labov (1972) point out, dialects such as African-American English vernacular have a logic and a set of rules every bit as complicated as that of Standard English. The differences between dialects have to do with how they negotiate the trade-off between work a speaker has to do (for example, mark plurality twice, once on the pronoun, once on the verb: *he comes* versus *they come*) and the work a listener has to do (listen carefully and catch each point in the conversation where information is not presented redundantly). African-American English vernacular has some redundancies that Standard English does not (for example, negatives must be marked at least twice, as in *I ain't never lost a fight*) and omits some redundancies required by Standard English (for example, omitted copulas, as in *Stan here right now*).

Many speakers of English learn to switch their dialects to suit the occasion, talking Standard English at school, for example, and their home dialect among friends and family. In fact, linguists may be the only people who perceive dialects to be equivalent. The 1997 controversy over the Oakland, California, school system's adoption of Ebonics (more technically known as African-American vernacular English, or AAVE) as a primary language has made this difference in the perceived prestige of dialects painfully clear. On a less-explosive level, George Bernard Shaw explored the difference in the prestige of dialects in his famous play, *Pygmalion*, and its musical version, *My Fair Lady*.

TRY IT OUT! #4 (Chapter 2)

Passage 1

Linguistic scholars engage in a study of our ability to communicate and the means we employ to that end *for its own sake*. The roots of this study are found in the basic philosophical quest into the nature of knowledge itself. How do we know what we know? How do we organise our experience? How do we communicate with others? This study is sufficient unto itself for most modern linguistic scholars.

The teacher of English deals with the more immediate task of applying the findings of the language scholars to the training of the young in more effective and more efficient use of their innate language gifts. Linguistic scholars are interested in the teacher's task – as they are interested in all facts of language and its use – but for the language scholars it does not loom so large in importance. The teachers are, by the same token, interested in language study, but only as one facet of their primary function, which is to help students learn.

The linguistic scholars bear a relationship to teachers of English that is analogous to the relationship of the research scientist to the general practitioner of medicine. One seeks information; the other seeks to apply that information to the more efficient handling of specific problems. (From Herndon, 1970, p. 5)

Passage 2

The rationalist notes that on an abstract level, all languages work in the same way – they all have words and sentences and sound systems and grammatical relations – and he attributes these universals of language to the structure of the brain. Just as birds inherit the ability to fly, and fish to swim, men inherit the ability to think and to use language in a manner which is unique to their species. A given language, English, for example, has to be learned, but the capacity to learn languages is inherited. The child is not a passive agent in language acquisition; he actively goes about learning the language of his environment. Language use becomes almost automatic, but what a person learns is more than a set of conditioned habits. If you read all the books in the English language, you will find very few sentences which are habitually used and are exact duplicates of each other – otherwise you would suspect quotation or plagiarism. Knowledge of a language allows a person to

TRY IT OUT! (*cont.*)   #4 (Chapter 2)

understand infinitely many new sentences, and to create grammatical sentences which no one else has ever pronounced but which will be understood immediately by others who know the language.   (From Diller 1971, p. 7)

TRY IT OUT!   #5 (Chapter 3)

Look at these three sample questions. Identify the subject, limiting word(s) and direction word(s) in each.

1. **Subject:** the development of pidgins and creoles
   Limiting words: the differences between; some of the factors that lead to
   Direction words: (Using examples), explain; discuss
2. **Subject:** language processing in brain-damaged people
   Limiting words: what we can learn
   Direction word: Describe
3. **Subject:** expressing politeness
   Limiting words: through the structure of what we say or write
   Direction words: Explain (with the help of examples)
4. **Subject:** child language acquisition
   Limiting words: the role of motherese
   Direction words: Discuss

TRY IT OUT!   #6 (Chapter 3)

Adjectives precede those nouns they modify which are adjacent to them.

Our research suggests a correlation between previous language-learning experience and speed and success in learning a new language.

There is clear evidence of a relationship between gender and the use of certain kinds of question tags.

TRY IT OUT!   #7 (Chapter 3)

1. Linguists today recognise the shortcomings of the behaviourist view of language acquisition.
2. Audiolingualism and Communicative Language Teaching had little in common.
3. CLT's principle of 'function over form' meant that, in the early days at least, the teaching of grammar was far less evident in language classrooms.

4. The evidence suggests strongly that, for someone beginning to learn a second language post-puberty, it is highly unlikely that they will achieve native-like proficiency.

5. The fact that we can sometimes understand a concept without being able to express it in words calls into serious question the idea that all thought is constrained by language.

TRY IT OUT! #10 (Chapter 5)

(possible answers, with thesis statement in italics at the beginning and end)

This essay considers some of the key factors that lay behind the shift away from structurally to functionally based approaches to language teaching that saw language as communication rather than as a set of rules and procedures to be learnt and applied – often in unauthentic contexts. This shift, like most of its precedents, reflected important changes in the way linguists and applied linguists thought about language and the social – even political – contexts of the time, and it was the result of a series of key developments. Chomsky's fatal undermining of the empiricist theory of learning in favour of a rationalist one was certainly fundamental. However, this coincided with other important developments within the disciplines of philosophy, psychology, anthropology and sociology, each of which promoted a new perspective on language as a complex social and cognitive phenomenon that could not be understood or learnt except within the context of purposeful and meaningful interaction. Furthermore, it keyed into social, political and technological developments of the 1960s and 70s – in particular the establishment of a European Union, the increased movement of people across national and linguistic boundaries, and the resultant need to be able communicate effectively and 'get real world business done' with language. As a result, the goals of learning moved away from a concern with grammatical accuracy and the ability to demonstrate a grasp of linguistic rules to the ability to actually do things with language according to communicative need.

In the late 1960s and early 70s an important shift occurred in the way language was viewed such that so-called structuralism gave way to functionalism and the view that language was fundamentally communication and competence in language far more than merely the ability to understand grammar and demonstrate a knowledge of rules. This shift changed the way in which language was taught and it was the result of a series of key developments. Chomsky's fatal undermining of the empiricist theory of learning in favour of a rationalist one was certainly fundamental. However, this coincided with other important developments

TRY IT OUT! (cont.)   #10 (Chapter 5)

within the disciplines of philosophy, psychology, anthropology and sociology, each of which promoted a new perspective on language as a complex social and cognitive phenomenon that could not be understood or learned except within the context of purposeful and meaningful interaction. Furthermore, it keyed into social, political and technological developments of the 1960s and 70s – in particular the establishment of a European Union, the increased movements of people across national and linguistic boundaries, and the resultant need to be able communicate effectively and 'get real world business done' with language. As a result, the goals of learning moved away from a concern with grammatical accuracy and the ability to demonstrate a grasp of linguistic rules to the ability to actually do things with language according to communicative need.

Given their significance, the forces underlying the emergence of functionalism forty years ago warrant an in-depth analysis.

TRY IT OUT!   #11 (Chapter 5)

(possible answer)

Without doubt, Krashen's Monitor Model was one of the most prominent, influential and controversial of all second-language acquisition theories. It had enormous intuitive appeal for both theorists and pedagogues, and in many ways was perfectly in tune with a communicative movement that was flourishing during the 1980s. The discussion that follows will offer an in-depth appraisal of the approach by first placing it within the theoretical context of the time and describing the five central hypotheses of which it was comprised. It will then go on to explain its influence on pedagogy and its appeal to language teachers and materials developers alike. Finally, it will detail those weaknesses that ultimately saw its decline and consider the extent of its impact on the field.

TRY IT OUT!   #12 (Chapter 7)

Conclusion

The unique features of metaphor clusters in conciliation talk, as well as features shared with other discourse types, help to generalise from the various cases studied so far[1]. It appears that metaphor clusters occur when some intensive interactional work linked to the overall purpose of the discourse is being carried out. In lectures, lessons and sermons, the discourse work was mainly explanations of difficult or unfamiliar topics, carried out through extended use of one or two root metaphors. In conciliation talk, the central discourse work of reducing alterity is pushed forwards through metaphor clusters, in which metaphors, as 'ways of seeing one thing in terms of another' (Burke, 1945), are also tried out and gradually appropriated across speakers. Other clusters occur as speakers explore alternative ways of feeling and acting, helping participants contemplate and reject often very negative alternatives[2]. In extending what we know about the role of metaphor clusters and how to identify them, this article offers researchers a heuristic tool to use in exploring discourse. Faced with discourse data, a researcher can seek out clusters of metaphors and investigate the interaction around and inside them, with the expectations that the metaphor clusters indicate points where intensive and important discourse work is carried out. Where large amounts of data are involved, identifying and investigating clusters at the various levels of scale gives a way of 'cutting into' data which can help understand the overall dynamics of the discourse while at the same time identifying particular episodes worth investigating in more detail[1].

Summary and conclusion

At the beginning of this paper, we proposed a general scheme intended to capture and accommodate all kinds of turn continuation – from prospective to retrospective ones, and within the latter, from TCU extensions to new TCUs. Our focus, however, has been firmly on retrospective turn continuations and how these are done in Chinese conversations[3].

The general scheme is based on four inter-related but distinct parameters all having something to do with an utterance's structure, meaning, and information status relative to their host. The four parameters are: syntactic continuity vs. discontinuity, main vs. subordinate intonation, prospective vs. retrospective orientation, and information focus vs. non-focus. As we have attempted to show, these parameters interact in interesting ways. Together they define different turn continuation methods located along a continuum ranging from the tightly integrated to the loosely linked[2].

As far as syntax is concerned, continuity or discontinuity is certainly a very important consideration. But it would be wrong to regard it as the only consideration. We have tried to show how syntax interacts in complex ways with prosody and intonation. The two work hand in hand some of the time, but at cross purposes at other times. In the case of Right Dislocation, for example, syntactic discontinuity is off-set by subordinate intonation. Syntax may even on occasion be over-ridden by prosody. A unit may be syntactically continuous with a prior unit, but this alone does not preclude it from attaining the status of a new, separate TCU, provided that it comes with full intonation and is supported by appropriate features of rhythm and tempo[2]. We believe that the study of turn continuation can proceed on a firmer footing if these four parameters are kept

TRY IT OUT! (*cont.*)   #12 (Chapter 7)

conceptually distinct, even though their interaction and combination are clearly very important[1].

Regarding the communicative functions of turn continuation, within our limited corpus we have been unable to find any systematic mapping between particular forms and particular functions, except the general observation that all retrospective turn continuations offer a means of supplementing or commenting upon the information conveyed in the just-completed TCU. We did find in our small data collection a range of interactional motivations for further talk after the possible completion of a TCU, e.g. pursuing recipient uptake (FFT 2002), showing affiliation, upgrading one's stand in face of potential disagreement, etc.[2] However, as our corpus contains only Chinese data, and a limited amount of data at that, this question must be left to further research[4].

TRY IT OUT!   #13 (Chapter 8)

(possible answer)

LoCastro (2001) notes that class size is generally considered by language teachers across the world to be negatively correlated with their ability to develop learners' language proficiency. However, what constitutes a 'large class size' is, she argues, largely subjective and contingent upon the individual's perceptions and experience. For instance, a teacher who is used to teaching classes of around ten students may balk at the prospect of teaching twenty or more, whereas those familiar with class sizes of forty will be less likely to consider this a large group.

TRY IT OUT!   #14 (Chapter 8)

(possible answer)

The question of whether or not language is peculiar to humans has been the subject of debate for many years, with some writers claiming there is sufficient evidence to suggest that it is a trait shared by animals – most notably chimpanzees and dolphins. Increasingly, however, linguists question whether the kind of animal behaviour these writers cite as evidence can legitimately be termed 'language'. Fromkin and Rodman, for example, observe:

> Despite certain superficial similarities to human language, the communicative systems of various animal species are fundamentally different. This is true, for example, of the gestures that make up the courtship rituals of spiders, the dance of the honeybee that

indicates the direction and distance of food sources, and of bird calls and songs. In all such cases, the number of messages that can be conveyed is finite, and the messages are stimulus controlled
(Fromkin and Rodman, 1998, p. 25).

TRY IT OUT!   #15 (Chapter 8)

Bailey, L. (2010, March 19). Pronoun position. Message posted to http://www.englishforums.com/English/PronounPosition/nrqwz/post.htm

Ehrlich, S., & King, R. (1992). Feminist meanings and sexist speech communities. In K. Hall, M. Bucholtz, & B. Moonwomon (Eds.), *Locating power: proceedings of the second Berkeley women and language conference* (pp. 100–107). Berkeley: Berkeley Women and Language Group, Department of Linguistics, University of California at Berkeley.

El Zawawy, A. M. (2009). Rethinking construction grammar: contributions and outstanding questions. *Web Journal of Formal, Computational & Cognitive Linguistics*. Viewed 16 May 2010, http://fccl.ksu.ru/issue11/FCCL_09_4spanstyle='border:none'>Rethinking_Construction_Grammar.pdf

Johnstone, B. (1993). Community and contest: Midwestern men and women creating their worlds in conversational storytelling. In D. Tannen (Ed.), *Gender and conversational interaction* (pp. 62–82). Oxford: Oxford University Press.

Pahl, K. (2005). [Review of the book A critical discourse analysis of family literacy practices: Power in and out of print, by J. K. Kidd]. *Applied Linguistics*, 26, 131–134.

Slobin, D. (1966). Grammatical transformations and sentence comprehension in childhood and adulthood. *Journal of Verbal Learning and Verbal Behaviour*, 5, 219–227.

Travers, L. (2010, 17 August). *Why is RP not good enough anymore?* National Tribune, p. 3.

Trudgill, P. (1990). *The dialects of England*. Oxford: Blackwell.

TRY IT OUT!   #16 (Chapter 9)

(possible answers)

Informal	Formal
Like	*such as; similar to, comparable to*
totally	*very, considerably, highly*
low-down	*latest/most recent information/findings, update*

TRY IT OUT! (cont.)
#16 (Chapter 9)

cool	*interesting, intriguing, fascinating*
really	*very, considerably, extremely, highly*
OK	*good, excellent, satisfactory,*
the best of the lot	*most appropriate/satisfactory, best*
all right	*satisfactory,*
honestly	*really*
nice	*good, accurate, suitable, excellent, ideal*
cute (as in 'a cute idea')	*the most successful*
kind of/almost	*virtually, nearly,*
awesome	*impressive, excellent*

TRY IT OUT!
#17 (Chapter 9)

(possible answers)

1. Widdowson, Nunan and Wilson were *key proponents* of the communicative movement in the 1970s and 80s.
2. Research around a natural order of acquisition of grammatical morphemes progressed *significantly/considerably* in the mid-1980s.
3. Publishers of language-teaching materials – and particularly English language-teaching materials – were quick to *take advantage of* the Communicative Language Teaching *boom* in the 1980s and 90s.
4. Traditionalist grammarians, who see themselves as gatekeepers of the English language, have always *been in dispute with/at odds with/disagreed* with scholars and academics who see language evolution and change as inevitable and not subject to rigid rules and standards.

TRY IT OUT!
#18 (Chapter 10)

1. comparison and contrast
2. classification/description
3. comparison and contrast
4. stability/comparison and contrast
5. description
6. description/time/comparison and contrast
7. description/cause-effect
8. description

TRY IT OUT! #20 (Chapter 10)

Key: Background (B), Aims (A), Samples (S), Methods (M), Results (R), Conclusions (C)

Abstract – example 2

A study of the impact of a major recent language education reform project in Italy employed a combination of qualitative and quantitative data collection methods, some of which could inform other studies of language learning and teaching (B, A and M). Impact study findings suggested interesting differences between the perceptions of learners and teachers on some of the activities in their foreign language classes. While both sides agreed in general on the virtues of communicative approaches to language teaching, there were interesting differences in the perceptions of learners and teachers on the prominence of grammar and pair work in their classes (R). These differences may indicate potential problem areas of lesson planning and implementation which could usefully be given attention on teacher support programmes (C).

TRY IT OUT! #23 (Chapter 10)

Participants assigned to groups according to experience (judged according to feedback from questionnaire)

31 novice raters (mainly students enrolled in or recently completed pre-service or teacher-training programs in ESL, no ESL teaching or rating experience);
29 experienced raters (graduates and/or ESL instructors with 5+ years' experience of teaching and rating writing, plus MA/MEd and training in assessment and essay writing)
From various universities in Ontario, Canada
Varied gender, age and L1 background
Native or highly proficient non-native English speakers

References

Aitchson, J. (2003). *Words in the mind: An introduction to the mental lexicon.* Wiley-Blackwell.

Baldauf, R., & White, P. (2010). Participation and collaboration in tertiary language education in Australia. In A. Liddicoat & A. Scarino (Eds.), *Languages in Australian education: Problems, prospects and future directions.* Newcastle-upon-Tyne: Cambridge Scholars.

Barkaoui, K. (2010). Do ESL essay raters' evaluation criteria change with experience? A mixed-methods, cross-sectional study. *TESOL Quarterly, 44*(1), 31–57.

Bennett, K. (2010). Academic discourse in Portugal: A whole different ballgame? *Journal of English for Academic Purposes, 9,* 21–32.

Bretag, T., Horrocks, S., & Smith, J. (2002). Developing classroom practices to support NESB students in information systems courses: Some preliminary findings. *International Education Journal 3* (4), 37–69.

Brown, J. D., & Ross, J. A. (1996). Decision dependability of subtests, tests and the overall TOEFL test battery. In M. Milanovic & N. Saville (Eds.), *Studies in language testing 3. Performance testing, cognition and assessment: Selected papers from the 15th Language Testing Research Colloquium, Cambridge and Arnhem.* Cambridge: Cambridge University Press.

Brown, K., & Miller, J. (1991). *Syntax: A linguistics introduction to sentence structure* (second edition). London: HarperCollins.

Cameron, L., & Stelma, J. (2004). Metaphor clusters in discourse. *Journal of Applied Linguistics, 1*(2), 107–136.

Cook, G. *Discourse.* (1989). Oxford: Oxford University Press.

Cordone, P. (n.d.). *Discuss some ways in which English has been shaped as a tool for work.* http://www.paolo.rhumbo.com/files/U210TMA3.pdf Accessed 5 January 2011.

Coster, C. (2002). The translator in between texts: on the textual presence of the translator as an issue in the methodology of comparative translation description. In A. Riccardi (Ed.), *Translation studies: Perspectives on an emerging discipline*. Cambridge: Cambridge University Press.

Diller, K. (1978). *The language teaching controversy*. Rowley, Massachusetts: Newbury House.

Dingwall, W. O. (1998). The biological bases of human communicative behavior. In Gleason, J. & N. Ratner (Eds.), *Psycholinguistics* 2nd Edn. Fort Worth: Harcourt Brace.

Fox, J. (2005). Rethinking second language admission requirements: Problems with language-residency criteria and the need for language assessment and support. *Language Assessment Quarterly*, 2(2), 85–115.

Freeman, R., & McElhinny, B. (2003). Language and gender. In S. McKay & N. Hornberger (Eds.), *Sociolinguistics in language teaching*. Cambridge: Cambridge University Press.

Fromkin, V., & Rodman, R. (1998). *An introduction to language*. Fort Worth: Harcourt Brace.

Gass, S., Svetics, I., & Lemelin, S. (2003). Differential effects of attention. *Language Learning*, 53(3), 497–545.

Gennari, S. (2005). Acquisition of negation and quantification: Insights from adult Production and Comprehension. *Language Acquisition*, 13(2), 125–168.

Gleason, J. B., & Ratner, N. B. (1998). *Psycholinguistics*. Fort Worth: Harcourt Brace.

Hawkey, R. (2006). Teacher and learner perceptions of language learning activity. *English Language Teaching Journal*, 60(3), 242–252.

Her, O. S. (2009). Apparent subject–object inversion in Chinese. *Linguistics*, 47(5), 1143–1181.

Herndon, J. (1976). *A survey of modern grammars*. New York: Holt, Rinehart and Winston.

Heugh, K. (1999). Languages, development and reconstructing education in South Africa. *International Journal of Educational Development*, 19, 301–303.

Heugh, K. (2003). *Language policy and democracy in South Africa: The prospects of equality within rights-based policy and planning. Centre for Research on Bilingualism, Stockholm University*. Stockholm: Elanders Gotab.

Hobbs, D. (2006). Ethnography. In D. Jupp (Ed.), *The SAGE dictionary of social research methods*. London: Sage Publications.

Ionin, T., & Montrul, S. (2010). The Role of L1 Transfer in the Interpretation of Articles with Definite Plurals in L2 English. *Language Learning*, 60(4), 877–925.

229

Kang-kwong, L. & Zhang, W. (2007). Retrospective turn continuations in Mandarin Chinese conversation. *Pragmatics, 17*(4), 605–635.

Leaver, B. L., & Shekhtman, B. (2002). *Developing professional-level language proficiency.* Cambridge: Cambridge University Press.

Lévi-Strauss, C. (1963). *Structural anthropology.* New York: Basic Books.

Liao, Y., & Fukuya, Y. (2004). Avoidance of phrasal verbs: The case of Chinese learners of English. *Language Learning, 54*(2), 193–226.

LoCastro, V. (2001). Large Classes and Student Learning. *TESOL Quarterly, 35*(3), 493–496.

Lyons, J. (1981). *Language and linguistics.* Cambridge: Cambridge University Press.

McCabe, A. (1998). Sentences combined: text and discourse. In J. Gleason & N. Ratner (Eds.), *Psycholinguistics* 2nd Edn. New York: Harcourt Brace.

Murray, N. (2010). Considerations in the Post-Enrolment Assessment of English Language Proficiency: Reflections from the Australian Context. *Language Assessment Quarterly, 7*(4), 343–358.

Murray, N. & Beglar, D. (2009). *Inside track to writing dissertations and theses.* Harlow: Longman.

Papathanasiou, E. (2009). An investigation of two ways of presenting vocabulary. *ELT Journal, 63*, 313–322.

Pollitt, A. & Murray, N. (1996). What raters really pay attention to. In M. Milanovic & N. Saville (Eds.), *Studies in language testing 3. Performance Testing, Cognition and Assessment: Selected papers from the 15th Language Testing Research Colloquium, Cambridge and Arnhem.* Cambridge: Cambridge University Press.

Ransom, L. (2009). Implementing the post-entry English language assessment policy at the University of Melbourne: Rationale, processes, and outcomes. *Journal of Academic Language & Learning, 3*(2), A13–A25.

Ratner, N. B., Gleason, J. B. & Narasimhan, B. (1998). An introduction to psycholinguistics: What do language users know? In J. Gleason & N. Ratner (Eds.), *Psycholinguistics* 2nd Edn. New York: Harcourt Brace.

Saunders, G. (1988). *Bilingual Children: From Birth to Teens.* Philadelphia: Multilingual Matters.

Scarino, A. (2010). Language and languages and the curriculum. In A. J. Liddicoat and A. Scarino (Eds.): *Languages in Australian education: Problems, prospects and future directions.* Newcastle-upon-Tyne: Cambridge Scholars.

Schiffrin, D. (2003). Interactional sociolinguistics. In S. McKay & N. Hornberger (Eds.), *Sociolinguistics in Language Teaching*. Cambridge: Cambridge University Press.

Swales, J. M. (1990). *Genre analysis: English in academic and research settings*. Cambridge: Cambridge University Press.

Taylor, C. (1996). A study of writing tasks assigned in academic degree programs: a report on stage 1 of the project. In M. Milanovic & N. Saville (Eds.), *Studies in language testing 3. Performance testing, cognition and assessment: Selected papers from the 15th Language Testing Research Colloquium, Cambridge and Arnhem*. Cambridge: Cambridge University Press.

Wardhaugh, R. (2010). *An introduction to sociolinguistics*. Oxford: Wiley-Blackwell.

Weiten, W. (2010). *Psychology: themes & variations*. Wadsworth: Cengage Learning.

Wiley, T. G. (2003). Language planning and policy. In S. McKay & N. Hornberger (Eds.), *Sociolinguistics in language teaching*. Cambridge: Cambridge University Press.